QuickTest Professional Unplugged

By Tarun Lalwani

QuickTest Professional Unplugged

By *Tarun Lalwani*

ISBN: *978-0-578-02579-7*

Editor: *Siddharth N Kanoujia*

Technical Editor: *Terry Howarth*

Reviewer: *Mark, QTP Forum Moderator, SQAForums.com*
Terry, QTP Forum Moderator, SQAForums.com

Printing History:

        May 2009: First edition

Contents

Preface

I started with Web testing Automation in mid 2004 by creating a project in Visual Basic 6 using the Internet explorer COM Automation. The project was a great success but with every change to the application the Automation Code had to be updated and recompiled. Trying to find a solution to this maintenance issue I stumbled upon QuickTest Professional 8.0 (QTP).

QuickTest Professional is a Test Automation tool and uses VBScript as its scripting language. QTP is a record and playback tool which can record events we perform on an application and replay them back. QTP is an object based tool which recognizes each element of the application as an object and provides various methods to work on them. All this makes look QTP an easy to use test tool. The myth about Record & Playback is that it makes people think that they do not need development skills for QTP, but to create effective Automation Frameworks one needs to view QTP as a development tool and not as a testing tool. This book presents QTP as a development tool rather than a mere test tool.

One of my problems while evaluating the tool led to me to join www.SQAForum.com, without knowing that I will specialize in the use of this tool in future. After sometime I launched KnowledgeInbox.com for sharing my articles on QTP with the larger group. Dealing with day to day automation problems faced by people on the QTP forums, I tried solving those problems for them and learnt a few new things on my own. Observing the patterns of queries being asked on the QTP forums, I thought what the QTP community was missing is a book which can guide the amateur automation engineers in becoming a professional in the use of this tool. I took up this responsibility and started writing this book in May 2005. I spent an year on the research of the undocumented QTP features and solving the unsolved queries of QTP.

Being a first time author, I had a very hard time getting this project completed. It was an additional responsibility, over and above my office work, QTP forum support, writing articles on KnowledgeInbox, creating tools for the community. It required a lot of motivation to keep myself on the project. But knowing what difference this book can make to the QTP community always kept me motivated.

I have organized the chapter in such a way that can make learning QTP an easier task. Each chapter is based on a QTP feature. The book is divided in two sections, Basics and Advanced. Chapter 1 to 18 cover features related to QTP while the chapters in the Advanced section cover integration/interaction of QTP with various external tools like Outlook, Word, Excel and Quality Center. The book discusses a lot of issues that are commonly faced while using various features of QTP and their resolution. This book discusses almost all the topics of QTP which one would require to create complex frameworks.

Who This Book Is For

This book is for Test engineers, Test Analysts, Test Consultants, Test Managers and anyone who is interested in learning advanced techniques of problem solving in QTP. This book is also for beginners who have just started with QTP and want to be experts in its use. The book assumes that one has the basic knowledge of QTP and VBScript, if not than it is advised that one should go through the basic help first. As the main focus of this book is to view the tool from a developer's eye, the book does not teach how to record and replay script in QTP. Also the book does not discuss about the Keyword view of QTP, which is for non-technical people who don't want to code in QTP.

Feedback and Queries

For any feedback or queries you contact the author at *http://KnowledgeInbox.com/contact-me* or post a query on the KnowledgeInbox forums – *http://Knowledgeinbox.com/forums/*

Acknowledgements

The following individuals deserve a special mention for reviewing my work in progress, and providing me with many useful comments and suggestions:

Mark smith, Terry Horwath and Siddharth N Kanoujia

Mark works as a freelance contractor and can be contacted on *Quicktest@gmail.com*

Terry has not only worked as a reviewer but also as a Technical editor for this book. Terry has worked with automated testing tools since the early 90's when he started designing solutions with Segue's QA Partner 1.0. He transitioned to Mercury Interactive tools in 1999 and has worked exclusively with QuickTest Professional since 2005. He can be contacted on *thorwath@lakefolsom.com*.

Siddharth has worked as a editor for this book and has done a great job making sure that contents of this book are lucid and unambiguous for the beginners. He is an Assistant Professor in the Department of English at Hindu College, University of Delhi. He can be contacted on *kandidsid@gmail.com*

I would especially like to thank my family and friends who have always motivated me while I was working on this book.

Quotes From Reviewers

"I find this to be a very pragmatic, hand's on book for those who want to extend their QTP skills beyond basic expert view programming. This book is written by a QTP master for those who wish to eventually become masters themselves." – **Terry**

"Tarun Lalwani has singlehandedly helped thousands of people to expand their knowledge of QuickTest Professional. Here is a book the automated testing community has been crying-out for. This book will help QTP practitioners, from beginner to expert. I have used QTP from V6.0 and during the review I learnt something from every chapter." – **Mark**

"After long brainstorming sessions with Tarun over almost each and every sentence, I realized that I am truly in the presence of a genius. Tarun has with his dedication and perseverance made possible a book which will go a long way in helping people understand the ins and outs of QTP." – **Siddharth**

Chapter 1

Introduction

What is Test Automation?

Software testing has always been an essential part of the software industry. With crunch in timelines and increasing scope of testing, Automation can play a key role for getting the Testing phase complete within the stipulated time. Test automation is the process of reducing, and whenever possible, removing human interactions from an existing manual testing process. There are different tools available in the market to achieve Test Automation of the Application under test (AUT). With variety of environment available in the market to develop an application, it gets difficult to get one tool which can cater to all the needs of the Applications. QuickTest Pro (QTP) does support a lot of environment through the use of Add-ins specified to the environment.

When Should Test Automation Be Used?

Automation is not a replacement of manual testing. 100% automation can be achieved only in certain case, not always. It is important in Automation to decide which test cases needs to be automated and which test cases need to be tested manually. Given below is the list of few parameters which makes manual test cases a good candidate for automation:

- The test must be repeated very often

- The test's workflow and its validation evolve and change slowly over time

- The test validates a business process or workflow, rather than validating the look and feel, color, table layout, etc.

- The test is very repetitive and/or has a lot of steps, and it is important that those steps be performed exactly the same way each time and where manual tester fatigue must be avoided

- The test produces results for a regulatory body that demands that those results be electronically recorded and archived as a formal evidence of compliance.

- The test's pass/fail results are reasonably easy to determine and capture with the selected automation tool

When Should Test Automation Be Avoided?

It is utmost important to make sure that test cases automated are right one. Not every manual test case is a good candidate for automation. Knowing which test cases are not to be automated is important. Some examples of test cases which should not be automated are listed below

- ◉ In the case of Ad hoc testing where a subject matter expert randomly prowls through a variety of combinatorial workflows

- ◉ In the case of One time testing or when testing is repeated only a few times

- ◉ In the case of testing which requires covering multiple functional areas so that the test travels through a small amount of virtually all of the product's functionality

- ◉ Testing where *look and feel*, color, table layout, etc. are validated

- ◉ Testing where pass/fail validation requires evaluating information from several different and unrelated systems and/or applications

- ◉ Test cases for which test data cannot be determined before hand

- ◉ Test cases for which automated version execution takes more time than manual execution

- ◉ Test cases for which development of the automated scripts takes more time

The Automated Testing Process

It is important to understand the various phases involved in the automated testing process in order to develop an effective framework and test cases. The image shown below describes the various phases involved in Automation testing

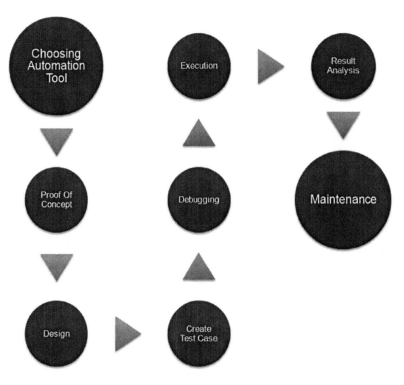

Figure 1-1. Automation Process

- **Selecting the "best fit" Automation Tool:** Before starting to automate testing in any application it is important to pick the best fit tool for the majority of our applications. The choice should be based on variety of factors such as cost, ease of use, capabilities and support

- **Proof of Concept (POC):** This activity involves creating a few sample scripts that validate a few important business workflows in one or two of our most important applications. This helps in identifying any major issues that might be encountered during future test case development. A proof of concept should also be used to select the best automation test tool for our applications

- **Requirements Analysis:** This activity involves analyzing the requirements of an application, studying the existing manual test cases and then defining the scope of the test automation project

- **Project Estimates:** Once the scope of automation is defined, estimates can then be made based on various factors like the number of test cases to be automated, their complexity, what re-usable components need to be developed, staffing requirements, etc.

- **Framework Design:** This activity involves creating the shared object repository(s), re-usable components, writing a best practices guideline document and completing other activities to create the base of software components that will be used to write the test scripts

- **Test Script Development:** Test cases are created by calling the re-usable components and adding appropriate validations to each workflow specific script

- **Debugging:** Completed test cases are debugged to make sure they work as designed. Make sure we force the code through all error handling paths during this debugging phase

- **Execution:** In this phase test cases are finally put to work, which involves regression testing and validating the application under test

- **Result Analysis:** Post process the results created by each executed test

- **Maintenance:** This phase involves updating scripts to fix any code related issues found during execution or for the inevitable changes that will be made to the application from time to time. A well designed framework and set of tests ensures that maintenance costs are kept to the minimum

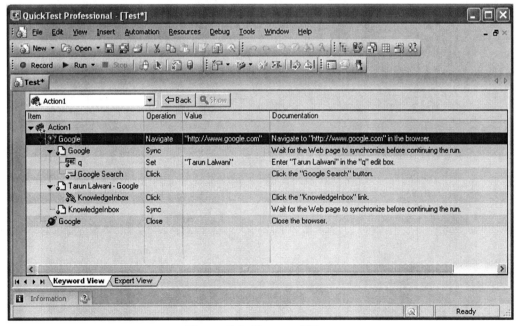

Figure 1-2. Keyword View

What is HP QuickTest Professional (QTP)

HP QTP is a functional test automation tool. It supports a Record and Playback framework out of the box, where we can record and capture our interactions with the application under test and then replay those actions later.

QTP has two modes in which to view and edit a test script: the Keyword View and the Expert View.

The Keyword View displays the script in the form of keywords arranged in a tree format and is targeted at subject matter experts with little or no programming background.

The Expert View exposes the script's underlying VBScript code and provides access to substantial capabilities not available in the Keyword view.

This book is targeted at automation engineers who want to exploit the power that QTP offers while working in the Expert View.

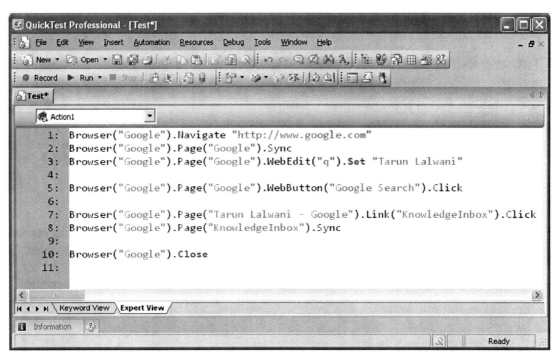

Figure 1-3. Expert View

 NOTE: QTP uses VBScript as its programming language. Virtually all VBScript functionality is available in the QTP Expert View. Conversely, all VBScript limitations are also present in QTP. It is important to learn what is related to QTP and what is VBScript related in a test's structure, and this book helps to clarify those aspects.

Reader's Note

Reader's Note

Chapter 2

Using QTP Help

QTP's online Help provides lot of useful information while we are working with QTP. But at times, especially for those new to QTP, finding specific information can be difficult. This chapter explains how to effectively search the Help file to find what we are looking for.

QTP Help file has four tabs as shown in the Figure 2-1

Figure 2-1. QTP Help tabs

We discuss each of the first three tabs in the remainder of this chapter.

Contents Tab

This tab provides a structured view of the Help file. The topics presented by this tab depend on what add-ins have been installed. As each add-in is installed its user's guide is added to this tab and its object model is added to the Object Model reference folder. We can use the content tab to perform the following tasks:

⦿ To look at new QTP features – Go to the "QuickTest New Features Guide" and go through each page to learn about all the new features

⦿ To read through each installed Add-in user's guide in a structured manner

⦿ Learning VBScript – We can learn VBScript in the VBScript reference folder. As it is written by Microsoft, it contains help for VBScript, Dictionary object, FileSystemObject object and Windows Script Host,

⦿ Understanding the QTP Object Model – This important folder explains all about the various QTP objects. We explore a couple of the key methods and properties from this folder next

Properties returned by the GetROProperty Function

The GetROProperty function returns a variety of runtime parameters for each unique QTP test object. To experiment with this, open the "Object Model reference" folder and expand the folder which describes all "Web" objects. Then drill down to *"WebList\Properties\WebList Identification properties"* Help then displays all the properties supported by the GetROProperty function for WebList as shown in the Figure 2-2

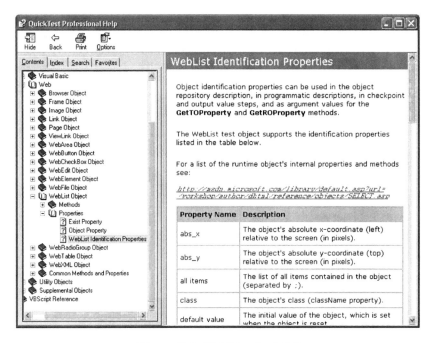

Figure 2-2. WebList GetROProperty

Methods provided by a Test Object

To determine all of the methods a WebTable supports, drill down to the *"Object Model Reference\ Web\WebTable Object\Methods"* folder in Help.

Index Tab

Use this tab when we know what individual topics or features we are looking for. For example, suppose we need details about using the InStr function; in that situation we should select the Index tab and then type "InStr" into the search field. Performing that set of steps produces the following Help information display on the right side of the help windows, as displayed below:

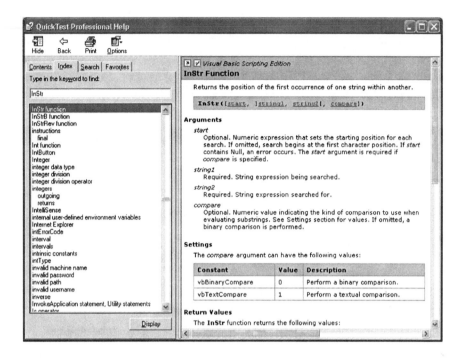

Figure 2-3. Index Tab – InStr function

Search Tab

Use the Search tab in situations where we have been unsuccessful in finding the needed information using the Contents and Index tabs. The Search tab allows us to enter free form text in an attempt to match the entered string in any part of the Help file. In the following example, when we enter the string, "Search a string", then it displays all Help file locations which contain that string, in the left pane.

We then apply some deductions to determine which location entry(s) to review for applicability to our problem. In this example we decide that it will be a VBScript function, so we can ignore all other entries except where Location indicates "Microsoft VBScript reference". In this example we find our way back again to the detailed Help page which describes the InStr functions:

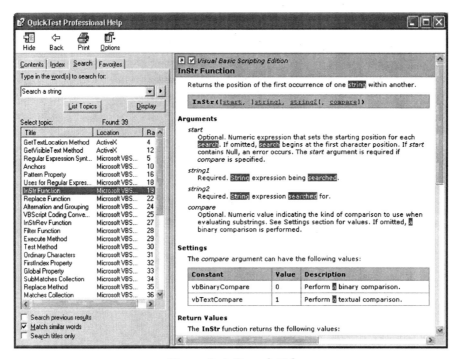

Figure 2-4. Search Tab

Reader's Note

Reader's Note

Chapter 3

Object Repository (OR)

QTP stores a definition for each test object in the Object Repository (OR). The definition contains values for various parameters which are used to uniquely identify an object at runtime in the AUT. The QTP Object Repository Manager is used to view and modify repository objects and their properties.

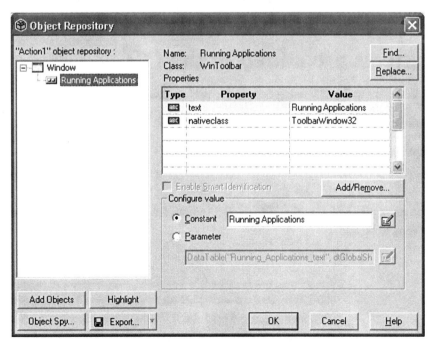

Figure 3-1. Object Repository Manager

Figure 3-1 shows a simple object repository. This OR has a WinToolbar object which is identified with the Logical Name of "Running Applications" and has two property definitions: "text" and "nativeclass". We can add and/or remove the properties by clicking the *Add/Remove...* button. Figure 3-2 shows the Add/Remove Properties dialog which can be used to add or remove any of the properties from object identification.

 NOTE: Selecting an object from the tree view and clicking the *Highlight* button will highlight the button in the application (that needs to be open). The same can be done in the code for highlight objects at run-time Window(**"Window"**).WinToolbar(**"Running Applications"**). Highlight

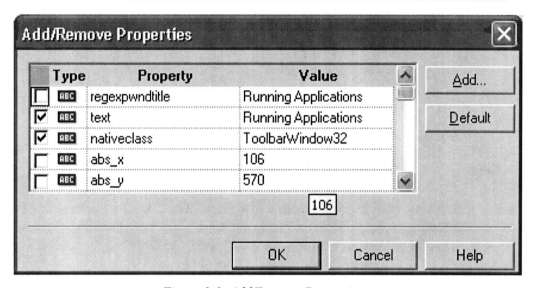

Figure 3-2. Add/Remove Properties

How objects are added to the OR

Objects can be added to the OR using one of the two methods:

⊙ By recording interactions against the application under test

⊙ By manually adding one or more objects

Object can be manually added to the OR by clicking on *Add Objects* button and then clicking on the object that needs to be added.

 NOTE: In case the object we want to add appears after a mouse click, then press and hold the CTRL key prior to that mouse click. This temporarily disables the object selection mode and allows us to perform mouse click operations to navigate. Then, when we are ready to add the object to the OR, release the CTRL key and click on the object.

In case we need to switch between applications, first press CTRL +
ALT to disable the object selection mode. Then we can switch between
different applications and use key combinations like ALT + TAB etc.
Once done, press the CTRL + ALT key to enable the object selection
mode and add the object.

Once the object is selected QTP displays the object selection window

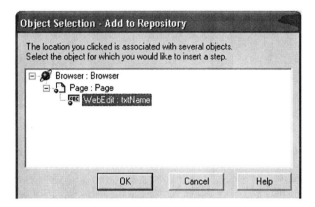

Figure 3-3. Object Selection

The object selection window displays the complete hierarchy of the objects on the web page. Select
the object which needs to be added and click the OK button.

 NOTE: The object hierarchy displayed might not be the same as
the one recorded in the OR. QTP only keeps the hierarchy which is
necessary for it to identify the object. This also reduces the length of the
code line generated when the object reference is used in a test script.

If we select the page object and continue, QTP will ask if we want to add all its child objects

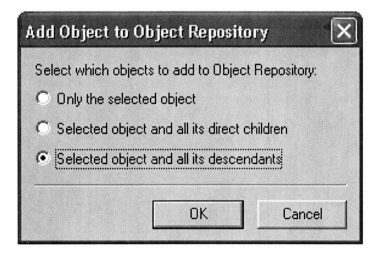

Figure 3-4. OR Object Selection options

Selecting the *Selected object and all its descendants* radio button and then clicking *OK* will add all the objects present on the page

> **NOTE:** QTP does not add hidden objects present on the page.

Test and Run-time Objects

Test Objects (TO): Test objects are QTP defined classes used to represent the various objects in the application under test (AUT).

Run-time objects (RO): Run-time objects are the actual AUT object which a Test Object refers/points to during test execution.

Comprehending the difference between these two object types is very important. Consider two cars; Car A and Car B. QTP would represent both cars using a Car Test Object in the script. In addition, each Test Object also provides methods and properties used to interact with its associated Run-time Object. For example, methods like Start, Run and Stop would be useful methods provided by a Car Test Object.

TO Properties

Test Object properties are those properties that QTP maintains in the OR for identifying a Run-time object during test execution. QTP allows enumeration of all TO properties using GetTOProperties. GetTOProperty and SetTOProperty are used to read or modify the TO property values respectively.

Problem 3-1. Working with Test Object properties

```
'Get the webedit object
Set oWebEdit = Browser("").Page("").WebEdit("")

'Get the TOProperties collection
Set TOProps = oWebEdit.GetTOProperties()

Dim i, iCount
iCount = TOProps.Count - 1

'Loop through all the properties
For i = 0 To iCount

    'Get Name of the property
    sName = TOProps(i).Name
```

```
'Get the value of the property
sValue = TOProps(i).Value

'Is the value a regular expression
isRegularExpression = TOProps(i).RegularExpression

'Display the values
Msgbox sName & "->" & sValue & "->" & isRegularExpression
Next
```

Problem 3-2. Changing Test Object properties at run time

```
'Get the webedit object
Set oWebEdit = Browser("Browser").Page("Page").WebEdit("txtName")

'Get the name test object property
oldName = oWebEdit.GetTOProperty("name")

'Change the test property
oWebEdit.SetTOProperty "name","new value"

'Get the modified property
newName = oWebEdit.GetTOProperty("name")


MsgBox newName
```

Problem 3-3. Getting Run-time Object properties during test execution

We use GetROProperty to read the value of any Run-time Object property, and save the value into a variable:

```
'x will have the text present the Search edit box.
x = Browser("").Page("").WebEdit("").GetROProperty("value")
MsgBox x
```

NOTE: QTP does not provide a method to set Run-time Object properties i.e. there is no SetROProperty. Also each different test object has a different list of supported property values which is defined in the object model reference in QTP help.

Object Repository Modes

There are 2 types of object repositories or rather the object repository modes

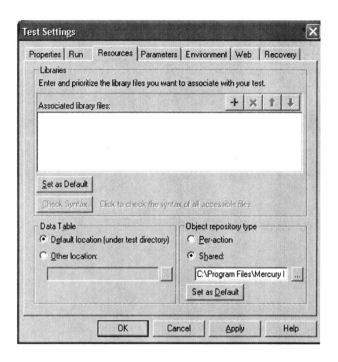

Figure 3-5. Per Action OR Setting

Per-Action versus Shared Object Repository

Table 3-1. Per-Action versus Shared Object Repository

Per-Action Object Repository	Shared Object Repository
Objects are added to the action object repository in case it doesn't already exist in the OR	Objects are added to the shared object repository in case it doesn't already exist in the OR
Renaming an object in the OR does not affect any other script. The current script is automatically updated with renamed object.	Renaming an object does not update all the scripts which are using the shared object repository. It can have serious impacts as the change is not updated on other scripts.
Changes need to be made to all scripts in case if the object identification property changes.	Changes to the object identification properties are reflected in all the scripts
Should be used when not many test cases are working on the same screens of the applications	Should be used when there are different scripts interacting with the same type of the object.
	The object repository can grow huge and needs to be backed-up regularly to avoid corruption risks.

The Object Spy

The Object Spy is a tool used to interrogate methods and properties supported by an object. To launch object spy go *Tools→Object spy…*

Click on the pointer button to select an object. When the Test Object Properties radio button is selected, it will display all the available TO properties in the Properties tab and all available methods in the Methods tab as shown in the Figure 3-6

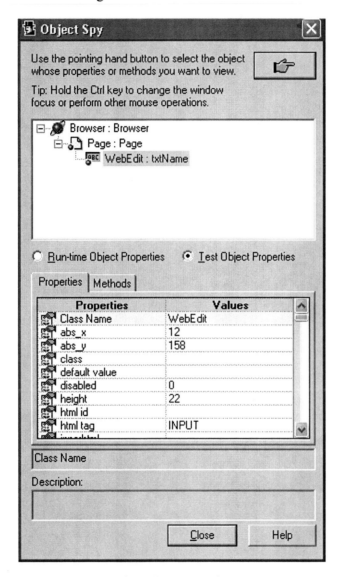

Figure 3-6. Object Spy Test Object Properties

Selecting the Run-time Object Properties radio button displays the actual properties/methods of the object as shown in the Figure 3-7

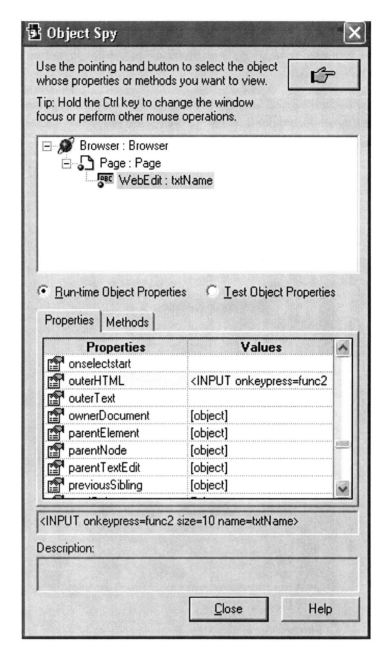

Figure 3-7. Object Spy RO properties

Most of these properties can be accessed using GetROProperty methods. To know about all the supported properties refer to the QTP Manual

```
'Get the outer html of the webedit
sOuterHTML = Browser("").Page("").WebEdit("").GetROProperty("outerhtml")
```

 NOTE: The Object Spy does not display any of the ordinal identifier properties such as CreationTime, index or location. They can only be evaluated after adding the object to the OR.

Object Identification

Object identification is a crucial part of a test case. QTP does not record properties arbitrarily, rather there is a configuration that QTP follows while recording a selected combination of properties. We can change these properties in case the application requires a different combination. To change these settings go to *Tools→Object Identification...*.

There are three types of properties that QTP uses for object identification

⦿ Mandatory properties – These are always captured and saved for the object even if it's possible to identify the object without some of these properties

⦿ Assistive properties – In case mandatory properties are not enough for uniquely identifying an object, QTP adds the assistive properties one by one, in the order specified, until the object can be uniquely identified

⦿ Ordinal identifier – If, after using all the mandatory and assistive properties, the selected object still can't be uniquely identified, QTP then uses the ordinal identifier. There are three types of ordinal identifiers:

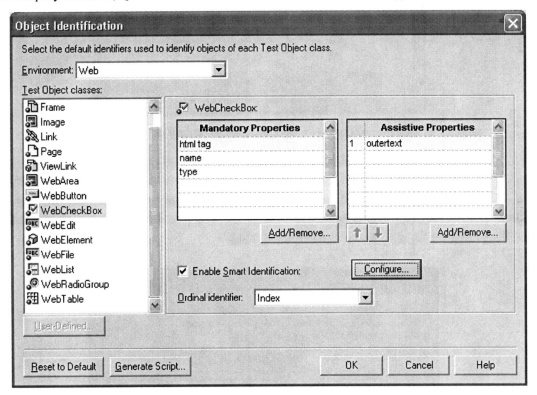

Figure 3-8. Object identification settings

Figure 3-8 shows the Mandatory and assistive properties of the WebCheckBox test object on my machine.

 NOTE: These settings are not based on the script but are generic settings for QTP as a whole. We can add/remove properties as needed.

User-defined Objects

QTP uses the class name of the Window to identify which type of test object it is. In case our application does not use standard Window classes QTP might be unable to correctly identify the object. Consider the Windows search dialog box which has certain checkboxes under the more advanced section. When we try to add them to QTP OR it would identify the checkbox as a WinObject as shown in the Figure 3-9. This occurs because QTP does not identify these checkboxes as a generic Test Object class.

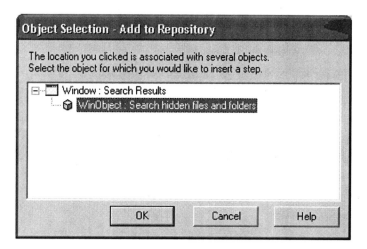

Figure 3-9. Search window checkbox identified as WinObject

Therefore we need to map this checkbox to a WinCheckBox in QTP settings. *Go to Tools→Object Identification* and select the Environment as *Standard Windows*. Now click on the *User Defined* button. This displays the mapping dialog box. Click on the hand arrow button and then click on the checkbox. The class name would be populated and we can map it to the checkbox as shown in the *Figure 3-10.* Click on the *Add* button to add the mapping.

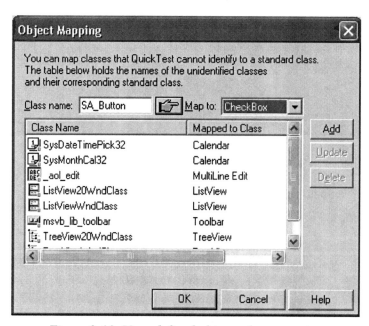

Figure 3-10. User-defined objects class mapping

Once mapped QTP will thereafter be able to identify the object as a WinCheckBox as shown in the Figure 3-11.

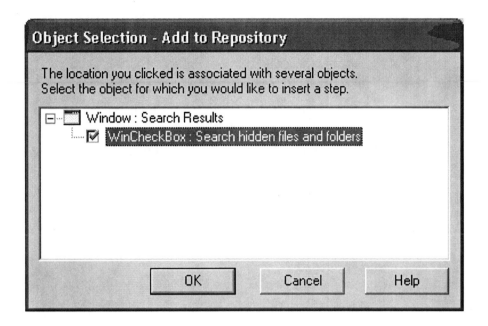

Figure 3-11. User-define object identified as checkbox

Object Repository Shortcomings

In my opinion the QTP 8.x object repository has some shortcomings

- The OR Manager does not allow mass update of various object properties

- Objects cannot be moved/copied under other objects

- It is necessary to re-record the entire test case in the situation where a Frame is added to the AUT

- Duplicate objects are often added when re-recording on a Page/Window which was previously recorded on—thereby creating duplicate Page/Window's in the form: Page_1, Page_2 etc. Sometimes this issue can be fixed by changing QTP web settings. Go to *Tools→Options...→Web (Tab)→Page/Frame Options...* and change the settings as shown in the Figure 3-12

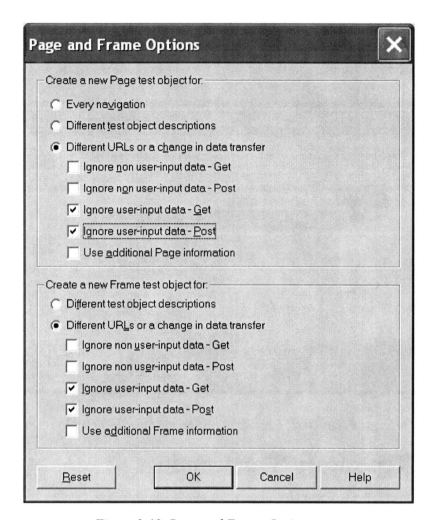

Figure 3-12. Page and Frame Options

 NOTE: Most of these shortcomings have been resolved in QTP 9.x version

Reader's Note

Reader's Note

Chapter 4

DataTables

A DataTable provides a way to create data driven test cases. It is similar to MS Excel spreadsheets and can be used to run an Action multiple times. Each test case has one global data sheet which is accessible to all actions inside that test case and each action has its own private data table also known as local data table. The name local data table is somewhat misleading because it is in fact possible to access any action's local data table from any other action, but the way of accessing the data becomes a bit different.

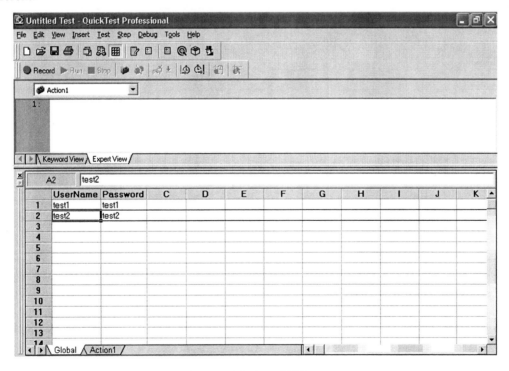

Figure 4-1. DataTable

Figure 4-1 shows a sample DataTable with 2 parameters, Username and Password.

We can use most of the formulas that work inside a typical Excel spreadsheet. But there are some differences between a DataTable and an Excel spreadsheet. In fact a DataTable is wrapped around an Excel spreadsheet—which provides access functionality to the values but does not expose the Excel spreadsheet object model.

```
'gives the value of Parameter1 stored in
'the Global data table.
DataTable("Parameter1",dtGlobalSheet)

'gives the value of Parameter1 stored in
'the current's action local data table.
DataTable("Parameter1",dtLocalSheet)
```

The same DataTable cannot have duplicate parameter names but we can use the same name parameters in different sheets (Global DataTable and Local DataTable). Each DataTable has only 1 row enabled even when it is blank and the other rows get enabled when data is entered into a new row. A DataTable is stored as "Default.xls" file in the test folder. Figure 4-2 shows how the stored file looks like

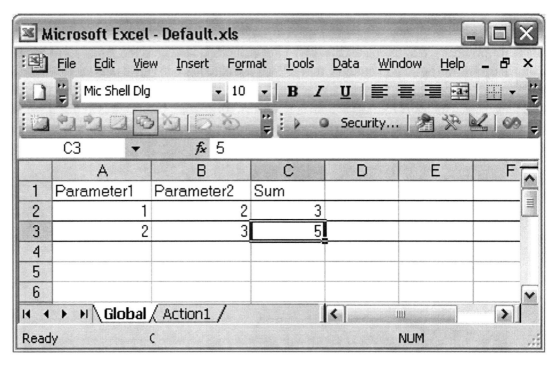

Figure 4-2. Default.xls Data table

When viewed in Excel, the first row of the sheet contains the parameter names, while QTP displays the parameter as the column titles. Therefore, when viewed using Excel, the 2nd row starts the 1st row of data in the DataTable. The DataTable shown above has only 2 data rows enabled. Note that QTP makes a data row enabled by marking the borders of the row in the actual spreadsheet. A row with no data but with marked borders is still considered as an enabled row by QTP. To delete an enabled row we must select the row and delete it from the context menu which appears on right clicking the row.

Design and run-time data table

Design time data table

As the name suggest the data table during the script design time is known as design time data table. Any changes to this are saved when the script is saved.

Run-time data table

The run-time data table contains a copy of the design time data table when a script is executed. It may contain values that are changed during script execution and are presented in the test result summary. The changes made to the data table during run-time are not saved to design time data table. Figure 4-3 shows a run-time data table from the test results summary

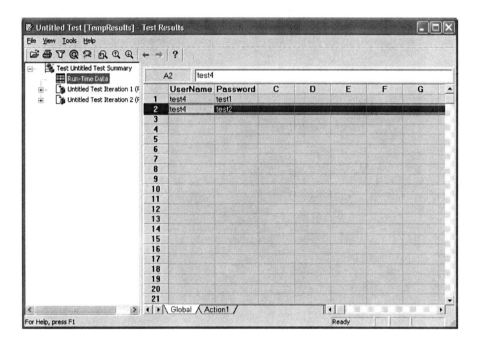

Figure 4-3. Run-time data table

When to use the global or a local data table

It is important to understand in what situations the global or a local data table should be used. Consider the following two scenarios

> Scenario 1 - Log into the application, book 1 ticket, log out. Repeat the scenario for many users

> Scenario 2 - Log into the application, book 3 tickets, and log out

Scenario 1

The Global data table is better suited for this scenario where we have the user name, password and tickets details as the parameters and we execute the scenario using a single action (which does everything) or multiple actions (Login, booking and logout).

Scenario 2

A Local data table is better suited for this scenario. Here a good approach would be to split the test into three actions: login, booking and logout. Login and logout can use the username and password parameters from the global data table and booking can use ticket detail parameters from its local data table and the action will be executed for all rows in its local data table.

Setting data table iterations

To run a test case for some number of iterations we need to set the iterations of global data table in the Test Settings dialog, which is invoked using *Test→Settings...→Run (Tab)* Figure 4-4 shows the iteration settings for the global table. These settings are specific to script.

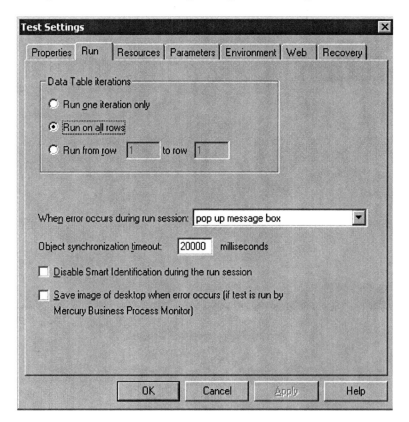

Figure 4-4. Global data iterations

 NOTE: We can use an external spreadsheet as a Data table by specifying the location of the file in the *Resource (Tab)* as shown in the Figure 4-4

We can set the iteration settings for an Action call by going into the keyword view and then right clicking on the Action and selecting *Action Call Properties...* as shown in the Figure 4-5

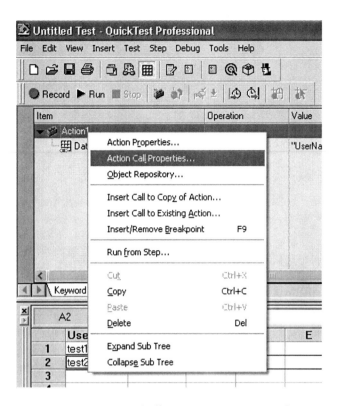

Figure 4-5. Action Call Properties - Keyword View

The Action call properties dialog can be used to set the iterations as shown in the Figure 4-6

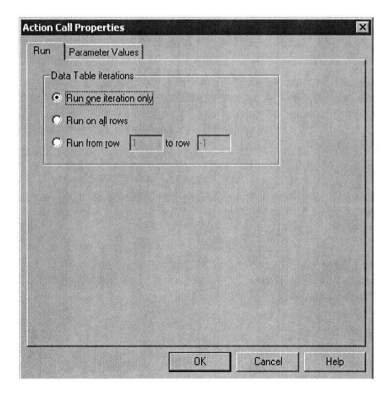

Figure 4-6. Action Call Properties dialog

Data table object model

QTP provides an object model to access various properties and methods in a data table:

There are three types of objects

- ⊙ DataTable – Represents all the global and local data tables in the test

- ⊙ DTSheet – Represents a single sheet in the test

- ⊙ DTParameter – Represents a single column in a sheet.

Each object has certain functions available and certain properties associated with it. These are explained in detail in the QTP user manual.

Data table formatting

When data is entered into the data table it automatically formats the value using the best possible matching format. For example, if "12345678901" is entered into a cell then it would be auto formatted to "1.23456789E+010". In situations where the formats are important the data should be entered with care. If data entered in the cell start with a single quote (') then it is always treated as a text and no format conversion is performed.

We can also define a specific format by right clicking the cell or an entire column and then picking a specific format from the popup context menu.

Problem 4-1. How to access a parameter from the global data sheet

There are a variety of ways to access a parameter from the global data table, most of which are presented in the following code snippet:

```
'Methods of getting a Data Table value
val = DataTable.Value("ParamName",dtGlobalSheet)
val = DataTable.Value("ParamName","Global")

'By giving the sheet index starting from 1 for the global sheet
val = DataTable.Value("ParamName",1)

' Sheet name or id is a optional parameter and is assumed
' to be as for global data sheet in case not provided
val = DataTable.Value("ParamName")

' Value property is the default property of the DataTable object
' so DataTable("ParamName",dtGlobalSheet) is
' equivalent to DataTable.Value("ParamName",dtGlobalSheet)
val = DataTable("ParamName",dtGlobalSheet)
val = DataTable("ParamName")

'Using the data table object model
val = DataTable.GlobalSheet.GetParameter("ParamName").Value

'Using the data table object model
val = DataTable.GlobalSheet.GetParameter("ParamName").ValueByRow(1)
```

Problem 4-2. How to access a parameter from a Local data sheet

```
'Various methods to get data table value
val = DataTable.Value("ParamName",dtLocalSheet)
val = DataTable.Value("ParamName","<LocalActionName>")
val = DataTable("ParamName",dtLocalSheet)
Val = DataTable("ParamName","<LocalActionName>")

'The local sheet of the action which is executing this statement
val = DataTable.LocalSheet.GetParameter("ParamName").value
```

Problem 4-3. How to check if a Sheet exists

```
'Function to check if DataTable sheet exists
Function isSheetExists(sheetName)
   On error resume next
    isSheetExists = TRUE
    Err.clear
    Set objSheet= DataTable.GetSheet(sheetName)
    'In case error occured sheet does not exist
    If err.number<>0 then
        isSheetExists = FALSE
    End if
End Function
```

Problem 4-4. How to preserve format of data output to a data table

```
'This would be modified to 1.23456789E+010 due to auto formatting
DataTable("ParamName") = "12345678901"
'This will not be auto formatted and will be treated as text
DataTable("ParamName") = "'" & "12345678901"
```

Problem 4-5. How to check if a parameter exists in a specific sheet

```
'Check if a parameter exists in data table
Function isParameterExists(sheetName, paramName)
   On error resume next
    isParameterExists = TRUE
    Err.clear
    ParamTotal = DataTable.GetSheet(sheetName).GetParameter(paramName)
    'In case of error the parameter does not exist
    If err.number<>0 then
        isParameterExists = False
    End if
   End if
End Function
```

Problem 4-6. How to export contents of a WebTable to a data sheet. Let's assume that the first row of the data table contains the columns heading. We then add those as parameters of the data table:

```
'Variable declaration
Dim i,j
Dim rowCount,colCount
Dim cellText, objTable
```

```
'Get table object
Set  objTable = Browser("").Page("").WebTable("")

'Get the row count of the webtable
rowCount = objTable.RowCount

'Get the column count of the webtable header row
colCount = objTable.ColumnCount(1)

'create a output sheet
Set outSheet = DataTable.AddSheet ("Output")

'Create Parameters based on the 1st row of the web table
For i = 2 to colCount
   cellText = objTable.GetCellData(1,i)

   'Note in case the CellText contains space in between
   'then QTP will automatically convert it to a "_" character
   outSheet.AddParameter cellText,""
Next

'Skip first row as we assumed it to be a header row
For i = 2 to rowCount
   outSheet.SetCurrentRow i-1

   're-calculate the column count as some rows
   'have different column sizes
   colCount = objTable.ColumnCount(i)

   For j = 2 to colCount
         cellText = objTable.GetCellData(i,j)


         'We are using index here to avoid the problem of
         'the "_" issue if cell text has spaces or new line chars
         'then we will get an error. to overcome that we can also use
         'outSheet.GetParameter(Replace(cellText," ","_")).Value
         outSheet.GetParameter(j-1).value = cellText
   Next
Next
```

Problem 4-7. How to get value of a parameter from any specific row in the data table

We use the ValueByRow method to get value for any row

```
'Get a value by row
DataTable.GetSheet("SheetName").GetParameter("ParameterName").
ValueByRow(RowNumber)
```

Problem 4-8. How to execute a script for all Global Data Table iterations, when the script is set to run for only one iteration:

In case we want to manually repeat the code for each iteration, we need to write a bit code.

```
'Declare variable
Dim i, iCount

'Get the global sheet object
Set oGlobal = DataTable.GlobalSheet

'Get # of rows
iCount = oGlobal.GetRowCount

For i = 1 to iCount
    'Set the current row
    oGlobal.SetCurrentRow i
    'Execute the code to be repeated here
    Msgbox DataTable("UserName")
Next
```

Problem 4-9. How to get the number of columns that contain data:

To solve this problem we need to utilize the excel formula COUNTA. We add a parameter to the data table with the formula and then read its value:

```
'Add a new parameter with the formula
'For Columns 1 of data table use A1:A65536
'For column 2 of data table use B1:B65536 and so on
DataTable.GlobalSheet.AddParameter "New","=COUNTA(A1:A65536)"
'Get the new value
Msgbox DataTable("New")
```

 NOTE: The above code won't work when there are no columns in the data table or all the columns have been used

Reader's Note

Chapter 5

Actions

Actions are used to divide scripts into logically related groups of QTP statements. They are similar to VBScript functions, but with a few differences. Actions are unique to QTP while functions are supported by both VBScript and QTP. Actions can optionally pass and receive input and output parameters. When used, input parameters must be passed first, followed by output parameters. A parameter cannot serve both as an input as well as an output parameter. In addition to supporting output parameters, Actions can also return a value. Lastly, an object/array can't be used as an action parameter.

Input and Output Parameters

The next step shows how input and output parameters are used by both the calling Action and the called Action:

Create a new blank test and right click in the expert windows and then go to *Action → Insert Call to a New...* as shown in the Figure 5-1

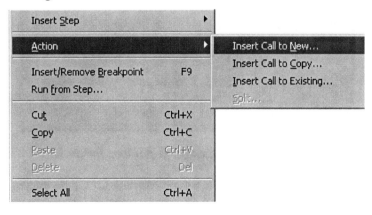

Figure 5-1. Insert call to New Action in Action1

Select "*After the current step*" radio button and click Ok as shown in the Figure 5-2

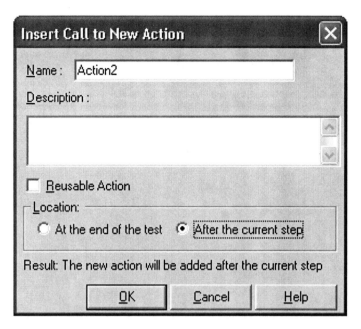

Figure 5-2. Insert Call to New Actions dialog in Action1

After clicking the OK button, the expert view will display Action 2. Now go to *Step → Action properties* and set the input and output parameters for Action 2 as shown in the Figure 5-3

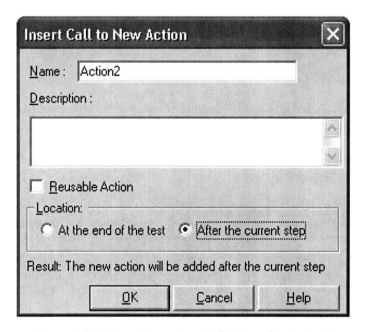

Figure 5-3. Action Properties Definitions for Action2

Next, browse back to Action1 in expert view and we will see that QTP has added a call to Action2 in the following line of code:

RunAction "Action2", oneIteration

Next, we add two input parameters, *input1* and *input2*, as well as one output parameter, output1, to the above Action call:

```
'Input to the action
input1 = 1
input2 = 3
Dim output1

'Run the action with parameters
actionOutput = RunAction ("Action2", oneIteration, input1, input2, output1)

'Display the output
MsgBox output1
MsgBox actionOutput
```

Next, browse back to Action2 and add the following code that uses the new parameters being passed by Action1:

```
'Assign value to the output parameter
Parameter("Output")= Parameter("Input1") + Parameter("Input2")

'Exit the action with below status
ExitAction ("The sum of the input parameters is :" & Parameter("Output"))
```

In Action2 we access the parameters passed by Action1 using Parameter ("name") statements (we can also use the Parameter Item statement as well). In our example we also use the ExitAction statement to terminate Action2 execution as well as return a string value to the calling Action.

Let's look again to line 3 in the calling action, Action1:

```
'Run the action with parameters
actionOutput = RunAction ("Action2", oneIteration, input1, input2, output1)
```

After this line of code executes, which occurs when Action2 terminates, the output1 variable contains the two numbers added by Action2, and the actionOutput variable contains the string returned by Action2 in its ExitAction statement.

We can also pass literal values in place of the input parameters:

```
'Run the action with parameters
actionOutput= RunAction ("Action2", oneIteration, 1,  3, output1)
```

For more details on the RunAction statement refer to the QTP manual.

In our example Action1 only called Action2 for a single iteration. But it is also possible to invoke RunAction as described below to iterate on a data table, thereby calling Action2 multiple times.

```
'The code below runs Action2 for all iteration in the local data table
RunAction "Action2", rngIterations, rngAll

'The code below runs Action2 for 1st, 2nd and 3rd data table row
RunAction "Action2", rngIterations, "1-3"

'The code below runs Action2 for only the 2nd data table row
RunAction "Action2", rngIterations, "2-2"
```

Action run iterations can also be configured in the Keyword view by right clicking on the action call and selecting *"Action call properties..."* from the context menu. Then we can set the iteration properties as shown in the Figure 5-4

Figure 5-4. Action Call Properties – Iterations

Types of Actions

There are three types of actions:

⦿ Normal/Non-reusable action – An action that can be called only in the test in which it resides and can be called only once

⦿ Reusable action – An action that can be called multiple times by the test in which it resides and can also be called by other tests

⦿ External reusable action – A reusable action stored in another test. External actions are read-only in the calling test, but we can choose to use a local, editable copy of the Data Table information for the external action

Inserting Calls to Actions

There are three types of actions calls that can be inserted

⦿ An "Insert Call to New..." will create a new action in the current test

⦿ An "Insert Call to Existing..." allows insertion of a call to a reusable action present in the current test or in another test

⦿ An "Insert Call to Copy..." inserts a copy of the specified action into the current test. If the copied action uses checkpoints and OR objects, these are also copied

Insert Call to New...

Refer to the Figure 5-2.

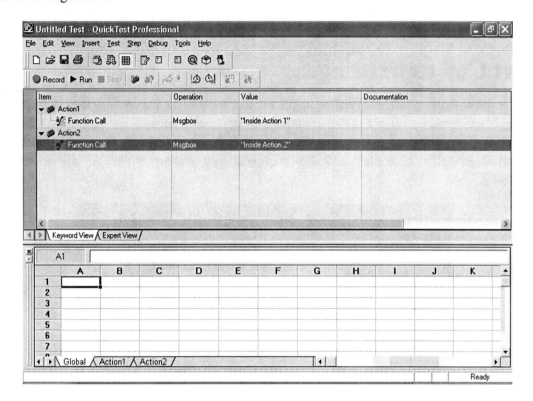

Figure 5-5. Keyword view – Action calls

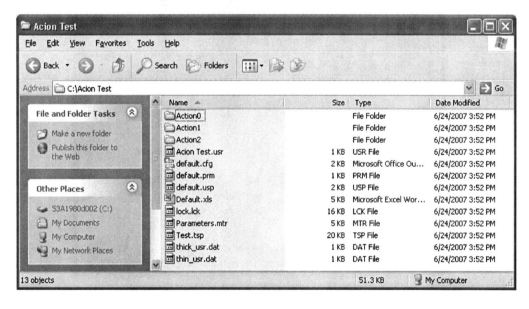

Figure 5-6. Saved Script Folder

```
'Code for TestFlow
RunAction "Action1", oneIteration
RunAction "Action2", oneIteration
```

Before the first action is executed in the test, a code can be executed in two ways

⊙ Add the code to a library file and associate it with the test

⊙ Or else we can open the Script.mts file present in Action0 manually in the notepad and add the code before the first RunAction call

Insert Call to Existing...

To insert a call to existing re-usable action, select a line of code in the expert view then right click and select the *Action→Insert Call to Existing...* from the context menu choices. By default the invoked Select Action dialog shows all the reusable actions present in the current test. To select a shared action from a test not yet called, click the "..." button to browse to another test. Figure 5-7 shows the Select Action dialog.

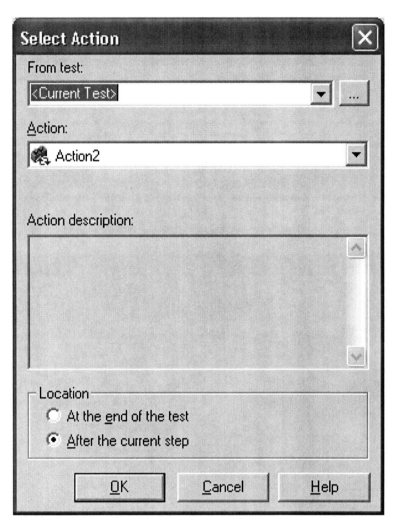

Figure 5-7. Insert Call to existing Action

Using the above dialog selections generates a 'RunAction "Action2", oneIteration' line of code. Note that we can't arbitrarily add this line of code without first following the steps specified above. And deleting the code statement still keeps the action call information in the test. To completely delete all the information associated with the call, the Keyword view should be used.

NOTE: By default selected external actions are inserted using a fully qualified pathname. But we can override this default behavior and use path relative references like "..\CommonActions\Lib1" which searches one level above the including test's directory. If tests might be moved from one location to another, always use relative paths references when inserting actions.

Insert Call to Copy...

To insert a copy of an existing action, select a line of code in the expert view, right click and then select the *Action→Insert Call to Copy...* from the context menu choices. This call works for both reusable and non-reusable action and a new action is created in the current test.

When we insert a call to a copy of an action into a test, the selected action is copied in its entirety, including checkpoints, parameters, the corresponding action tab in the Data Table, plus any defined action parameters. If the test we are copying from uses per-action object repository mode, the copied action's object repository is also copied together with the action.

If the test into which we are copying uses a shared object repository, the copied action will then use that shared object repository. Before running the test, confirm that the shared object repository contains all the objects that are referenced in the copied action, and if necessary add any object references needed by the copied action not yet in the test's shared object repository.

The action is inserted into the test as an independent, non-reusable action, even if the original action was reusable. Once the action is copied into our test, we can add to, delete from, or modify the action just as we would with any other non-reusable action. Any changes that we make to this action after we insert it affects only this action, and changes we make to the original action do not affect the copied action.

Reader's Note

Chapter 6

QTP Environment Variables

QTP environment variables are special types of variables whose values persist across and are shared by all actions in a test. These values persist for the life of the test's runtime execution. QTP environment variables can be used to share information across actions, recovery scenarios and libraries. These environment variables are different from Windows environment variable. Windows environment variable are available to all the programs running on the machine while QTP environment variables are only available to a test script running at run-time.

Types of Environment variables

There are three types of Environment variables in QTP:

- **Built-in** – QTP provides a variety of environment variables that define information such as the currently executing test's name, the test's path, the operating system type and its version, and the local host name. We can check the available built-in environment variables by going to *Test→Settings...→Environment (Tab)* as shown in the Figure 6-1

- **User defined Internal** – These variables are defined in a test and saved with the test. These variables can be modified during run-time

- **User-defined external** – These variables are defined in an external environment file. These variables are read-only and cannot be modified at run-time. The external file can be associated with the test and can also be loaded at run-time using the LoadFromFile method discussed later in the chapter

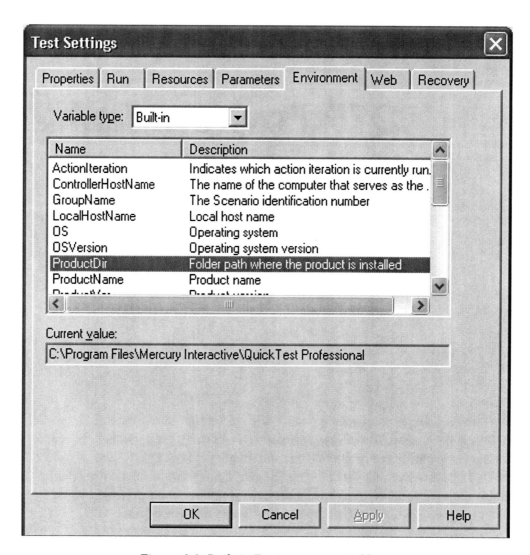

Figure 6-1. Built-in Environment variables

Environment Object

The Environment object provides access to the values of environment variable. Its methods and properties are given below.

- **ExternalFileName Property** - Returns the name of the loaded external environment variable file specified in the Environment tab of the Test Settings dialog box. If no external environment variable file is loaded, this property returns an empty string

- **LoadFromFile Method** - Loads the specified environment variable file

- **Value Property** - Sets or retrieves the value of environment variables. We can retrieve the value of any environment variable. We can only set the value of user-defined internal environment variables using this property

Problem 6-1. How to access an environment variable?

```
'Get the value to Environment variable TestName
sTestName = Environment.Value ("TestName")

'Since .Value is the default property of the Environment
'object, we can also use shorthand as follows:
sTestName = Environment ("TestName")
```

Problem 6-2. How can we check if an environment variable exists?

QTP throws an error if we try to access an environment variable that does not exist. . Therefore we use the following code to check if the error exists without throwing a QTP exception:

```
'Function to check if an environment variable exist
Public Function IsEnvExist(ByVal varName)
    IsEnvExist = True

    'In case of error resume execution of next statement
    On Error Resume Next

    Dim envVal
    envVal = Environment(varName)

    'Check if any error occured
    If err.number<>0 Then
        'If error occured assume the variable does not exist
        IsEnvExist = False
    End If

    'Enable the error popups
    On Error Goto 0
End Function
```

The code shown below demonstrates the usage of the IsEnvExist method.

```
'Check if "Invalid" environment variable exist
MsgBox IsEnvExist("Invalid")
```

Problem 6-3. How is an environment variable defined at run time?

The act of assigning a value to a non-existent environment variable causes QTP to implicitly create and initialize the variable. So building on the previous example:

```
'Check if "Invalid" variable exists in QTP environment
MsgBox IsEnvExist("Invalid") 'this returns False

'Create and set the environment variable ar run-time
Environment("Invalid") = "Not invalid any more"

'Check if "Invalid" variable exists in QTP environment
MsgBox IsEnvExist("Invalid") 'this now returns True
```

Problem 6-4. How can environment variables be exported to an XML file?

There are two ways to do this. First method is to write text strings to generate XML statements and second is to use the XMLUtil object to create XML objects and then export their statements. In the next example, we use a simpler method by writing strings. Working with the XMLUtil object will be covered in a later chapter.

Here is the XML code we want to create:

```
<Environment>
      <Variable>
            <Name>FirstName</Name>
            <Value>Tarun</Value>
      </Variable>
      <Variable>
            <Name>LastName</Name>
            <Value>Lalwani</Value>
      </Variable>
</Environment>
```

And here are the QTP statements to generate that XML code in an external file:

```
'Function to get XML tags for a variable with name and value
Public Function GetVarXML(varName,varValue)
   GetVarXML ="<Variable>" & vbCrLf & _
                          "<Name>" & varName & "</Name>" & vbCrLf & _
                          "<Value>" & varValue & "</Value>" & vbCrLf & _
              "</Variable>" & vbCrLf
End Function

'Function to write the file to a string
Public Sub WriteStringToFile(fileName, varXML)
   Dim fso, file
   Set fso = CreateObject ("Scripting.FileSystemObject")

   'Create the file
   Set file = fso.CreateTextFile (fileName,True)

   'write the text
   file.WriteLine(varXML)
   file.close

   Set file = nothing
   Set fso = nothing
End Sub
```

```
Dim strXML

'Create the envriontment XML start
strXML = "<Environment>"

'nodes for variables
strXML = strXML & GetVarXML("FirstName","Tarun")
strXML = strXML & GetVarXML("LastName","Lalwani")

'Create the envriontment XML end
strXML = strXML & "</Environment>" & vbCrLf

'Create the XML file from the string
WriteStringToFile "C:\Testing.xml",strXML

'Load the XML to test it
Environment.LoadFromFile "C:\Testing.xml"

'Read the variables
Msgbox Environment("LastName") & ", " & Environment("FirstName")
```

 NOTE: The environment variable names are case sensitive, so FirstName and Firstname are treated as different variables

Problem 6-5. How are QTP record and run settings changed using Environment variables?

When we start a web test, environment variables can be used to define the browser type and the URL QTP uses. The environment variables used to control this are BROWSER_ENV and URL_ENV respectively. In QTP 8.2 the possible values for BROWSER_ENV are IE, NS or NS6 and modifying these values in test script code won't work. Rather we need to add these statements to a library file and then associate that library with the test so that the code is executed before the test is invoked.

Add the following two lines of code to a text file and save it as "c:\LaunchURL.vbs"

```
'Change the browser to launch as IE
Environment("BROWSER_ENV") = "IE"

'Change the URL to be navigated
Environment("URL_ENV") = "http://www.mywebsite.com"
```

Now associate the LaunchURL.vbs file by browsing to *Test→Settings…→Resources (Tab)* as shown in the Figure 6-2

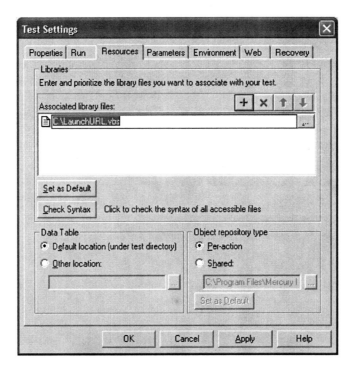

Figure 6-2. Associated library file

Now set the Record and Run setting to launch a new browser with the mercury website as shown in the Figure 6-3

Figure 6-3. Record and Run settings

When we execute this script we will notice that the browser will open and navigate to http://www.google.com instead of http://newtours.mercuryinteractive.com.

NOTE: In case the option "Record and run test on any open Web browser" is selected then these changes would not make any difference, they won't make QTP launch a browser and navigate to the desired URL. So proper test settings are necessary for the code to work as described.

Problem 6-6. How is an environment variable cleared or destroyed?

QTP does not provide any method to delete an environment variable, but we can always put nothing or Empty into it to differentiate it with having or not having a value

```
'Delcare the firstname
Environment("FirstName") = "Tarun"

'Check if FirstName exists
'Displayes True
MsgBox IsEnvExist("FirstName")

'Change it to nothing
Environment("FirstName") = Nothing

'Check if the first name exist
'Displays False
MsgBox IsEnvExist("FirstName")
```

NOTE: The error generated when the variable does not exist and when the value is set to Nothing is different but since we are only checking if any error occurred while accessing the environment variable in the function IsEnvExist this method will work fine.

Problem 6-7. How an object is passed using an environment variable?

If we try to use the Set operator to assign an object to the Environment variable a 'Type mismatch' exception is raised. There are two ways to deal with this. One is to use a string definition of the object and then convert it to an object and another is to simply assign the object to the variable without using the Set operator.

Method 1

```
'String form of the object we need
Environment("BrowserObj") = "Browser(""creationtime:=0"")"

Dim objBrowser

'Execute the code Set objBrowser=Browser("Browser")
Execute "set objBrowser = " & Environment("BrowserObj")

objBrowser.close
```

Method 2

```
'String form of the object we need
Environment("BrowserObj") = Browser("creationtime:=0")

Dim objBrowser

Set objBrowser = Environment("BrowserObj")

objBrowser.close
```

> **WARNING:** In case the "Browser" is a part of the Action1 OR then using the code given above in Action2 may not work as the OR for two actions are different. So the code must always be executed within the scope of the Action.

Problem 6-8. How an array is passed using Environment variables?

QTP throws a "This array is fixed or temporarily locked" exception, if we try to pass a fixed length array using an environment variable. To pass a fixed length array we need to first assign it a variable and then assign it back to the environment variable:

```
'Create a fixed array
Dim fixedArr(3)

For i = LBound(fixedArr,1) to UBound(fixedArr,1)
   fixedArr(i) = Cstr(i)
Next

Dim dynArr

'Assign it to another variable to make it dynamic
dynArr = fixedArr

'Assign the dynamic array to the environment variable
Environment.Value("PassArray") = dynArr

MsgBox Environment.Value("PassArray")(2)

'Get the array from the environment variable
retArr = Environment.Value("PassArray")
Msgbox retArr(1)
```

Problem 6-9. How are environment variables loaded from an external XML file?

```
'Variables in Env_Dev.xml are now available
Environment.LoadFromFile "C:\Env_Dev.xml"

'Variables in Env_Test.xml are now available.
Environment.LoadFromFile "C:\Env_Test.xml"

'Variables in Env_Dev.xml no longer available.
```

The above example highlights the limitation of loading multiple environment files, as the earlier XML variables are destroyed. There will be a workaround to the issue presented in "Working with XMLs" in a later chapter.

Reader's Note

Reader's Note

Chapter 7

Utility Objects

QTP provides several utility objects to enhance the power of scripting. Below is a list of all QTP utility objects:

Crypt, DataTable, Description, DTParameter, DTSheet, Environment, Extern, OptionalStep, Parameter, PathFinder, Properties (Collection), QCUtil, RandomNumber, Recovery, Reporter, Services, Setting, TextUtil, TSLTest, XMLUtil

The remainder of this chapter only discusses those objects not covered in the other chapters of this book.

The Crypt Object

This object encrypts strings in a format that the QTP SetSecure function understands. Encrypt is the only method provided by this object:

```
'Encrypt the string
myVar = Crypt.Encrypt ("Tarun Lalwani")
```

The above statement will assign myVar a value which looks something like:

"45249373c5a4ec489211eda2314133751e8a5cbd529ac9060aee041a38f75636".

This value produced by Crypt.Encrypt is not constant because encrypting the same string again generates a different encrypted string. Now the question arises that when should this capability be used? Consider a script which is executed on a tester's PC with the results sent to others. If the script has a step to enter a password:

```
'Set the text in the WebEdit
Browser("Browser").Page("Page").WebEdit("password").Set "tarun"
```

Then this step will appear in the test result summary and will include the "tarun" value. This could compromise security, so let's replace the above statement with a new one:

```
'Encrypt and then set the password
sEncryptePassword = Crypt.Encrypt("tarun")
Browser("Browser").Page("Page").WebEdit("password").SetSecure sEncryptePassword
```

Now the password won't appear in the test results summary as we are using the secure mode of setting a password.

 NOTE: We can also create an instance of the Crypt object in VBScript using the following code statement: Set myCrypt = CreateObject("Mercury.Encrypter")

The OptionalStep Object

This object is used to make a statement optional in situations where the statement might fail. Consider the following statement:

```
'Click Yes on the security warning dialog box
Browser("Browser").Dailog("Security Warning").WinButton("Yes").Click
```

This statement could have been recorded with a browser where security warnings were enabled, but then run on another PC who's browser does not have those warnings enabled—in that scenario the statement will fail. So when a statement depends on the system state, it should be made optional using the OptionalStep object:

```
'Click Yes on the security warning dialog box.
'In case the step fails proceed to next step without
'failing the status in test result summary
OptionalStep.Browser("Browser").Dailog("Security Warning").WinButton("Yes").
Click
```

The PathFinder Object

This object can be used to find the absolute path to a file. QTP allows setting folder paths in the *Tools→Options→Folders (Tab)* as shown in the Figure 7-1 and in situations where we want to determine which particular folder a file resides in we can use PathFinder.Locate method. Consider the following example:

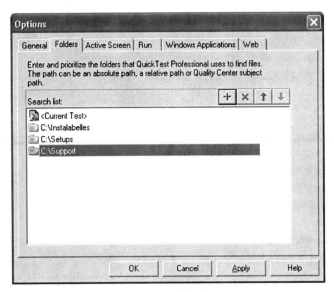

Figure 7-1. Folder Settings

Let's say we want to find the key.txt file located in the "C:\Setups" folder.

```
'This will assign "C:\Setups\key.txt" to x
x = PathFinder.Locate("key.txt")
```

Even if "C:\Support" folder also has a "key.txt" file the Locate method will still return "C:\Setups\key.txt" as the "C:\Setups" folder has a higher priority than the "C:\Support" folder.

The RandomNumber Object

This object provides a method to get a random number between two specified values

```
'This will randomly assign a number to x between 1-200
x = RandomNumber.value(1,200)
```

Since value is the default property for RandomNumber object, we can also use the following syntax:

```
'This will randomly assign a number to x between 1-200
x = RandomNumber (1,200)
```

The Setting Object

This object provides the following properties and methods to modify test properties at run-time:

- Add Method

- Exists Method

- Remove Method

- Item Property

The Add Method

This method is used to add user-defined settings to the object:

```
'Add the setting to QTP
```

```
Setting.Add "LogErrors","Yes"
Msgbox Setting.Item("LogErrors") 'Will return "Yes"
'Since Item is the default property for
'Setting object we can also use the following syntax:
Msgbox Setting ("LogErrors") 'Will return "Yes"
```

The Exists Method

This method is used to check if a setting is currently defined:

```
'Check if LogErrors setting exists or not
If Setting.Exists("LogErros") then
  MsgBox Setting ("LogErrors") 'Will return "Yes"
Else
  Setting.Add "LogErrors","Yes"
  Msgbox Setting ("LogErrors") 'Will return "Yes"
End If
```

The Remove Method

This method is used to remove any user-defined settings from the object:

```
'Will return False
MsgBox Setting.Exists ("LogErrors")
Setting.Add "LogErrors","Yes"

'Will return True
MsgBox Setting.Exists ("LogErrors")

Setting.Remove "LogErrors","Yes"

'Will return False
Msgbox Setting.Exists ("LogErrors")
```

 NOTE: We will see how useful the Setting object is in the "Advanced QTP" chapter

QTP also provides the following built-in Setting object values:

- AutomaticLinkRun
- DefaultLoadTime
- DefaultTimeOut
- ReplayType
- SnapshotReportMode
- WebTimeOut

Refer to QTP online help for more details on these setting values.

The WebUtil Object

This object provides an undocumented method to delete browser cookies:

```
'Delete cookies
WebUtil.DeleteCookies
```

 NOTE: The WebUtil object is implicitly available after installing QTP Plus, and it can be explicitly instantiated using the following statement:

```
'Create the WebUtil object
Set oWebUtil = CreateObject("Mercury.GUI_WebUtil")

'Delete cookies and destory the object
oWebUtil.DeleteCookies
Set oWebUtil = Nothing
```

The SystemUtil Object

This object is used to run and close processes. Below are few examples of starting processes:

```
'Run internet explorer
SystemUtil.Run "iexplore.exe"

'Run internet explorer and pass the starting URL
SystemUtil.Run "iexplore.exe", "http://www.yahoo.com"
```

Below are few examples of closing a process:

```
'Examples of closing a process
'Give # of closed processes
numClosed = SystemUtil.CloseProcessByName ("iexplore.exe")

'Title with a regular expression
SystemUtil.CloseProcessByWndTitle "Microsoft Internet Explorer.*", True

'Title without a regular expression
SystemUtil.CloseProcessByWndTitle "Notepad"


'Closing a process by window handle
hWnd = Browser("creationtime:=0").GetROProperty("hwnd")
SystemUtil.CloseProcessByHwnd hwnd

'Close process by the process id
SystemUtil.CloseProcessById processID

'Close all processes opened by QTP
SystemUtil.CloseDescendentProcesses
```

The RegisterUserFunc Object

This object is used to add new methods to a test object or to override existing ones. The syntax is:

```
RegisterUserFunc TOClass, MethodName, FunctionName, SetAsDefault
```

If we want to override the Set Function for the WebEdit test object then we need to create a new function and then assign it using the RegisterUserFunc object as follows:

```
'New set method for WebEdit objects
Sub NewSet(Object, newValue)
   Object.Set Ucase(newValue)
End Sub

RegisterUserFunc "WebEdit", "Set", "NewSet"

Browser("...").Page("...").WebEdit("...").Set "tarun"
```

The last statement in the above example now calls our NewSet function and changes the input value to upper case and then sets the value.

If we want to use the NewSet function to handle different types of test objects, then we can use GetTOProperty function to determine which type of object has been passed to the function

If we want to define a new Set method for all objects like "WebEdit", "WebCheckBox", "WebList", "WebRadioButton" etc, then we can create a function like one shown below

```
'Generic set method for various objects
Sub GenericSet(Object, newValue)
  'Get the type of the object
  sObjectType = Object.GetTOProperty("micclass")

  Select Case sObjectType
    Case "WebEdit", "WebCheckBox"
      WebSet Object, newValue
    Case "WebList", "WebRadioButton"
      WebSelect Object,newValue
  End Select
End Sub
```

WebSet and WebSelect functions used in the code given above are user defined functions that are being used to do operation on specific types of object.

Reader's Note

Reader's Note

Chapter 8

Checkpoints

A checkpoint is used to verify a runtime value against an expected value predefined in a Test. Checkpoints allow setting Pass/Fail status in the Test Results File.

Types of checkpoints

QTP provides the following types of checkpoints:

- **Standard checkpoints:** Standard checkpoints are used to verify a set of properties for standard objects. This checkpoint can be used on objects like Buttons, Images, Radio buttons etc.

- **Image checkpoint:** It compares the various property values of an Image like source file location, width, height etc.

- **Bitmap checkpoint:** This checkpoint compares an on screen bitmap image and compares it pixel by pixel against a **previously** recorded bitmap

- **Table checkpoint:** Validates data presented in a screen table against the predefined values

- **Text checkpoint:** Validates that a text string is presented at an expected place in the application

- **Textarea checkpoint:** Validates that a text string is displayed in an expected area in the application

- **Accessibility checkpoint:** Checks for the areas in a web application that do not comply with W3C accessibility standards

- **Page checkpoint:** Validates properties on a web page like number of links, page load time, etc

- **Database checkpoint:** Validates the contents of a database entry specified in the checkpoint

- **XML Checkpoint:** Validates the content of an XML document or a Web XML document

> **NOTE:** XML and Database checkpoints can be added in recording/design mode. All other checkpoints can be added in recording mode or through active screen objects.

Refer to the QTP user's manual for the steps needed to insert checkpoints into a test case.

Problem 8-1. How can we check if a checkpoint passed or failed?

When a checkpoint is executed its result are placed in the Test Results File. A checkpoint statement looks like below:

```
'Execute the checkpoint
Browser("").Page("").Link("test").Check CheckPoint("TestLink")
```

Here "TestLink" is the name of the checkpoint and "test" is the object on which the checkpoint is being executed. We can check the status of a checkpoint by evaluating the return value of a Checkpoint call:

```
'Save the retrurn value of the checkpoint call
cpStatus = Browser("").Page("").Link("test").Check (CheckPoint("TestLink"))

If cpStatus Then
    MsgBox "Checkpoint Passed"
Else
    MsgBox "Checkpoint Failed"
End if
```

In cases where we don't want the status of checkpoint reported in the Test Results File, we use the Filter property of the Reporter object as follows:

```
'Disable all events reporting
Reporter.Filter = rfDisableAll

'Get the status of the checkpoint
cpStatus = Browser("").Page("").Link("test").Check (CheckPoint("TestLink"))

'Enable all reporting
Reporter.Filter = rfEnableAll
```

Problems with QTP built-in checkpoints

It's important to understand some of the problems that are encountered while using QTP checkpoints:

⦿ Checkpoints are not very flexible. For example, QTP does not allow the expected value of a checkpoint to be changed through the code—but we can achieve this by using DataTable variables or Environment variables to specify the checkpoint's expected values

⦿ Checkpoints can't be created at run-time

⦿ Checkpoints can't be renamed in QTP 8.x

⊙ Checkpoints can't be deleted in QTP 8.x

⊙ Checkpoints are stored using a proprietary binary format in the Object Repository—and they are not visible

⊙ Existing checkpoints can't be copied from one Action to another

QTP checkpoints are most suitable when the application being tested is static in nature like an informational website which contains static content that rarely changes.

Alternatives to QTP checkpoints

Using inline VBScript statements to validate runtime values against expected results generally proves to be a more effective and flexible alternative to using QTP checkpoints. In this section we convert the previous checkpoint into this type of inline code validation:

```
'Get a reference to the object we want to validate
Set objLink = Browser("").Page("").Link("Sign out")

'Read the actual property values we want to validatre from that object
actualHREF = objLink.GetROProperty("href")
actualTEXT = objLink.GetROProperty("text")

'Define the values we expect these properties to contain
expectedHREF = "http://www.mysexpected.com"
expectedTEXT = "Sign out"

'Validate that the rutnime values match the expected values
If actualHREF = expectedHREF AND actualTEXT = expectedHREF then
    Reporter.ReportEvent micPass, "Sign out checkpoint", "Checkpoint passed"
Else
    strReport = " href - Actual:" & actualHREF & ", Expected: " & expectedHREF & vbCrLf
    strReport = strReport & " text - Actual:" & actualTEXT & ", Expected: " & expectedTEXT
    Reporter.ReportEvent micFail, "Sign out checkpoint", strReport
End if
```

We can simulate any QTP checkpoint using this technique, except a bitmap checkpoint.

NOTE: Equivalent Database checkpoints can be simulated using ADODB. We will find more information about ADODB in the "Working with Databases" chapter. XML checkpoints can be simulated using the XMLUtil object. We will find more information about using the XMLUtil object in the "Working with XMLs" chapter.

Updating Checkpoints at run-time

QTP does not allow modifying checkpoint properties at run-time though it is possible to configure a checkpoint to use a DataTable value or an Environment variable. Also there are some properties that we can modify using the code also. Usually a checkpoint statement would look like this

```
'Check the checkpoint
Browser("Google").Page("Google").Check CheckPoint("the web")
```

Here CheckPoint("the web") is an object which contains all information about that checkpoint. There are two hidden functions that the CheckPoint object supports and those are SetProperty and GetProperty. Let's see what properties we can use with these functions.

Table 8-1. Checkpoint property description

Checkpoint	Property	Description
Standard	micclass	Mercury internal class for checkpoint This will have a value "VerifyObj" for a standard checkpoint
	step_type	Type of checkpointThis will have a value "Checkpoint" for a standard checkpoint
	step_timeout	The timeout value In case the checkpoint is failing
Text	micclass	Mercury internal class for checkpoint This will have a value "TextVerObj" for a standard checkpoint
	step_type	Type of checkpoint This will have a value "Text Checkpoint" for a standard checkpoint
	step_timeout	The timeout value In case the checkpoint is failing
	Text	The text to be searched between "Text Before" and "Text After"
	Text Before	The text to be searched between "Text Before" and "Text After"
	Text Before	The text before the search text
	Indexoftextbefore	Number of occurrences of text before
	Text After	The text after the search text
	Newindexoftextafter	Number of occurrences of text after
	text not found	Text not found checkbox

NOTE: micclass, step_type, step_timeout are three common properties that we can get for any checkpoint. Checkpoints other than the above two are complex and cannot be modified at run-time.

An example on how to use these checkpoint properties is given below

```
'Display the new expected value of checkpoint
MsgBox "Expected value of text is: " & Checkpoint ("the web").
GetProperty("Text")

'Change the expected value
Checkpoint ("the web").SetProperty "Text", "New Text value"

'Display the new expected value of checkpoint
MsgBox "Expected value of text is: " & Checkpoint ("the web").
GetProperty("Text")
```

WARNING: It is not recommended to change the checkpoint properties using the method discussed above as these are undocumented methods and might not work in later version of QTP

Reader's Note

Chapter 9

Library Files

Library files are plain text files, containing VBScript code. They are used to declare functions, variables, classes etc. Library files can be stored with any extension; the most commonly used extension is VBS or TXT. Library files help organizing the code into distinguishable functionalities. They provide a way to share code between various QTP scripts. There are two ways to load a Library file as discussed in the next two sections.

Associating a Library globally with a Test

By using this method the same instance of the library is shared and accessed by all Actions included in a test. Go to *Test→Settings...→Resources (Tab)* and add the library as shown in Fig 9-1:

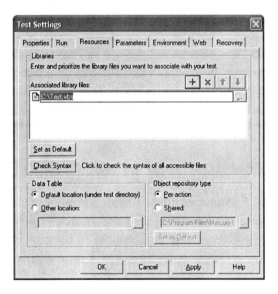

Figure 9-1. Test Resource Settings

NOTE1: These libraries are loaded from the bottom entry to the top entry. In case two different libraries have the same defined function then the one nearer the top in the list will be used.

NOTE2: In the case where Library B depends on definitions in Library A, then Library A needs to be nearer the bottom of the list.

NOTE3: QTP will use the fully qualified pathname while placing the library in the list. As a recommended option we can use a relative path of the file, for example "..\test.vbs".

Dynamically Loading libraries locally at run-time

QTP provides the ExecuteFile function to dynamically load a library at run-time. When this method is used the library and its contents are only visible in the Action in which the ExecuteFile is used. Below are the few examples:

```
'Load a file using absolute path
ExecuteFile "C:\Test.vbs"

'Load a file using relative path
currentTestDir = Environment("TestDir")
vbsFilePath = currentTestDir & "\..\..\CommonLibs\Test.vbs"
ExecuteFile vbsFilePath

'Load a file Library from Quality Center
ExecuteFile "[QC-ATTACH];;Subject\CommonLibs;;\Test.vbs"
```

NOTE: If ActionA and ActionB both load test.vbs using the ExecuteFile command, and ActionA calls ActionB, note that they will both be using their own copy and separate instance of all test.vbs variables and functions.

Dynamically Loading libraries globally at run-time

As just described above, using ExecuteFile directly in an Action only makes that library visible within the Action. But every QTP Script can have a set of global libraries which are available to all test's Actions. So instead of loading a library using the ExecuteFile directly in an Action, if we load it through a function in one of the global libraries, then it will be available to all the test's Actions:

```
'C:\LibLoader.vbs
Public Function ExecuteFileGlobal(ByVal fileName)
    ExecuteFile fileName
End Function
```

We should save the code given above into a VBS file and associate it with the test and thereafter call the ExecuteFileGlobal in any action to load the file. Files loaded using ExecuteFileGlobal function will be available for the all the actions.

```
'Load file in global scope
ExecuteFileGlobal "C:\Test.vbs"
```

But when there are multiple Action iterations the call to ExecuteFileGlobal will reload the library multiple times, thus destroying the current state of the library's global variables each time the library is reloaded.

This issue can be solved by using the following code. We add a reload flag to ExecuteFileGlobal function and when it is False the library will not be reloaded. This is achieved by creating a global dictionary of all loaded files using ExecuteFileGlobal. The file path is used to determine if the library has already been loaded.

```
'C:\LoadLibrary.vbs
Dim loadedFiles
Set loadedFiles = CreateObject("Scripting.Dictionary")
loadedFiles.CompareMode = vbTextCompare

'ExecuteFileGlobal function to load a file at run-time
'Inputs - strFile: The complete filename which needs to be loaded
'          reLoad: Reload the file in case already loaded
Public Function ExecuteFileGlobal (ByVal strFile,ByVal reLoad)
        'If reLoad is False then check if file is already loaded or not
   If reload = False and loadedFiles.Exists(strFile) then
      'If already loaded then exit the loading function
         ExecuteFileGlobal = False
         Exit Function
         End if

   'Load the library
   ExecuteFile strFile
   'Add the file to loaded list
   loadedFiles(strFile) = True
   ExecuteFileGlobal = True
End Function
```

To better understand the above code let's take an example. First create a library file which we will load at run-time

```
'C:\TestA.vbs
Dim X
X = 2
```

The code shown below demonstrates the usage of ExecuteFileGlobal function

```
'Load testa.vbs in global scope
ExecuteFileGlobal "C:\testa.vbs", False
Msgbox X 'displays 2
X = X + 2

'Load testa.vbs in global scope, don't
'reload if already loaded
```

```
ExecuteFileGlobal "C:\testa.vbs", False
Msgbox X 'displays 4

'Load testa.vbs in global scope
ExecuteFileGlobal "C:\testa.vbs", True
Msgbox X 'displays 2
```

Problem 9-1. How are global variables defined at run-time?

Sometimes it's necessary to share values across two or more Actions at run-time. Using the same concept we used for loading the libraries we can create global variables at run-time

Declare.vbs

```
'C:\Declare.vbs
Sub ExecuteGlobalCode (sStatement)
   ExecuteGlobal sStatement
End Sub
```

Action1:

```
'Execute code in global scope
ExecuteGlobalCode "Dim strText"
strText = "Tarun Lalwani"
```

Action2:

```
'Will display "Tarun Lalwani"
MsgBox strText
```

Understanding Execution Scope

It is important to understand and differentiate between Global and Local scope of a test script.

- ⊙ Global Scope is a place where QTP loads all the resource and recovery scenario libraries. This is accessible to all actions present in the test

- ⊙ Local scope is an action scope where anything defined within the Action is not accessible to anything present outside the Action

Figure 9-2 depicts the scope view of a QTP script with 2 actions. This is how the QTP works

- ⊙ When the script is started QTP creates a Global scope

- ⊙ QTP first adds all libraries for associated recovery scenarios. This is done in the order the recovery scenarios are associated from Top to bottom

- ⊙ After loading all associated Recovery scenario's library files, QTP then loads all the files associated in the Test→Settings…→Resources (Tab). These files are loaded from Bottom to the Top

- ⊙ After this QTP calls each action in the order defined in the Test Flow. For each action QTP creates a local scope which is private to that action. The scope gets created and destroyed on each Action's iteration

- ⊙ A function written in Action1 would not be accessible in any other Action or the Global scope

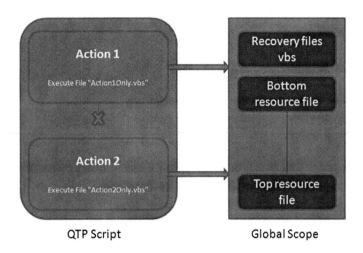

Figure 9-2. QTP Execution Scope: Local and Global scope

 NOTE: If more than one library in the global scope contains a function with same name then the last one loaded would be called

Applicability of Option Explicit

Option Explicit statement at the top of a library file allows a programmer to enforce variable declaration for all used variables. We might observe that even having *Option Explicit* in some of our associated libraries is not enforcing errors for undeclared variables.

This happens because of the way Global scope is created. We cannot enforce Option Explicit on individual libraries in a global scope. It can be done only on the complete global scope. To enforce variable declaration Option Explicit should be put in the top most library of the Global scope. This would be the first associated Recovery VBS file associated with the Test or the bottom most file in the *Test→Settings...→Resource* (Tab) (whichever is applicable).

Executing code in Local scope from within Global Scope

We earlier saw how to load library files in local scope from within the local scope ("Dynamically Loading libraries locally at run-time") and how to load libraries in global scope from within local scope ("Dynamically Loading libraries globally at run-time").

At times, because of script maintenance we might need to add code to the start or the end of the Action. This maintenance might apply to multiple no. of scripts. QTP allows opening single script at a time, which makes editing multiple scripts a time consuming task. To avoid such situations we can call two special functions in our Actions as shown the following code

```
'Evaluate any code that needs to be executed at
'the start of this  Action
Execute GetActionStart()

'Code realted to Action

'Execute any code that needs to be executed at
'the end of this Action
Execute GetActionEnd()
```

GetActionStart and GetActionEnd function return either a blank string or some code that needs to be executed. Below is the implementation of the above two functions

```
'Function to be called at start of each action
'this function will allow dynamic execution of
'code in local scope of the action. function should
'be called in the below format at the start of action
'Execute GetActionStart()
Function GetActionStart()
    'By default no code to be executed
    GetActionStart = ""

    'Get the name of the Action which called this function
    sAction = LCase(Environment("ActionName"))

    If InStr(sAction,"main") Then
            GetActionStart = "ExecuteFile PathFinder.Locate(""Workaround.vbs"")"
    End If
End Function


'Function to be called at end of each action
'this function will allow dynamic execution of
'code in local scope of the action. Function should
'be called in the below format at the start of action
'Execute GetActionEnd()
Function GetActionEnd()
    'By default no code to be executed
    GetActionEnd = ""

    'Get the name of the action which call the script
    sAction = Environment("ActionName")
End Function
```

Reader's Note

Reader's Note

Chapter 10

Descriptive Programming (DP)

Descriptive programming provides a means to perform interactions with runtime objects which are not in the Object Repository. This technique also proves useful while developing test cases for applications which are not yet available for recording.

Object Identification

To identify an object during test script play back QTP stores one or more properties for that object in the Object Repository, which QTP then uses to uniquely identify the object at runtime. Figure 10-1 shows a simple Object Repository that contains descriptions for a web page and three of its control objects.

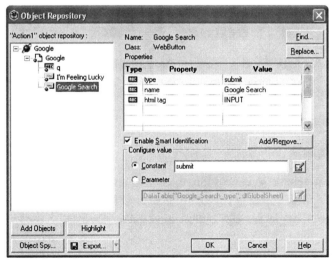

Figure 10-1. Object Repository

The "Google Search" object in the OR has 3 recorded properties: "type", "name", "html tag". Note that QTP recorded 3 properties, i.e. the mandatory properties defined for this test object, but not all of them may be needed to recognize the object at runtime.

Implicit Properties

When we define an object description using DP there are certain properties that we don't need to explicitly provide as QTP automatically assumes certain values based on the test object type being referenced. For example, the "Google Search" above is a WebButton, and as such QTP assumes that the "html tag" will be the INPUT and the "type" will be submitted. But in a situation where we reference a generic WebElement, it is necessary to explicitly define every property of importance

When to use Descriptive Programming

Below are some of the examples when Descriptive Programming is considered a good alternative to using a traditional Object Repository to define a test object:

- ⊙ When the objects in the application are dynamic in nature and need special handling to identify them at runtime. The best example would be of clicking a link which changes according to the user of the application, Ex. "Logout <<Username>>"

- ⊙ When the Object Repository is getting very large. If the size of Object repository increases too much then it decreases the performance of QTP during runtime playback

- ⊙ When we don't want to use an Object Repository at all. The following scenarios provide some rationale for why we might not use an Object Repository

- ⊙ When modification to an OR object is required but the Object Repository in which the object resides is either Read Only or it is located in a shared OR and the changes may affect other scripts outside of our control

- ⊙ When we want to take action on large number of similar/uniform objects, for example we have 20 textboxes on a page and their names are in the form of txt_1, txt_2, through txt_20. In this situation adding 20 entries to the Object Repository would not be a good programming approach, but using dynamically defined DP statements would be

Descriptive Programming Syntax

There are two ways to create descriptive programming statements:

- ⊙ Using description objects

- ⊙ Using description strings

Using description objects

By using this approach we create a description object and define the properties and values for identification. The description object is very similar to creating and initializing a Dictionary object. Using this technique the "Google Search" button can be described as:

```
'Create a description object
Dim btnGoogleSearch
Set btnGoogleSearch = Description.Create
```

```
'Add description identifiers
btnGoogleSearch("type").value = "submit"
btnGoogleSearch("type").RegularExpression = False
btnGoogleSearch("name").value = "Google Search"
btnGoogleSearch("html tag").value = "INPUT"
```

Descrition.Create creates a new object to store one DP description. Each description object property supports both a Value assignment and a RegularExpression flag. By default the regular expression flag is True indicating that its Value assignment string is interpreted using VBScript's Regular Expression syntax. To click the "Google Search" button using this DP syntax technique the codewill be:

```
'Click on the Button using description object btnGoogleSearch
Browser("Browser").Page("Page").WebButton(btnGoogleSearch).Click
```

NOTE: Once we start using any Descriptive Programming syntax in a statement, then the rest of the statement must continue to use DP syntax. The above code statement starts with OR references through the page reference, but at the WebButton reference we start using DP syntax.

In the code given above we saw that it took several lines of code to define the "Google Search" button using a DP description object. Now we provide a subroutine that does most of the assignment work for us:

```
'Function to convert a string or array to a description object
Sub CreateDescription(ByVal dpObjName, ByVal dpObjStringOrArray)
    'This will carry all the properties
    Dim propArray
    'This will carry the property name and it's corresponding value
    Dim valArray

    If VarType(dpObjStringOrArray)< vbArray Then
        'Convert the string into Array for creating the description
        propArray = Split(dpObjStringOrArray,",")
    Else
        'It's already an array
        propArray = dpObjStringOrArray
    End If

    'Create the description object
    ExecuteGlobal "Set " & dpObjName & " = Description.Create"

    Dim i
    For i = LBound(propArray) to UBound(propArray)
        'Split the propery and value from property:=value
        valArray = Split(propArray(i),":=")
        Execute dpObjName &"(""" & valArray(0) & """).Value = " & valArray(1)
    Next
End Sub
```

The above can be used in following way

```
'Usage
descArray = Array("html tag:=INPUT", "Name:=Submit")
descStr1 = "Name:=Submit"
descStr2 = "Name:=Submit, html tag:=INPUT"

CreateDescription "dpSubmit1", descArray
CreateDescription "dpSubmit2", descStr1
CreateDescription "dpSubmit3", descStr2
```

The micclass Identifier

The micclass is an identifier that describes the type of QTP Test Object. For example the "micclass:=WebButton" is an implicit property of the WebButton object. When there is only a single button on a page we don't need to use any property description other than "micclass:=WebButton". We can use GetTOProperty with the micclass on any QTP test objects to determine its test object type:

```
'Displays Browser
MsgBox Browser("Browser").GetTOProperty("micclass")

'Displays Page
MsgBox Browser("Browser").Page("Page").GetTOProperty("micclass")
```

NOTE: "Class Name" is not a property for the type of test object as QTP object spy shows it. micclass is mapped to the class name in object spy.

Using Description Strings

In this method of descriptive programming we don't need to create a description object, instead we use a description string to recognize the "Google Search" button in Figure 10-1. We use the following three description strings in the second line of code:

```
'Get the page obect reference
Set oPg = Browser("Google").Page("Google")

'Get the button object using string description
Set oButton = oPg.WebButton("html tag:=INPUT", "type:=submit", "name:=Google
Search")
```

But as we said earlier it is not necessary to define all the properties in order to identify the object:

```
'Get the button using a single property
Set oButton = oPg.WebButton("name:=Google Search")
```

Enumerating ChildObjects

QTP provides the ChildObjects method which is used to enumerate child objects. To enumerate all the textboxes on a page we can use the following code:

```
'Create a description object
Set dpAllTxt = Description.Create

'Set the description for WebEdit only
```

```
dpAllTxt("micclass").value = "WebEdit"

'Get all the objects macthing the description
Set allTextboxes = Browser("Google").Page("Google").ChildObjects(dpAllTxt)

'Loop through all of them
iCount = allTextboxes.Count - 1
For i = 0 to iCount
   Set oTxt = allTextboxes.item(i)

   oTxt.Set "This is Text box #" & (i+1)
Next
```

ChildObjects enumerates all the child objects when we pass it an empty description object:

```
'Create a description object
Set dpAllChilds = Description.Create

'Get all the objects on the page as a blank description is used
Set allChilds = Browser("Google").Page("Google").ChildObjects(dpAllChilds)

iCount = allChilds.Count - 1

'Loop through all the objects on the page
For i = 0 To iCount
   MsgBox allChilds.item(i).GetTOProperty("micclass")
Next
```

Converting an OR-based script to a DP-based script

Converting an OR-based script to a DP-based script demands the careful selection of each OR object's properties required for each DP statement to uniquely identify the intended runtime object. Consider the OR-based statements below, recorded when interacting with the Windows calculator to multiply 2 times 5:

```
'Launch the calculator application
SystemUtil.Run "calc.exe"

'Activate the window
Window("Calculator").Activate

'Perform various operations
Window("Calculator").WinButton("2").Click
Window("Calculator").WinButton("*").Click
Window("Calculator").WinButton("5").Click
Window("Calculator").WinButton("=").Click

'Check the results
Window("Calculator").WinEdit("Edit").Check CheckPoint("Edit")
```

The OR for the above script is shown in the Figure 10-2

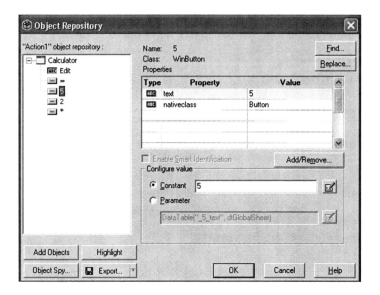

Figure 10-2. Calculator Object Repository

Inspecting the OR we notice the objects are recognized based on their text labels. The DP-based converted script will then use the following statements:

```
'Run the calculator application
SystemUtil.Run "calc.exe"

With Window("regexpwndtitle:=Calculator")
  'Activate the window
  .Activate

  'Perform various operations
  .WinButton("text:=2", "nativeclass:=Button").Click
  '* is regular expression and we should use a \ before that
  .WinButton("text:=\*","nativeclass:=Button").Click
  .WinButton("text:=5","nativeclass:=Button").Click
  .WinButton("text:==","nativeclass:=Button").Click

  'Check the results. We cannot create checkpoint object using
  'DP but we can run a already created checkpoint on a object
  'identified using DP
  .WinEdit("nativeclass:=Edit").Check CheckPoint("Edit")
  .Close
End With
```

 NOTE: We have used the regexpwndtitle:=Calculator to recognize the calculator window. We could have also use regexpwndclass:= SciCalc which looks unique to the calculator application. In case the application window title keeps changing it is always a better option to choose just the window class or some other property.

It's important to select the correct property (or properties) to identify an object in DP. Selecting properties like x, y, abs_x, etc., is never a good choice as they are subject to change with each run of the AUT. Properties like title, regexpwndtitle etc. are in most cases much more reliable.

Using a VBScript DP object repository

Placing our DP object definitions in a VBScript library file logically emulates a QTP Object Repository:

UserForm.vbs

```
'Delcare DP string definitions
Const dpBrowser = "micClass:=Browser"
Const dpPage = "micClass:=Page"
Const dpFirstName = "name:=txtFirstName"
Const dpLastName = "name:=txtLastName"
Const dpSubmit = "name:=Submit"
```

There are two ways to include the above file in one or more scripts:

⊙ Associate the VBS file on the Test Settings Resource tab

⊙ Use the ExecuteFile statement to load the file into one or more test Actions

Script

```
'Run the internet explorer application
SystemUtil.Run "iexplore.exe"

Browser(dpBrowser).Sync

'Enter data
Browser(dpBrowser).Page(dpPage).WebEdit(dpFirstName).Set "Tarun"
Browser(dpBrowser).Page(dpPage).WebEdit(dpLastName).Set "Lalwani"

'Click on the submit button
Browser(dpBrowser).Page(dpPage).WebButton(dpSubmit).Click
```

This technique can also be used to implement a multi-language testing script. To do this create different VBS files for each language, for example, dpOR_EN.vbs, dpOR_FR.vbs, dpOR_DN.vbs etc. and then use the following code to select the proper file, based on the language specified:

```
'Set the environment variable. This should be loaded
'through a external file
Environment.Value("LanguageToTest") = "FR"

'Check for which environment to execute in
Select Case Environment.Value("LanguageToTest")
  Case "EN"
        ExecuteFile "dpOR_EN.vbs"
  Case "FR"
        ExecuteFile "dpOR_FR.vbs"
  Case "DN"
        ExecuteFile "dpOR_DN.vbs"
End Select
```

```
'...
'The rest of the script goes here
'...
```

Problems with Ordinal Identifiers

QTP only uses ordinal identifiers when there are multiple object matches for a given description.

```
'Check if a second browser exist
MsgBox Browser("micclass:=Browser","index:=1").Exist(0)
```

The above code statement will tell whether there is a 2nd browser instance open or not. But that is not always the case because QTP will first see the above statement as:

```
'Check if a browser exist
MsgBox Browser("micclass:=Browser").Exist(0)
```

In situations where QTP is able to resolve the object based on just the above description then it will return the True/False value. But in situations where there are multiple browsers that exist then QTP must use the ordinal identifier index or CreationTime property to uniquely identify each instance. For example, the following code:

```
'Check for existence of various browser
bBrowser1 = Browser("CreationTime:=0").Exist(0)

bBrowser2 = Browser("CreationTime:=1").Exist(0)

bBrowser3 = Browser("CreationTime:=2").Exist(0)
```

Return values from the of the above code statements are shown in the Table 10-1

Table 10-1. CreationTime Exist values

No. of Open Browser	Variable Value		
	bBrowser1	bBrowser2	bBrowser3
0	False	False	False
1	True	True	True
2	True	True	False

These results make it clear that in case of 0 or 1 open browser, the CreationTime property was never used for identification. This creates a problem if we need to determine if a 2nd browser exists or not, because we can't use the code below to make this determination:

```
'Check if second browser exists
Browser("CreationTime:=1").Exist(0)
```

Therefore we can use the following code to reliably test for a 2nd browser. This code uses window handles, which are always unique for each browser. By comparing the handles returned by both CreationTime:=0 and CreationTime:=1 statement we will know that a 2nd browser exists if and only if the handles differ:

```
'Check if browser with creation time 0 exists
If Browser("CreationTime:=0").Exist(0) Then
    'There might be a possibility that one one browser exists
    'To make sure we can check the handle of 1st and 2nd browser
    hwnd1 = Browser("CreationTime:=0").GetROProperty("hwnd")
    hwnd2 = Browser("CreationTime:=1").GetROProperty("hwnd")

    'Check if the handles are equal
    If hwnd1 <> hwnd2 then
        MsgBox "The 2nd Browser exists"
    Else
        MsgBox "The 2nd Browser does not exist"
    End if
Else
    Msgbox "No browser exists"
End if
```

And, because there can't be a browser with CreationTime:=-1, the following statement will return a False value when there is 0 or more than 1 browsers open:

```
'Check for non existent browser
bNonBrowser = Browser("CreationTime:=-1").Exist(0)
```

So here is the complete code to reliably determine if 0, 1 or multiple browsers are open:

```
'Check if non existent browser exists. this trick
'helps us determine if the ordinal identifier was
'used during recogniztion of the object. If the
'return value is True then we are sure that the
'property was not used
bNonBrowser = Browser("CreationTime:=-1").Exist(0)

'Check for the 1st browser
bBrowser1 = Browser("CreationTime:=0").Exist(0)

'If bNonBrowser was true that means only 1 browser
'Can exists
If bNonBrowser then
    'Only 1 Browser
    Msgbox "Only 1 browser exists"
Else
'If bNonBrowser is false then we have either
'no browser existing or multiple browsers
    If bBrowser1 then
            'If the first one exist then there
            'are multiple browsers
            Msgbox "Multiple browser exists"
    Else
            'None Exists
            Msgbox "No browser exists"
    End if
End if
```

NOTE: When there is only one browser then the Browser("CreationT ime:=0").Exist(0) statement takes 10 seconds to return.. This is a known issue with QTP. The only workaround for this issue is to avoid using such DP statements in situations where only one browser is open. This can be accomplished by intentionally launching a dummy browser to make the statements work faster.

Working with Multiple Browser

QTP provides ordinal identifiers index and CreationTime for web browsers that can be used to differentiate between the browsers at runtime.

Consider the following script:

Script 1

```
'Launch internet explorer
SystemUtil.Run "iexplore.exe"

'Naviagte to www.mywebsite.com
Browser("micClass:=Browser").Navigate "http://www.mywebsite.com"
```

The above code statement creates a new browser and opens the specified website in that browser. Now let's launch another browser:

Script 2

```
'Launch internet explorer
SystemUtil.Run "iexplore.exe"

'Launch a dummy intenet explorer
SystemUtil.Run "iexplore.exe"

'Wait for the process to load
Wait 10

'Navigate to www.mywebsite.com. this time we
'cannot use micclass:=Browser as there are
'multiple browser so we need to creation time
Browser("creationtime:=0").Navigate "http://www.google.com"
```

The wait statement lets both browsers launch properly. But the 4th statement that specifies the web site will produce a "multiple matches of object found" error because the Browser ("micclass:=Browser") statement is valid for both browsers.

To differentiate between the two browsers we must use the index or CreationTime property unique to each browser:

```
'All of the following statements refer only to the 1st Browser:
Browser("micClass:=Browser","index:=0").Navigate "http://www.google.com"
Browser("micClass:=Browser","creationtime:=0").Navigate "http://www.google.com"
Browser("index:=0").Navigate "http://www.google.com"
Browser("creationtime:=0").Navigate "http://www.google.com"
```

```
'All of the following statements refer only to the 2nd Browser:
Browser("micClass:=Browser", "index:=1").Navigate "http://www.google.com"
Browser("micClass:=Browser", "creationtime:=1").Navigate "http://www.google.com"
Browser("index:=1").Navigate "http://www.google.com"
Browser("creationtime:=1").Navigate "http://www.google.com"
```

Browser identification Issue

Use of the CreationTime or index property to identify multiple browsers may cause problems in the following situations:

- Before running the script there are one or more browsers already open

- The script is not able to close browsers it spawns on subsequent iterations

- Running the script from QC. In this particular situation the QC browser might get counted as one of the script browsers and that might cause the script to fail

Here are few ways to avoid these situations:

- Close all the internet explorer processes before launching any browser. This can be accomplished using the next statement:

```
'Kill all internet explorer processes
SystemUtil.CloseProcessByName "iexplore.exe"

'This may not work well when the script is running from QC as it might
'kill the QC browser as well.
```

- In the case where a script is using an Object Repository Browser object with the CreationTime property defined, we can use SetTOProperty to update the CreationTime at run time (Note: Smart identification should be disabled for this to work properly). For example the following line of code sets the Browser object to point to the 3rd browser:

```
'Change the creationtime use for Browser identification
Browser("Browser").SetTOProperty "creationtime", 2
```

But the above methods do not always provide reliable browser references. Now we discuss some of the additional browser identification techniques.

Browser identification using OpenTitle

The browser's OpenTitle property defines the browser's initial title when the browser is first launched:

```
'description string for the browser
dpBrowser = "OpenTitle:=Google"

'Launch internet explorer and navigate to www.google.com
SystemUtil.Run "iexplore.exe", "www.google.com"

Browser(dpBrowser).Navigate "www.gmail.com"
```

But we need to know the page title that corresponds to the opening URL and running the above code twice causes an error because as there will then be two browsers with the same OpenTitle property. So this method is still not a foolproof method for browser identification, unless these issues are avoided.

Browser Identification using a unique OpenURL Property

The following method specifies nonsense (but valid) opening URL that includes a unique integer:

```
'Generate a random URL every time
browserID = RandomNumber.Value(10000,99999)

'Get the open url string
dpBrowser = "OpenURL:=about:" & browserID

'Launch a new browser with opening url based on the random number
SystemUtil.Run "iexplore.exe", "about:" & browserID

Browser(dpBrowser).Navigate "www.google.com"
```

 NOTE: We used a "about:#####" format of the URL because if we had used a constant string then the browser would try to search the website with the string used.   The above code is independent of the number of browsers already open. The only limitation it has is in the case of the popup windows. When we know the URL/title of the popup then we can use OpenTitle/OpenURL

The above code provides a reliable method for browser identification and has none of the disadvantages of the other methods described earlier. It also does not encounter any 10 second delay while using a single browser.

Reader's Note

Reader's Note

Chapter 11

Debugging in QTP

This chapter covers the following debugging topics:

- ⊙ Establishing our Debugging Configuration

- ⊙ Using Breakpoints

- ⊙ Working with the Watch Expressions Tab

- ⊙ Working with the Variables Tab

- ⊙ Working with the Command Tab

Establishing our Debugging Configuration

QTP must be configured before we can start debugging. Go to *Tools→Options→Run (Tab)* and make sure that Run Mode is selected as Normal as shown in the Figure 11-1

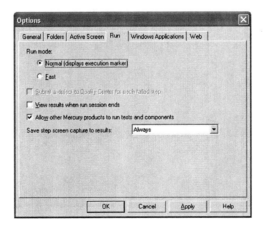

Figure 11-1. Run Mode - Normal

If this radio button is disabled it means that Microsoft Script Debugger is not installed on the machine. Download and install the Microsoft Script Debugger to enable this option.

Using Breakpoints

Breakpoints are inserted into a script to cause the execution to switch from the normal mode to debug mode. We add a breakpoint in QTP by pressing the F9 key or by right clicking and choosing *Insert/ Remove breakpoint*…from the context menu on the line of code where we want to place a stop code execution.

A red dot appears to the left of the line where a breakpoint has been set. Once the breakpoint is set we can run the program. Consider the code below with a breakpoint set on the 3rd line:

```
'Code to be debugged
Dim X
X = "This is a test"
y = Left(x,4)
MsgBox y 'Put a break point here
```

When this code is executed, QTP pauses at our breakpoint. Make sure we have the debug window visible (If not then go to *View→Debug viewer*). There are three tabs in the debug window which we will discuss in the next three sections.

Working with the Watch Expression Tab

In this tab, we add variable names and statements in the left column, thereafter QTP keeps the contents of the variables and the results of these statements updated in the right column. Let's add few entries to Watch Expressions tab as shown in the Figure 11-2

Figure 11-2. Watch Expressions Tab

We can see in the Watch pane that x has a value "This is a test" and y has a value "This". We can also change the actual value stored in the variable by double clicking on value cell and changing the value.

 NOTE: Changing of values will only apply when the expression being watched is a variable and not an evaluated value (Ex – Len(x))

Working with the Variables Tab

Now select the variable tab. This tab displays the name and values of all variables currently visible in the local scope as shown in the Figure 11-3

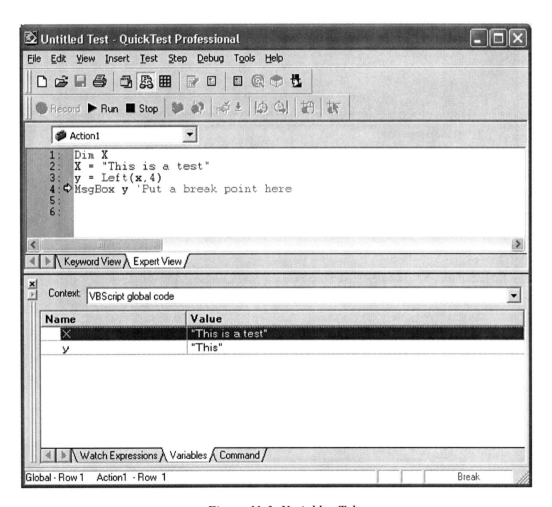

Figure 11-3. Variables Tab

Working with the Command Tab

This tab is used to interactively execute VBScript statements. Select the Command tab and then type y = "Changed from command tab" and press the Enter key. Then re-select the Variables tab and note that this new string is now assigned to variable y:

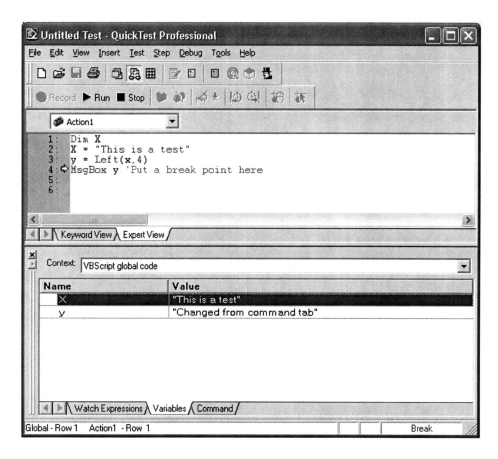

Figure 11-4. Updated value after command tab operation

 NOTE: QTP 8.x does not allow debugging VBScript library files associated on the Test Settings, Resource tab, nor does any version of QTP support debugging library files referenced using the ExecuteFile function. The best way to debug such a file is to a put a message box or to write information to a text file.

Reader's Note

Reader's Note

Chapter 12

Recovery Scenarios

QTP recovery scenarios provide a method for scripts to recover from different types of runtime error conditions. This is required for an unattended test case execution.

This chapter does not discuss how to create different types of recovery scenarios because that is well explained in the QTP Manual. Rather, the focus of this chapter is on when and where to use a recovery scenario.

When not to use recovery scenarios?

Consider the following code, which has the potential to generate a divide by zero error exception:

```
'Sample code with error probability
y = z - 2
x = 4 / y
```

We can handle this class of error using the On Error statement:

```
'Handling predictable errors
z = 2
y = z - 2
On Error Resume Next
x = 4 / y

If Err.Number = 11 Then
    MsgBox "Error code divide by zero handled"
Else
     'Unknown error. Handler for unknown errors.
    Msgbox err.Description & " , " & err.source
End if
```

The above scenario produces a predicted specific error in a specific location in the code. This type of situation can only be handled using the "On Error Resume Next" statement, rather than a recovery scenario.

> **NOTE:** QTP Recovery scenarios are NOT activated by VBScript errors; rather they are activated on any error involving QTP test objects.

When to use recovery scenario?

We can use a recovery scenario when we know what type of error can occur, but don't know when or where it might occur.

A recovery scenario consists of following components:

A Trigger Event – It is an event that unexpectedly interrupts script execution. This event can be any one of the following:

Pop-up window

Object state

Test run error

Application crash

A Recovery action – This specifies what action needs to be taken after the associated trigger event has occurred, and it can be any one of the following:

Keyboard or mouse operation

Close application process

Function Call

Restart Microsoft Windows

Post Recovery – This specifies what should be done once the recovery action has been successfully completed, and this can be any one the following:

Repeat current step and continue

Proceed to next step

Proceed to next action iteration

Proceed to next test iteration

Restart current test run

Stop the test run

Here in an example of where we could use a recovery scenario. Consider a website that displays a modal dialog every 15 seconds. No application interaction can be performed while the dialog is open. Suppose our test case is to verify each link on the web page. If the dialog is presented while our script tries to perform some operation in the application, an error will occur because the browser is disabled while the dialog is displayed. So in this situation we can create a recovery scenario to automatically close the dialog when a script interaction error occurs due to its presence.

Let us create such an HTML page and a recovery scenario to handle this situation:

C:\ TestRecovery.html

```html
<html>
    <head>
        <script type="text/JScript">
        function showmsg()
        {
        var t = setTimeout("alert('Clicked Me!')",500)
        }
        </script>
    </head>

    <body>
        <form>
            <input type="button" value="Click Me" onClick="showmsg()">
        </form>
    </body>
</html>
```

Clicking the "Click Me" on the above page button will display a message box after 500 milliseconds. Let's create a QTP test script for the above HTML page

```
'Launch explorer.exe
SystemUtil.Run "iexplore.exe"

Browser("CreationTime:=0").Sync
Browser("CreationTime:=0").Navigate "C:\TestRecovery.html"
Browser("CreationTime:=0").Sync
Browser("CreationTime:=0").Page("micClass:=Page").WebButton("name:=Click me").
Click

'Now we know that this will display a Msgbox after 500 msec,
'so let's wait for 1 sec and try to click the button again
Wait 1
Browser("CreationTime:=0").Page("micClass:=Page").WebButton("name:=Click me").
Click
```

Running the above script will produce an error in the last step "Object is disabled". This is because the alert box disabled the browser. Now we will make a recovery scenario for the above test case and execute it again. Go to *Tools→Recovery Scenario Manager…* and click the *New scenario* button on recovery manager window. Create a Recovery scenario with following properties

> Trigger Event: Pop-up window.
>
>> Window title: "Microsoft Internet Explorer"
>>
>> Window text contains: "Click Me!"

Recovery Operation:

Operation type: Keyboard or Mouse operation

Operation: Click Default Button/Press the Enter key

Test Run options: Repeat current step and continue

Save the recovery scenario and add it to the current test.

Then re-run the script and notice a "Clicked Me!" Message box left at the end of the script. This is how the things work in this example.

The 1st Click event → A message box is displayed→The 2nd click event fails because of object being disabled→ Failure of the script causes activation of the recovery scenario → The trigger event is identified and the action is taken to press enter key→ Post recovery re-executes the 2nd click step again.→ The click causes another message box to be displayed and the script ends

The test results summary will show when a recovery scenario has been used:

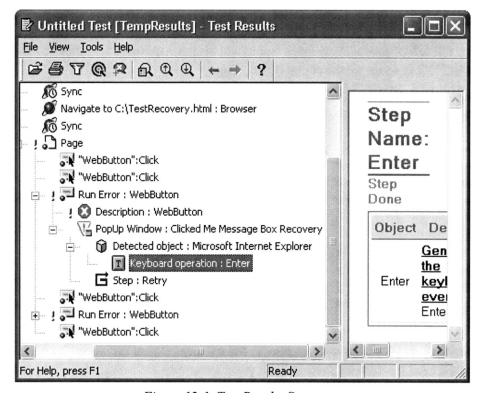

Figure 12-1. Test Results Summary

Situations in which a Recovery Scenario won't work

There are some situations in which a recovery scenarios won't work. Few of them are given below:

Case 1

Consider the script below:

```
'Recovery scenarios are only executed on statements
'containng QTP test objects
Dim x
x = 2

MsgBox x

Window("hwnd:=-1").Exist(0)
```

Even if we enable the recovery scenarios to be run on "On Every Step", it will not be activated on the first three steps, but it will be activated on the 4th step, because QTP only activates recovery scenarios on code statements which contain QTP test objects. Any pure VBScript code error can't be handled using recovery scenarios. So we can either use a dummy step like Window("hwnd:=-1").Exist(0) or we can use the statement below at any position to force the activation of recovery scenario:

```
'Activate the recovery scenario
Recovery.Activate
```

The above statement forces execution of all enabled recovery scenarios associated with current test.

Case 2

```
'Division by Zero
X = 2/0
```

As explained in Case 1 the above error will not cause a recovery scenario to be activated, and can only be handled using the "On Error Resume Next" statement as described earlier.

Case 3

```
'Access object not present in OR
Browser("BrowserNotInOR").Close
```

In the above situation the object is not in the Object Repository and therefore can't trigger any recovery scenario. This type of exception occurs before QTP has a chance to execute the script's recovery scenario(s).

Case 4

A recovery scenario cannot close a dialog box initiated by code statement inside QTP. Consider the following code statements:

```
'Display a message box
MsgBox "Go to next statement"

'The next message box will not be displayed
'until user manually clicks the Ok button or
'some non-QTP program closes the dialog
MsgBox "Passed"
```

When the above statements are executed in a script which has a recovery scenario to dismiss unexpected modal dialogs, the scenarios won't be activated. Neither Recovery.Activate nor QTP recovery itself can close these message boxes. They either need to be closed manually or they need to be closed by some other process outside QTP. Note that we will write a VBScript in "Working with APIs" chapter to achieve this.

Problem 12-1. How can we get the status of an Action as Pass/Fail at the end of the action?

The key here is to execute a recovery scenario whose recovery action is a function call and mark the Action as failed when the function gets called. Create a recovery scenario as given below

Trigger Event: Test-Run error.

Error: Any Error

Recovery Operation:

Operation type: Function Call

Function:

```
'Recovery function call
Function StatusUpdate(Object, Method, Arguments, retVal)
    'Don't want to cause any error inside
    'a recovery action function
    On Error Resume Next

    'Get the current action name. This is a user defined
    'environment variable and has to be populated in every
    'Action
    sCurrentAction = Environment.Value("CurrentAction")

    'Create a environment variable for current action as failed
    Environment.Value(sCurrentAction) = "Failed"

    'Set the status for current test as failed
    'This again is a user defined variable
    Environment.Value("RunStatus") = "Failed"
End Function
```

Test Run options: Proceed to next step

Now in every action we start the action with code as given below

```
'Disable all error messages
On error resume next
sCurrentActionName = DataTable.LocalSheet.Name
'Environment values cannot take a name with space or special
'chracters. Remove all special characters
sCurrentActionName = Replace(sCurrentActionName ," ", "_")
sCurrentActionName = Replace(sCurrentActionName ,"[", "_")
sCurrentActionName = Replace(sCurrentActionName ,"]", "_")
```

```
'Save the old action so that in case we call another action
'then the current action name is not lost
sOldAction = Environment.Value("CurrentAction")
Environment.Value("CurrentAction") = sCurrentActionName

'Initialize the status as Passed for the action
Environment.Value(sCurrentActionName) = "Passed"
On error goto 0
```

And we end the action with below code as given below

```
'Once the action is completed make sure we set the
'action name back to earlier action
Environment.Value("CurrentAction") = sOldAction
```

Now we can access the status of action as given below

```
'Access the status of the current action
DataTable("Status",dtGlobalSheet) = Environment.Value(sCurrentActionName)
```

Recovery Scenario for IE Authentication window

Figure 12-2 shows a typical IE authentication window in Windows XP.

Figure 12-2. IE Authentication window

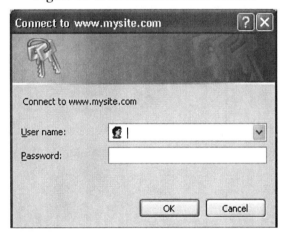

The full window title changes with the site being accessed. But it always starts the "Connect to" string. So we need to first create a recovery scenario on a popup dialog which contains a title matching the regular expression "Connect to .*". The recovery action will execute a script function which in turn will fill in all the dialog details. Here is the recovery function to enter the details of login:

```
'Recovery function to login on a proxy password
'window
Function Recovery_LoginProxy(Object)
    'The object represents the popup window
    'Get the handle of the window
    hwndPwdWindow = Object.GetROProperty("hwnd")

    'Now get the window test object for the same
    Set pwdWindow = Window("hwnd:=" & hwndPwdWindow)
```

```
      wndTitle = pwdWindow.GetROProperty("title")

      'Set the user ID here. By observation the Set method does
      'not work here so we will use the Type method.
      pwdWindow.WinEdit("attached text:=.*","index:=1").Type  "USER ID"

      'Set the password
      sPwd = Crypt.Encrypt("PASSWORD")
      pwdWindow.WinEdit("attached text:=&Password:").SetSecure sPwd

      'Click the OK button
      pwdWindow.WinButton("text:=OK").Click
End Function
```

We can make the function configurable by putting the User ID and password in an environment variable instead of hard coding them in the function. One more enhancement that can be made is to define different UID/PWD for different domains. We could get the domain name using this code:

```
   'Will contain "Connect to domain
   strDomain = pwdWindow.GetROProperty("title")
   strDomain = Mid(strDomain, Len("Connect to")+1)

   userID = GetUserIDForDomain(strDomain)
   password = GetPasswordForDomain(strDomain)
```

"GetUserIDForDomain" and "GetPasswordForDomain" functions need to be implemented.

Default Recovery Scenarios

QTP comes with some default scenarios that can be found in "\Program Files\Mercury Interactive\ QuickTest Professional\recovery\WebRecovery.qrs". This contains various recovery scenarios for the following pop-up dialogs:

Internet Redirect

Security Warning

Security Information

Security Alert

File download

There are other recovery scenarios as well. We can look up for all them using the recovery scenario manager. It's a good idea to add all these scenarios to any web application test script, instead of creating our own.

The Recovery object

The Recovery object provides various methods to control recovery scenarios using code at run-time. This object provides the following methods:

Activate – Forcibly activates the recovery scenarios

GetScenarioName

GetScenarioPosition

GetScenarioStatus

SetScenarioStatus

It also provides the following properties:

Count – Retrieves total number of recovery scenarios associated with the test.

Enabled – This is the default property. It sets/retrieves the current state of the whole recovery mechanism. We can disable all the recovery scenarios at once by using one of the following statements:

Recovery.Enabled = False

or

Recovery = False

We have already looked at the Activate method and I won't be discussing the other methods here. Each usage is well described in the QTP user manual.

Recovery Function Calls

A Recovery function call can use one of the following prototypes, depending on the type of associated trigger:

Trigger - OnRunStep

Function RecoveryFunction1(Object, Method, Arguments, Results)

Object - The object of the current step.

Method - The method of the current step.

Arguments - The actual method's arguments as arrays.

Result - The actual method's result code.

Trigger - Pop-up window and Object state triggers

Function RecoveryFunction2(Object)

Object - The detected object.

Trigger - Application crash trigger

Function RecoveryFunction2(ProcessName , ProcessId)

ProcessName - The detected process's Name.

ProcessId - The detected process' ID

Functions which do not use one of the above mentioned prototypes cannot be used as a recovery function.

There are some things that can be done in legal recovery functions. Here are the few examples:

```
'Recovery function
Function RecoveryFunction1(Object, Method, Arguments, Results)
  Select Case Method

    Case "Check"
      'It's check point that cause an issue

    Case "Set"
      'It's a Set function that cause issue

    Case "Select"
      'It's a Select function that caused the issue.
      typeOfObject = Object.GetTOProperty("micclass")
      Select Case typeOfObject

        Case "WebList"
          'Try and run recovery for weblist selection
          'Arguments(0) will give the value passed

        Case "WinList"
          'Recovery action for WinList Select method
      End Select
  End Select
End Function
```

To get the complete object definition from the QTP object we can use the following function:

```
'Get object description from an object
Public Function GetObjectSTR(pObject)
  'Get the type of the objecy
  sClass = pObject.GetTOProperty("micclass")

  'Get all the test object identification properties
  Set oTOProps = pObject.GetTOProperties
```

```
    Dim sProps()
    ReDim sProps(0)

    iCount = oTOProps.Count - 1
    'Loop through and create a array for string description
    For i = 0 to iCount
            sProps(UBound(sProps)) = oTOProps(i).Name & ":=" & oTOProps(i).Value
            ReDim Preserve sProps(UBound(sProps) + 1)
    Next

    ReDim Preserve sProps(UBound(sProps)-1)

    'Create the string object description of current object
    sObjectStr = sClass  & "(""" & join(sProps,""",""") & """)"

    'Check if the object is a top level object
    If TypeName(pObject.GetTOProperty("parent")) = "Empty" Then
            GetObjectSTR = sObjectStr
    Else
        'Get the parent object of the current object
            Set    oParent = pObject.GetTOProperty("parent")
            'Recursivly call the function to get the complete description
            GetObjectSTR = GetObjectSTR(oParent) & "." & sObjectStr
    End If
End Function
```

Here is an example of how to use the above function

```
'Example
Set oPg = Browser("micclass:=Browser").Page("micclass:=Page")

Set oWebEdit = oPg.WinEdit("name:=username")

MsgBox GetObjectSTR(oWebEdit)
```

Error Handling

Let's take another look at the On Error handling method:

```
'Disable error popups
On Error Resume Next
'....
'Code lines to be executed
'....

If Err.Number <> 0 Then
   MsgBox "Error Occured. Source = " & Err.Source & _
          ", Number = " & Err.Number & _
          ", Description = " & Err.Description
End If
```

On error resume next statement disables the standard error pop-up dialogs that are normally presented. We should use the 'err.number' to check for any known error situation and then handle them. Whenever an error occurs it is propagated to the top of the call stack order until a function or code scope with "on error resume next" is found. And if none of these have been found then VBScript displays the error message.

```vbscript
'Disable error popups
On Error Resume Next
Call ErrorFunc()

If Err.Number <> 0 Then
   MsgBox "Error occured inside function"
End If

Public Function ErrorFunc()
   'This function contains an error and the
   'error should be trapped in the calling function
   x = 3 / 0
   MsgBox "Function completed"
End Function
```

In the above code the MsgBox "Function Completed" will not be executed. The ErrorFunc raises an error which is then passed to the calling module and also where we have the code handling the errors.

VBScript does not support 'on error goto' statements because it does not support labels. But there is workaround that we can use to achieve the same functionality:

```vbscript
'Global error handler
Dim globalErrHanlder

Function FuncWithError()
   'This function contains the main code that needs to be executed
   Dim x, y
   x = 2 + 4
   y = x - 2 - 4

   x = x/y
End Function

'Error wrapper function. This is really helpful
'when creating frameworks.
Function FuncWithErrHanlder()
   On Error Resume Next
   Call FuncWithError()
   If Err.Number <> 0 Then
         Call globalErrHanlder()
   End If
End Function

'This updated ths global error hanlder module function
Public Function OnErrorGoTo(byVal FunctionName)
```

```
    Set globalErrHanlder = GetRef(FunctionName)
End Function

Public Function errHandler()
    'Here some generic code for recovery can be used
    Msgbox "Source = " & Err.Source & ", # = " & err.number & ", Desc = " & err.
description
End Function
'Method2
'Set the global errHandler code
OnErrorGoTo "errHandler"

'Execute the Error wrapper function
Call FuncWithErrHanlder()
```

The above technique can be used when we are building frameworks where external sheets are used to run keywords

Reader's Note

Chapter 13

Regular Expressions

Regular expressions are strings containing special meta characters used to match patterns inside the strings. Text editors use this feature for doing color syntax highlighting and other operations. This chapter covers the basics of regular expressions in VBScript and how to use them in QTP. Table 13-1 summarizes the most often used meta characters:

Table 13-1. Regular Expression Characters

Meta Character	Description
.	Matches Any Single Character (.)
[xyz]	Matches Any Single Character in a List ([xy])
[^xyz]	Matches Any Single Character Not in a List ([^xy])
[x-y]	Matches Any Single Character within a Range ([x-y])
*	Matches Zero or More Specific Characters (*)
+	Matches One or More Specific Characters (+)
?	Matches Zero or One Specific Character (?)
( )	Groups Regular Expressions (( ))
|	Matches One of Several Regular Expressions (|)
^	Matches the Beginning of a Line (^)
$	Matches the End of a Line ($)
\w	Matches Any Alphanumeric Character including the Underscore (\w)
\W	Matches Any Non-Alphanumeric Character (\W)
\	Escape character, useful when a meta characters needs to be represented literally
{}	Matches X number of occurrences

Regular Expression Characters

Match Any Single Character (.)

The "." character matches any single character. For example, "..." will match "12B", "B3B", "123", "ABC", "$g%" etc…

Match Any Single Character in a List [xyz]

A character list inside square brackets matches any of the single characters in the list. For example, "[abc][12]" will match "a1", "a2", "b1", "b2", "c1" and "c2".

Match Any Single Character Not in a List [^xyz]

The "^" character is a negation character used to exclude a pattern from the regular expression. For example, "[^a][12]" will not match "a1" and "a2", but will match "11", "12", "c1" etc…

Match Any Single Character within a Range ([x-y])

The "[d-h]" construct will match any character ranging from d to h. For example, "[abcdef][123]" can also be written as "[a-f][1-3]"

Match Zero or More Specific Characters (*)

The "*" character is used to match zero or more occurrences of a regular expression that precedes the star. For example, "a*" will match a blank string, "a", "aa", "aaa" etc, while ".*" matches any pattern of characters. Additional examples are:

"aa*" will match "a", "aa", "aaa" etc..

"[abc][1-4]*" will match "a", "b", "c", "a1", "b1", "a12", "a1234344" etc…

"User.*" will match any string starting with text "User".

NOTE: Many people make mistake and use "User*" to match a string starting with "User" but "User*" will only match strings like "Use", "User", "Userr" etc…

Match One or More Specific Characters (+)

The "+" character is used to match one or more occurrences of a regular expression that precedes the plus sign. For example, "aa*" can also be written as "a+".

"123+" will match "123", "1233", "12333" etc…

"[123]+" will match "1", "2", "3", "12", "23" etc…

Match Zero or One Specific Character (?)

A "?" character is used to match zero or one occurrences of a preceding regular expression. For example, "a[123]?" will match "a", "a1", "a2" and "a3"

Regular Expression Groups (( ))

Use matching parenthesis, "()", to group a regular expression. For example, "(123)+" matches "123", "123123", "123123123", etc., which makes it different from how "123+" is interpreted.

Match One of Several Regular Expression Phrases (|)

The "|" character provides a logical OR operation in regular expressions. For example, [(123)|(abc)] will match "123" or "abc".

Match the Beginning of a Line (^)

A "^" character at the beginning of a regular expression is used to match the start of a line. For example, "^abc.*" matches any line starting with "abc".

Match the End of a Line ($)

A "$" character at the end of a regular expression is used to match end of a line. For example, "abc$" matches "abc", "123abc", "aabc" etc, at the end of the line, while "^abc$" only matches "abc" on its own line.

Match Any AlphaNumeric Character Including the Underscore (\w)

A "\w" expression matches any character including underscore. This is equivalent to using the regular expression"[A-Za-z0-9_]". For example, "\w\w" will match "A_", "a1" etc…

Match Any Non-AlphaNumeric Character (\W)

A "\W" expression matches any non-word character. This is the negation/opposite of "\w" and is equivalent to "[^A-Za-z0-9_]". For example, "\W" will match "$", "%", "@" etc…

Using the Escape Character (\ )

A backward slash allows the next character to be treated as a literal character or as a special character instead of literal. For example, a "." will match any character, but to represent it as a literal period character we use "\." to escape the period's special meaning. Normally the "t" character is treated as a literal but placing a backward slash before it allows tab characters "\t" to be matched.

Match a Number of Occurrences ({})

The "{}" braces allows matching X number of occurrences of a regular expression. There are multiple ways to use this capability as shown in Table 13-2

Table 13-2. Multiple occurrence matches

Character	Description	Example
{M}	Matches M occurrences of a pattern.	A{2} will match only "AA"
{M,}	Matched M or more occurrences of a pattern	A{1,} will match "A", "AA" etc… which is equivalent of using "A+". A{0,} will be equivalent of using "A*"
{M, N}	Matches at least M and at most N times occurrence of a pattern	A{1,3} will match "A", "AA" and "AAA"

Other Regular Expression Characters

Although the QTP user manual does not list all regular expression characters, it does support all VBScript regular expression characters. Shown next are the other regular expression characters which can be used:

Table 13-3. Miscellaneous regular expression character

Character	Description	Example
\d	Matches any digit. Equivalent to using "[0-9]"	"\d{2}" will match all numbers from 01 to 99. Though it won't match 1 to 9 as they are single digits
\D	Matches any non-digit characters. Equivalent to using "[^0-9]".	"\D" will match "A", "&", "$" etc…
\num	Matches num, where num is a positive integer. A reference back to captured matches	"(\d)\1\1" will match numbers "111", "222", "333" etc…
\s	Matches any white-space character. Equivalent to "[\f\n\r\t\v]".	
\S	Matches any non white-space character. Equivalent to "[^ \f\n\r\t\v]".	

Problem 13-1. What will the regular expression be for a domain which can have possible value of " test.app.com", "qa.app.com", "www.app.com"

The ".app.com" is constant in both the string, so we can use the regular expression for that part as "\.app\.com" (a "\" character is used before "." so that the "." character is treated literally as character and not as a meta character). Now we need a regular expression which can have a value from test, qa or www. The regular expression for this would be (test|qa|www). So the complete regular expression would be "(test|qa|www)\.app\.com"

Problem 13-2. What will be the r.e. matching a date in the format MM/DD/YY?

MM can be from 1 to 12. So the regular expression would be ([1-9]|1[0-2]). For the DD it can be 1-31, so the regular expression would be "([1-9]|[1-2][0-9]|3[0-1])". For the YYYY part it will be [0-9][0-9]. The combined regular expression for the date would be "([1-9]|1[0-2])/([1-9]|[1-2][0-9]|3[0-1])/[0-9][0-9]".

This actually matches a string containing the date inside it, to make it just match a string which is a date, we can add ^ at the start and a $ at the end. So the final regular expression would be "^([1-9]|1[0-2])/([1-9]|[1-2][0-9]|3[0-1])/[0-9][0-9]$".

When to use Regular Expressions in QTP

If the expected value of a property is dynamic, but follows a pattern then regular expressions are most often the best solution. For example, values NameID_233, NameID_256, NameID_290…… etc., follows a pattern where the value always starts with the string literal, "NameID_", and is always followed by a number. This pattern can be represented using a regular expression "NameID_.*", where "." and "*" are meta characters with special meanings as shown in Table 13-1. The "." characters specified here mean any character and the "*" character after the "." means zero or more occurrences of pattern matching ".".

Regular expressions can also be used to identify QTP Test Objects whose properties are dynamic or when there are many objects with similar identifying patterns. Let say a webpage contains text boxes where all their names start with the string literal "Name" and the actual name is a pattern like "Name1", "Name2", "Name3", etc.. To access these text box objects we can use Descriptive Programming (DP) and one of the following methods.

Method 1

```
'Create a description object for text box
Set oTextBox = Description.Create

'The regular expression to match a value starting Name
oTextBox("name").value = "Name.*"

'This property by default is True, so we could skip this line of code
oTextBox("name").RegularExpression = True

'To access the first text box whose name start with Name
oTextBox("index").value = 0

'Set the value of the text box
Browser("").Page("").WebEdit(oTextBox).Set "Value"
```

Method 2

```
'Set the value of first text box whose name start with "Name"
Browser("").Page("").WebEdit("name:=Name.*","index:=0").Set "Value"
```

In this method we can also avoid using the regular expression by generating the name at runtime as given here.

```
'The text box to be set
i = 1

'Set the text box value
Browser("").Page("").WebEdit("name:=Name" & i).Set "Value"
```

If our object is in the repository then we need to change the value using the Object Repository Manager. Using that tool, open the object repository and browse to the object as shown in the Figure 13-1. Click on the "Constant value options" button. Now check the checkbox for "Regular Expression" and enter the appropriate text in its input field as shown in the Figure 13-2.

NOTE: If we click the regular expression after entering the text then QTP will ask if we want to add '\' to all the special characters. We should choose Yes incase we want to match the string literally or No if .we want to match it as a pattern.

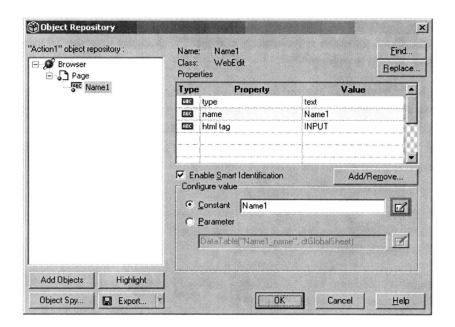

Figure 13-1. Object Repository

If we are unsure what would be the literal regular expression, e.g. a URL like "http://www.testapp. com/Test%20Test.html". We can enter the URL in the text box and then check the regular expression checkbox. Clicking the checkbox would open the dialog for adding '\' to the special characters as shown in the Figure 13-3. The literal string generated by clicking Yes on the dialog would be *'http://www\.testapp\.com/Test%20Test\.html'*

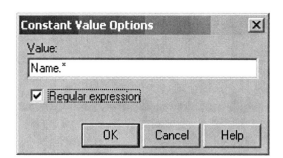

Figure 13-2. Regular Expression Checkbox

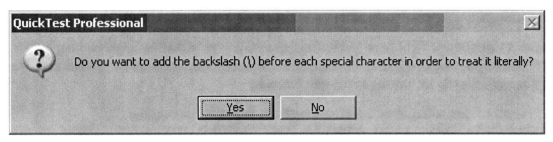

Figure 13-3. Regular Expression Escape character

Testing a Regular Expression Using Code

QTP, through the Microsoft VBScript engine, provides the RegExp class which is used for general regular expressions evaluation and processing. Below is a function that tests a pattern within a string:

```
'Function to check if a string matches a regular expression pattern
Function IsRegEqual(s_Text, s_Pattern, MatchCompleteString)
    Dim regEx, retVal

    'Create regular expression object.
    Set regEx = New RegExp

    'Set pattern.
    regEx.Pattern = s_Pattern
    'Ignore case
    regEx.IgnoreCase = True
    'Match complete string or not
    regEx.Global = MatchCompleteString

    'Test the regular expression
    IsRegEqual = regEx.Test(s_Text)
    Set regEx = Nothing
End Function
```

Usage:

```
'Will display True
Msgbox IsRegEqual("foos","foo|bar", False)

'Will display False
Msgbox IsRegEqual("foos","foo|bar", True)

'Will display False
Msgbox IsRegEqual("foo","fo(o|b)ar", True)

'Will display True
Msgbox IsRegEqual("Are you foo?","foo")

'Will display False, This is for a string starting and
'ending with foo which is foo only.
Msgbox IsRegEqual("Are you foo?","^foo$")
```

Using a Regular Expression to Select a WebList or WebRadioGroup Value

To select a value from a WebList or WebRadioGroup we first get all the list's values using its "all items" Test Object Property. The values returned are separated with a semicolon ";" character. We then place all values in an array using the split function:

```
'Function for selecting a value based on regular expression
'matchIndex is a 0 based value
Function WebRegSelectValue(ByVal oObject, ByVal Pattern, ByVal matchIndex)
    Dim allItemValues, matches

    matches = 0

    'Get all the items into an array
    allItemValues = Split(oObject.GetROProperty("all items"),";")

    'Loop through all the values in the array
    For i = LBound(allItemValues) to UBound(allItemValues)

            'See if the current value matches the pattern
            If IsRegEqual(allItemValues(i), Pattern, True) Then
                    'If match found is equal to the no. of matched then
                    'select the value
                    If matches = matchIndex Then
                            oObject.Select "#" & i
                            Exit Function
                    End If
                    matches = matches + 1
            End If
    Next

    'No matching value found. Raise error
    Err.Raise vbObjectError + 1, "WebRegSelectValue","Could not find the
specified value - " & Pattern & ", Index - " & matchIndex
End Function

'Register the new function
RegisterUserFunc "WebList","SelectReg","WebRegSelectValue"
RegisterUserFunc "WebRadioGroup","SelectReg","WebRegSelectValue"

'Select the 2nd value matching the pattern
Browser("Browser").Page("Page").WebList("Test").SelectReg "TEST.*", 1
```

Extracting Information Using a Regular Expression

Regular expressions are also used to extract information from a string. Consider the string "Your package will be shipped on 10/1/2008 and will be delivered by 15/1/2008". Now a regular expression to match a "DD/MM/YYYY" date pattern would be "(0[1-9]|[12][0-9]|3[0-1])/(0?[1-9]|1[0-2])/([0-9]{4})"

```
'Text from which data needs to be extracted
txtInformation = "Your package will be shipped on 10/1/2008 and will be
delivered by 15/1/2008."
```

```
'Pattern to find the data
datePattern = "(0[1-9]|[12][0-9]|3[0-1])/(0?[1-9]|1[0-2])/([0-9]{4})"

Set oRegExp = New RegExp

'Set the date pattern
oRegExp.Pattern = datePattern

'Set global to true as we want all matches
oRegExp.Global = True

'Fidn the matches
Set oMatches = oRegExp.Execute(txtInformation)

If oMatches.Count <> 2 Then
   MsgBox "Error could not find both dates"
Else
   shippingDate = oMatches(0)
   deliveryDate = oMatches(1)

   MsgBox "Shipping Date - " & shippingDate
   MsgBox "Delivery Date - " & deliveryDate
End If
```

This approach can also be used to be to extract information from web pages

Replacing Data from a String Using a Regular Expression

Regular expressions are also used to replace a substring matching a given pattern. The VBScript
LTrim and RTrim functions remove space characters from the start and end of the string respectively.
If we need a function that also removes additional whitespace characters like new line, tab, carriage
return etc., we can implement that by using the following code:

```
'Text from which data needs to be replaced
txtInformation = vbnewline & vbLf & vbTab & _
                       " This Is Great " _
                                & vbTab & vbLf & vbNewLine
'Function to trim white space characters from end of a string
Public Function RTrimW(ByVal Text)
   'String pattern ending with carriage return, tab, new line
   'or a space character
   RTrimPattern = "[\s]*$"

   Dim oRegExp
   Set oRegExp = New RegExp
   oRegExp.Pattern =RTrimPattern
   oRegExp.Global = False
   RTrimW = oRegExp.Replace(Text,"")
End Function

'Function to trim white space characters from start
'of a string
```

```
Public Function LTrimW(ByVal Text)
    'String pattern ending with carriage return, tab, new line
    'or a space character
    LTrimPattern = "^[\s]*"

    Dim oRegExp
    Set oRegExp = New RegExp
    oRegExp.Pattern = LTrimPattern
    oRegExp.Global = False
    LTrimW = oRegExp.Replace(Text,"")
End Function

'Function to trim white space characters from start
'and end of a string
Public Function TrimW(ByVal Text)
    TrimW = LTrimW(RTrimW(Text))
End Function

MsgBox (txtInformation)
MsgBox LTrimW(txtInformation)
MsgBox RTrimW(txtInformation)
MsgBox TrimW(txtInformation)
```

Reader's Note

Reader's Note

Chapter 14

VBScript

QTP uses Microsoft's VBScript for its native scripting language. While it is beyond the scope of this book to provide a full description of this language, this chapter provides a short overview of VBScript features often used when developing QTP scripts. For a full explanation of the functions covered, refer to the QTP Online HELP.

Strings

This section discusses functions used for string manipulation.

Lcase and Ucase

These two functions convert a string from lower top upper case or vice versa:

```
'Convert to lower case
x = LCase("aBc") ' this will assign "abc" to x

'Convert to upper case
x = Ucase("aBc") ' this will assign "ABC" to x
```

StrComp

This function compares two strings and returns 0 when they are equal:

```
'Compare strings
x = StrComp("abc","abc") ' this call returns 0
x = StrComp("abc","aBc") ' this call returns non-zero

'The following call returns 0, as an explicit case insensitive
' comparison is performed
x = StrComp("abc","aBc",vbTextCompare)
```

StrReverse

This function reverses a string's characters:

```
'this call returns "yhW"
x = StrReverse("Why")
```

Len

This function returns the length of a string:

```
'this call returns 3
x = Len("abc")
```

Left

This function returns the specified number of characters from the left side of a string:

```
'this call returns "This is"
x = Left("This is a test",7)
```

Right

This function returns the specified number of characters from the right side of a string:

```
'this call returns "test"
x = Right("This is a test",4)
```

Mid

This function returns the specified number of characters from the middle of the string. If the number of characters is not specified then it will return the string from the specified mid to the end

```
' this call returns "is a test"
x = Mid("This is as test",6)

'this call returns "is", as we specified 2 characters
'starting at the 6th character position
x = Mid("This is as test",6, 2)
```

InStr

This function returns the starting character position of a sub-string in another string. It returns 0 when the substring is not found, as character positions within a string starts from 1:

```
'this call returns 6
x = InStr ("Find abc in this","abc")

'this call returns 0
x = InStr ("Find abc in this","aBc")

'this call returns 6
x = InStr ("Find abc in this","aBc", vbTextCompare)

'We can also specify a character position to start the search
```

```
'Returns 6. This is equivalent to default behavior, as we are
'saying to start the search from the 1st position in the string
x = InStr (1, "Find abc in this","abc")

'This call returns 0 as the search begins at the
'7th character, meaning the search string to be
'considered is "bc in this"
x = InStr (7, "Find abc in this","abc")
```

Problem 14-1. How can we find the current page and the total page values from the string "Page 4 of 15"?

First, we search for the " of " phrase within the full string (with a space character at the start and the end).

```
'Original text
s_Text = "Page 4 of 15"

'Text to search for
s_Search = " of "

'returns 7, the start of " of "
i_Index = InStr (s_Text, s_Search)
```

Next, the length of our search string, " of ", is 4 characters. So to get the total pages value we need to read all characters after 4 + i_Index. We have two ways to extract this portion of the string—either use the Right function or use the Mid function. Both approaches are shown below, but the Mid function will produce a cleaner code:

```
'Get text right from the search string
s_AllPages = Right (s_Text, Len(s_Text) - i_Index  - Len(s_Search))

'We need to know the # of characters that we need to
'take from the Right of the string and Len(s_Text) will
'give the length of the string " of 15"
'and we need to subtract the length of " of "
'also to get the 3 of characters in the all pages count
s_AllPages = Mid (s_Text, i_Index + Len (s_Search))
```

Now the current page count always appears from the 6th position in the string and goes till the start of the " of " string:

```
'We took the string from the left of " of " and then took the
'string from the 6th position to get the current page no.
s_CurrentPage = Mid(Left(s_Text, i_Index - 1), 6)
```

Problem 14-2. How can we count the number of "if" phrases in the "if + if = 2 if" string?

```
'Original text
s_Text = "if + if = 2 if"

'text to search for
```

```
s_Search = "if"

' this variable is used to store the last index found
'and then search the string again from 1 character forward
'to the next found string position
i_IndexFound = 0

'this variable will store the # of "if" strings found
i_NumCount = 0

Do
   i_IndexFound = InStr(i_IndexFound + 1, s_Text, s_Search)

   'If found increase the counter
   If i_IndexFound > 0 then
     i_NumCount = i_NumCount + 1
   Else
     Exit Do
   End If
' An infinite loop ended by a condition inside the loop
Loop while (True)

'This will give a value 3
MsgBox i_NumCount`
```

There is another way of doing this:

```
'Original text
s_Text = "if + if = 2 if"

'Search string
s_Search = "if"

'Delete the "if" phrases from s_Text and note the difference in lengths
i_NumCount = (Len(s_Text) - Len(Replace(s_Text,s_Search,""))) / Len(s_Search)

' Will give 3
MsgBox i_NumCount
```

InStrRev

This function is also used to search for a sub-string in a string but searches from the end of the string. It does not reverse the string and then search it.

```
' this call returns 0
x = InStrRev ("abc","cba")

' this call returns 5
x = InStrRev ("abc abc","abc")
```

Below is an example which should make it clear when it is better to use InStr and when it is better to use InStrRev

Problem 14-3. Given a complete file path specification, extract the filename, file path and drive letter from the specification

The complete file path specification is "C:\Test\Strings\Function.vbs". We know that the file name must appear after the last "\" in the string and the drive letter must appear before the first "\"

```
'File name
s_File = "C:\Test\Strings\Function.vbs"

'Locate first slash
i_FirstSlash = InStr(s_File,"\")

'Locate last slash
i_LastSlash = InStrRev(s_File,"\")
```

Now we know the position of the first and the last slash:

```
'-1 in case we don't want the ":" in the resulting drive letter
s_DriveLetter = Left (s_File, i_FirstSlash -1)

'+1 as we want to ignore the "\" character and take
'the string from its right
s_FileName = Mid (s_File, i_LastSlash + 1)

'-1 as we want to ignore the "\" character
'and take the string from its left
s_FilePath = Left (s_File, i_LastSlash - 1)
```

LTrim, RTrim and Trim

These function removed white spaces from the left, right or both sides of the string:

```
' returns "test "
x = LTrim ("   test   ")

' returns " test"
x = RTrim ("   test   ")

' returns "test"
x = Trim ("   test   ")
```

Replace

This function is used to replace a substring with a string:

```
'returns "The value of 2 is 2" to x
x = Replace (" The value of 1 is 2", "1", "2")
```

This function is also useful in cases of parameterization. Suppose we input a XML to a system and want to parameterize some value in the XML. In that situation, use Replace function as follows:

```
'XML template string
s_XML= "<Variable><Name>%NAME%</Name></Variable>"

'Replace the parameter %NAME% with actual value
s_XML = Replace (s_XML,"%NAME%", "Tarun")
```

Space

This function generates specified number of space characters.

```
' This call returns a string containing 2 space characters
x = Space (2)
```

String

This function generates a string of specified length for the given character.

```
' This call returns a string containing 3 'A' characters
x = String (3, "A")
```

Array

This function returns the array containing a variable number of strings:

```
' returns an array containing 2 strings
x = Array("Tarun","Lalwani")
```

Join

This function joins the contents of an array into a string. Each array element placed in the string is separated by an optionally defined delimiter character—if none is specified a space character is used:

```
'Get an array
x = Array("Tarun","Lalwani","wrote","this","book")

' returns "Tarun Lalwani wrote this book"
s_Text = Join (x)

' returns "Tarun_Lalwani_wrote_this_book"
s_Text = Join (x, "_")
```

Split

This function performs the opposite actions of the Join function, thus creating an array of strings from an input string:

```
'Text to be split
s_Text = "Tarun_Lalwani_wrote_this_book"

'This will assign Array("Tarun","Lalwani","wrote","this","book")
'to x
x = Split (s_Text, "_")
```

Problem 14-4. Let's revisit the page number extraction problem again. How can we find the current page and the total page values from the string "Page 4 of 15"?

In this approach we use the Split function to place each non-space sub-string into an individual array element. Thereafter we can easily extract the 1st and 3rd array elements to extract the current page number and the total number of pages respectively.

```
'String page numbers
X = "Page 4 of 15"

'Split the string base on space as delimiter.
```

```
'This will return Array("Page","4","of","15")
pages = Split(x," ")


' returns a "4" string
MsgBox pages(1)


' returns a "15" string
MsgBox pages(3)
```

Problem 14-5. How can we split a string into words or lines?

The VBScript Split function of VBScript allows one delimiter character to be specified. In case we want to split a string into words we need multiple delimiters. Next we create an extended version of Split to achieve this task

```
'Parmeters
'pText - The text to be splited
'Delimiter - This is a set of characters which will be considered as
delimiters.
'each character in the delimiter string will be taken as a delimiter and not
the
'complete string
'IncludeDelimiter - If set to True the resulting array will contain delimiters
also
'revDelimiter - If this is set to True then any character other than specified
in
'delimiter are considered as delimiters
Public Function SplitEx(ByVal pText, ByVal Delimiter, ByVal IncludeDelimiter,
ByVal revDelimiter)
   'If a blank delimiter then split the whole string into array
   'of characters
   If Delimiter = "" Then
       iCount = Len(pText)
       ReDim outarray(iCount)

       For i = 1 To iCount
           sChar = Mid(pText, i, 1)
           outarray(i - 1) = sChar
       Next
   Else
       'Variable to store the word
       sword = ""

       iCount = Len(pText)
       ReDim outarray(0)

       'Loop through all characters in the string
       For i = 1 To iCount
         'Get the current character
           sChar = Mid(pText, i, 1)

           'If the character is one of the delimiters
```

```vbscript
            'and revDelimiter flag is false then
            'create the word and store it in the result array
            If (InStr(Delimiter, sChar) <> 0 And Not revDelimiter) Then
                'store the word in the array
                If sword <> "" Then
                    outarray(UBound(outarray)) = sword
                    sword = ""
                    'Increase the array size by 1
                    ReDim Preserve outarray(UBound(outarray) + 1)
                End If

                 'If IncludeDelimiter flag is true then add
                 'the delimiter as well to the array
                If IncludeDelimiter Then
                    outarray(UBound(outarray)) = sChar
                    ReDim Preserve outarray(UBound(outarray) + 1)
                End If
            ElseIf (InStr(Delimiter, sChar) = 0 And revDelimiter) Then
                'If the character is not in the delimiter string
                'and revDelimiter is TRUE then create the word
                If sword <> "" Then
                    outarray(UBound(outarray)) = sword
                    sword = ""
                    ReDim Preserve outarray(UBound(outarray) + 1)
                End If

                'The delimiter word is always added to the array
                outarray(UBound(outarray)) = sChar
                ReDim Preserve outarray(UBound(outarray) + 1)
            Else
                'Continue to capture the word
                sword = sword + sChar
            End If
        Next

        'In case word in not blank then add to the array
        If sword <> "" Then
            outarray(UBound(outarray)) = sword
            ReDim Preserve outarray(UBound(outarray) + 1)
        End If
    End If

    'Decrease the array size by 1 as we started with a array
    'of length 1 when we had not data at all
    ReDim Preserve outarray(UBound(outarray) - 1)

    'return the array
    SplitEx = outarray
End Function
```

Now to split a statement into words or line we can use the SplitEx function in following ways:

```
'Usage:
'Returns Array("You","can't","do","this","can","you")
x = SplitEx("You can't do this, can you?", " ,?;.",False,False)
'Returns Array("You", " ", "can't", " ","do"," ","this", "," , " ", "can", " ",
"you", "?")
x = SplitEx("You can't do this, can you?", " ,?;.",True,False)

'Returns Array("Line1","Line2", "Line3")
x = SplitEx("Line1" & vbCrLf & "Line2" & vbCrLf & "Line3", vbCrLf, False,False)
```

Filter

This function returns a sub-set array of the search array containing the specified substring:

```
'Get an array
X = Array("Tarun","Lalwani","wrote","this","book")

'This will assign Array("Tarun","wrote")
'to x as both of the elements contains "r" in that
x_Found = Filter (x, "r")
```

Escape/ UnEscape

This function converts all special characters to their escape values. For example a " " is converted into "%20" where 20 is ASCII code of " ". This is used in HTML to encode special character and pass it as a part of the URL. UnEscape method can be used to decode these string and convert the "%XXX" characters back to the actual character

```
'encode a string
'x="http%3A//mycompany. com/cart%3Faction%3DAdd%26ProdId%3D12%26QTY%3D2"
x = Escape("http://mycompany. com/cart?action=Add&ProdId=12&QTY=2")

'decode a encoded string
'x = http://mycompany.com/cart?action=Add&ProdId=12&QTY=2
x = UnEscape(x)
```

Conversion function

These functions convert one data type to another data type. Although VBScript uses Variant as its only primary data type, it does have a sub-type which can be dynamically changed by using the functions described in this section.

CBool, CByte, CCur, CDate, CInt, CLng, CSng, CStr

```
'Now x contains a date in string format
X = "12/13/2006"

'Now x contains a Date data type
X = CDate(X)
```

Asc

```
This function returns the ASCII value of character
' returns 65 decimal
x = Asc("A")
```

Chr

```
Converts a ASCII value to a string
'returns an "A" string
x = Chr(65)
```

Hex/Oct

Converts a number to its Hexadecimal or Octal string representations:

```
'returns F5 hexidecimal
x = Hex(245)

'returns 120 octal
x = Oct(80)
```

Date and Time functions

These functions are used get the current date, time or both:

Date

This function returns the current date:

```
'Get the current local system date
x = Date()
```

Time

This function returns the current time:

```
'Get the current local system time
x = Time()
```

Now

This function returns the current date and time:

```
'Get current local system Date and time
x = Now()
```

Day/Month/Year

These functions are used to extract different parts from a date:

```
' this will return 13
s_Day = Day ("12/13/2006")

' this will return 12
s_Month = Month("12/13/2006")

' this will return 2006
s_Year = Year ("12/13/2006")
```

Hour/Minute/Seconds

These functions are used to extract different parts from a time:

```
' this will return 22
s_Hour = Hour ("10:32:30 PM")
' this will return 32
s_Minute = Minute("10:32:30 PM")
' this will return 30
s_Seconds = Second ("10:32:30 PM")
```

Weekday

This function returns the number corresponding to the day of the week. For Sunday the value is 1 and for Saturday it's 7.

DateDiff

This function is used to determine the difference between two dates. The difference can be based on weeks, months, days etc…

```
' returns 2
x = DateDiff ("d", "12/13/2006","12/15/2006")
```

 NOTE: The later or newer date should be provided as second argument to produce a positive difference; otherwise the value returned will be negative.

Problem 14-6. How can the number of business/working days be calculated between two dates (i.e. difference should exclude the weekends)?

This problem can be broken down into two parts. The first is getting the difference between two dates, which is easy. The second, and the more difficult part is getting the number of weekdays only between the date intervals. We get the number of days by dividing the difference between the dates by 7 and what is left is to determine if the day exists in the interval which is left when the difference is not an exact multiple of 7. We know that the weekday function returns a numeric value representing the day of the week where Sunday is represented using 1 and Saturday as 7. Now let's create a small graph to understand how we can check if a weekday comes between a interval or not

10/1		10/3		10/5		10/7		10/9		10/11		10/12
Sun	Mon	Tue	Wed	Thu	Fri	Sat	Sun	Mon	Tue	Wed	Thu	Fri
I	2	3	4	5	6	7	I	2	3	4	5	6

The above table shows the days and their day values for an interval between 10/1 through 10/12. Now if we want to determine if Monday is present in the interval 10/3 to 10/7. Monday has a value 2 and my start date has a value 3 while the end date has a value 7, so if I check that 2 (Monday) exists between 3(Tue) to 7 (Sat) then I will be able to tell if that day is present in between the interval or not. Now the problem arises when the interval is say 10/5 to 10/9. Now my start date has a value 5 and the end date has a value 2 which is less than the value of start date. Now if I am looking to check for the existence of a day then I should be checking that the day does come between the 2 and 5 (i.e. 1, 3 and 4 are not present in this interval). So here is the HowManyWeekDays function:

```
'Function to check how many times a day appears between
'a given date interval
Function HowManyWeekDays(ByVal startDate, ByVal endDate, ByVal DayToCheck)
```

```
    Dim startWeekDay
    Dim endWeekDay

    'Get the no. of days between to 2 dates and divide by 7
    HowManyWeekDays = DateDiff("d", CDate(startDate),CDate(endDate)) \ 7

    startWeekDay = Weekday(startDate)
    endWeekDay = Weekday(endDate)

    'Check for boundary condition
    If endWeekDay >= startWeekDay Then
        If DayToCheck >= startWeekDay And DayToCheck <= endWeekDay Then
            HowManyWeekDays = HowManyWeekDays + 1
        End If
    Else
        If DayToCheck <= startWeekDay Or DayToCheck >= endWeekDay Then
            HowManyWeekDays = HowManyWeekDays + 1
        End If
    End If
End Function
```

 NOTE: It's a good habit to always use ByVal when ByRef is not needed as the default arguments are ByRef.

Day To Check variable will be 1 for Sunday and 7 for a Saturday

So here is the final function that computes how many business/working days exist between any two dates:

```
'Function to get business days between 2 dates
Function GetBusinessDays(ByVal startDate, ByVal endDate)
    GetBusinessDays = DateDiff("d",startDate,endDate) _
                    - HowManyWeekDays(startDate,endDate,vbSunday) _
                    - HowManyWeekDays(startDate,endDate,vbSaturday)
End Function
```

Timer

This function returns the number of seconds that have elapsed since 12:00 AM (midnight). It can be used to calculate the time difference between the start and the end of the task..

 NOTE: If the task starts before the 12:00AM and ends after the 12:00AM, the time difference calculated would be incorrect.

```
'Get the current timer
startTime = Timer()

' Do some time consuming task
```

```
'Get the current timer
endTime = Timer()

'gives the difference in seconds
MsgBox endTime - startTime
```

Misc

This section contains several useful miscellaneous functions:

TypeName

This function returns a string that provides the Variant subtype name of a variable:

```
'Covert to double
x = CDbl(4)

'returns "Double"
MsgBox TypeName(x)

'Convert to string
x = CStr(4)

'returns "String"
MsgBox TypeName(x)
```

VarType

This function returns a constant representing the Variant subtype of a variable:

```
'Convert to interger
x = CInt(4)

'Get the type of variable
If VarType(x) = vbInteger then
    Msgbox "It's a integer"
End if
```

Refer to the VBScript Online HELP for a full list of TypeName and VarType values.

GetRef

GetRef method can be used to create a pointer object to a function. The Code below shows the usage of the same

```
'Custom Function to do a text comparison
'we are worried about only first 5 characters
Function ComparePartText(Text1, Text2)
   If Left(Text1,5) = Left(Text2,5) Then
        ComparePartText = True
   Else
        ComparePartText = False
   End if
End Function


'Function to compare two string
```

```
Function CompareText(Text1, Text2)
   If Text1 = Text2 Then
        CompareText = True
   Else
        CompareText = False
   End if
End Function

'Function to compare 2 text based on comparison function
Function IsEqual(text1,text2, compareFuncPointer)
   IsEqual = compareFuncPointer(text1,text2)
End Function

Text1 = "TarunLalwani"
Text2 = "Tarun Lalwani"

'Displays True
MsgBox IsEqual(Text1,Text2, GetRef("ComparePartText"))

'Displays False
MsgBox IsEqual(Text1,Text2, GetRef("CompareText"))
```

In the above code we are passing a pointer to the comparison function to be used by *IsEqual* method when doing the text comparison.

CreateObject

This function returns a reference to a specified Automation object:

```
'Declare variable
Dim ExcelSheet

'Create an COM object for ProgID "Excel.Application"
Set ExcelSheet = CreateObject("Excel.Application")

sRemoteSever = "127.1.1.1"
'Create an COM object for ProgID "Excel.Application"
'on a remote server
Set ExcelSheet = CreateObject("Excel.Application", sRemoteSever )
```

GetObject

This function returns a reference to an Automation object from a file or an already open application:

```
'Get excel application form a running file
Set ExcelObject = GetObject("C:\Test\Default.xls")

'Get excel application running instance
Set ExcelObject = GetObject(,"Excel.Application")
```

Problem 14-7. Get a sub-string in a string between two specified characters.

For example, a string contains "DEL (DELHI)", and we want to get the text between the parenthesis "(" and ")". Our function will also take the start position in the string to start the search

```
'Function to get a sub-string in a string between
'to specified characters
Public Function GetStrBetweenChar(ByVal Start, ByVal s_Text, ByVal s_StartChar,
ByVal s_EndChar)

    GetStrBetweenChar = ""

    Dim i, Count, s_Char

    i = InStr(Start, s_Text, s_StartChar)

    If i <> 0 Then
        i = i + Len(s_StartChar)

        Count = InStr(i, s_Text, s_EndChar)

        If Count <> 0 Then
            GetStrBetweenChar = Mid(s_Text, i, Count - i)
        End If
    End If
End Function

'Usage:
' This will return "DELHI"
MsgBox GetStrBetweenChar(1,"DEL (DELHI)","(",")")
```

Problem 14-8. Function to get a substring from a start character in a string.

For example - For this string "DEL (DELHI)" the function should return "DELHI)" when the start character is "(". The algorithm for this is much the same as the function discussed above but the difference is that we don't look for an end string this time:

```
'Get a sub string starting from a character
Public Function GetStrFromChar(ByVal Start , ByVal s_Text , ByVal s_StartChar ,
ByVal ReturnSameForNotFound)
    If ReturnSameForNotFound = True Then
        GetStrFromChar = s_Text
    Else
        GetStrFromChar = ""
    End If

    Dim i , Count , s_Char

    i = InStr(Start, s_Text, s_StartChar)

    If i <> 0 Then
        i = i + Len(s_StartChar)
        GetStrFromChar = Mid(s_Text, i)
    End If
End Function
```

If the last argument, ReturnSameForNotFound=True, then the function returns the same string as if the start character is not found:

```
' This will return "(DELHI)"
MsgBox GetStrFromChar (1, "DEL(DELHI)","DEL", False)

' This will return "DEL(DELHI)"
Msgbox GetStrFromChar (1, "DEL(DELHI)","BEL", True)

' This will return ""
Msgbox GetStrFromChar (1, "DEL(DELHI)","BEL", False)
```

Problem 14-9. Write a function that reads a string word by word where two words would be separated by one or more spaces.

The trick here would be to trim the string from the specified start position and then search for a space character in the string and then return the string till that space character

```
'Function to Get a word starting from a position
Public Function GetWordFromPos(ByVal Start, ByVal s_Text)

    GetWordFromPos = ""

    Dim i, Count, s_Char, index
    i = Start

    Count = Len(s_Text)

    If Start >= Count Then
        GetWordFromPos = ""
    Else
        s_Text = Trim(Mid(s_Text, i))

        index = InStr(s_Text, " ")

        If index Then
            GetWordFromPos = Mid(s_Text, 1, index - 1)
        End If
    End If
End Function

'this will return "Tarun"
Msgbox GetWordFromPos (1,"Tarun      Lalwani      wrote this      book")

'this will return "arun"
Msgbox GetWordFromPos (2,"Tarun      Lalwani      wrote this      book")

'this will return "Lalwani"
Msgbox GetWordFromPos (6,"Tarun      Lalwani      wrote this      book")
```

Problem 14-10. Create a function TrimAll which trims not only spaces but other whitespace characters like new lines, carriage returns, and line feeds etc.:

```
'Function to trim all type of white spaces from start
'and end of a string
Function TrimAll(ByVal strText)
    Dim strLen
    Dim strChar
    strLen = Len(strText)
```

```
    TrimAll = ""

    Dim i
    For i = 1 To strLen
        strChar = Mid(strText, i, 1)
        Select Case strChar
            Case vbCrLf, vbNewLine, vbTab, vbLf, vbFormFeed, vbCr, " "
            Case Else
                Exit For
        End Select
    Next

    strText = Mid(strText, i)
    strLen = Len(strText)

    For i = strLen To 1 Step -1
        strChar = Mid(strText, i, 1)
        Select Case strChar
            Case vbCrLf, vbNewLine, vbTab, vbLf, vbFormFeed, vbCr, " "
            Case Else
                Exit For
        End Select
    Next

    strText = Left(strText, i)
    TrimAll = strText
End Function

x= vbCrLf + vbNewLine + "wTarun" + vbLf

'this will assign "Tarun" to x
x = TrimAll(x)
```

Problem 14-11. Create a FilterStr function which takes a string and character set as input and will filter the string based on the characters in the character set.

For example, using the string "212-203-9587", and the character set "0123456789", the function will return "2122039587" or "--" depending on the flag set. The algorithm evaluates each character in the string and checks if it is present in the character set and depending on the bInCharSet flag builds an appropriate return string:

```
'Function to filter a charset from a string
Function FilterStr(ByVal strText, ByVal strCharset, ByVal bInCharSet)
    Dim strLen
    Dim strChar
    strLen = Len(strText)

    FilterStr = ""


    Dim i
```

```
    If bInCharSet Then    'return each strCharSet chars found in strText
        For i = 1 To strLen
            strChar = Mid(strText, i, 1)
            If InStr(strCharset, strChar) <> 0 Then
                FilterStr = FilterStr + strChar
            End If
        Next
    Else                    'return each strCharSet chars NOT found in strText
        For i = 1 To strLen
            strChar = Mid(strText, i, 1)
            If InStr(strCharset, strChar) = 0 Then
                FilterStr = FilterStr + strChar
            End If
        Next
    End If
End Function

'this will return "2122122122"
Msgbox FilterStr("212-212-2122","0123456789",True)

'this will return "--"
Msgbox FilterStr("212-212-2122","0123456789",False)

'this will return "2122122122"
MsgBox FilterStr("212-212-2122","-",False)
```

Problem 14-12. Create two functions, one which returns the path portion and another the file name, when passed a fully qualified path or filename:

```
'Function to get file path from file name
Function GetFilePath(ByVal s_FileName)
    GetFilePath = ""
    On Error Resume Next
    GetFilePath = Left(s_FileName, Len(s_FileName) - InStr(StrReverse(s_
FileName), "\") + 1 )
End Function

'Function to get file name from path
Function GetFileName(ByVal s_FileName)
    GetFileName = ""
    On Error Resume Next
    GetFileName = Right(s_FileName, InStr(StrReverse(s_FileName), "\") - 1)
End Function


'Will return "Test.vbs"
Msgbox GetFileName("C:\Test\Test.vbs")

'Will return "C:\Test\"
Msgbox GetFilePath("C:\Test\Test.vbs")
```

Problem 14-13. Write a function that compares two string ignoring new line, line feeds, tab etc. whitespace characters:

```
'Function to clean up white space characters
'from inside a string
Function CleanText(s_Text)
    CleanText = s_Text
    CleanText = Replace(CleanText, vbCrLf, "")
    CleanText = Replace(CleanText, vbCr, vbLf)
    CleanText = Replace(CleanText, Chr(7), "")
    CleanText = Replace(CleanText, vbCrLf, vbLf)
    CleanText = Replace(CleanText, vbVerticalTab, vbLf)
    CleanText = Replace(CleanText, vbTab, "")
End Function


'Usage:
If CleanText(text1) = CleanText(text2) then
    Msgbox "String equal after cleaning"
End if
```

Problem 14-14. Write a function that replaces repeated occurrences of a given character by another character.

Example: this function will return "Tarun_Lalwani" when a input string "Tarun Lalwani" is given for replacing repeated <Space> characters with a single underscore,'_', character:

```
'Function to replace continous character occurance of
'a specified character by a replacement character
Function ReplaceMultipleByOne(ByVal strText, ByVal strSearch, ByVal strReplace)
    Dim i, strLen, strChar
    Dim bFlag
    bFlag = False
    strLen = Len(strText)
    For i = 1 To strLen
        strChar = Mid(strText, i, 1)

        If strChar = strSearch Then
            If Not bFlag Then
                bFlag = True
                ReplaceMultipleByOne = ReplaceMultipleByOne + strReplace
            End If
        Else
            bFlag = False
            ReplaceMultipleByOne = ReplaceMultipleByOne + strChar
        End If
    Next
End Function
```

Working with Arrays

VBScript provides two types of arrays – fixed length and dynamic.

Fixed length arrays

Sample code:

```
'create a 3 member fixed length array
Dim X(2)

X(0) = "This"
X(1) = "is a"
X(2) = "test"

For i = LBound (X) to UBound(X)
    Msgbox X(i)
Next
```

The LBound and UBound functions return the values of lower and upper bound of an array respectively, which in above example would be 0 and 2.

Dynamic Arrays

```
'create a dynamic array
Dim X()

'Before using the array the first time the array must be initialized with some
dimension
ReDim X(2)
X(0) = "This"
X(1) = "is a"
X(2) = "test"
```

We can ReDim a dynamic array to change its size as often as we want. But each time this is done, the values in the array are destroyed unless we use the 'preserve' keyword as shown here:

```
'Redimension the array
ReDim Preserve X(5)
```

The above statement resizes the array while preserving the values of the first 3 elements.

In the case of a multi-dimensional array, the Preserve keyword can be used if only the last dimension of the array is changing.

```
'Dynamic array
Dim X()

ReDim X(2,3)
'This will work fine as we are only changing
'the last dimension while preserving the array
ReDim Preserve X (2,5)

'This will throw an error due to the first
'dimension of the array being changed
ReDim Preserve X(3,5)
```

```
'This will work fine as normal ReDim does
'not have a restriction
ReDim X(4,5,6)
```

Problem 14-15. How can we get the UBound/LBound values of multi-dimensional array?

Consider the multi-dimensional array X(4,5,6). UBound(X) will return 4, the upper bound of the 1st dimension. To get the other dimension we can use the optional parameter of UBound

```
'returns 4, if the second argument is not
'specified it is defaulted to 1
MsgBox UBound(X, 1)

'returns 5, the upper bounds of the 2nd dimension
Msgbox UBound(X, 2)

'returns 6, the upper bounds of the 3rd dimension
Msgbox UBound(X, 3)
```

Execute Statement

VBScript provides a very useful statement, Execute, which is used to execute any statement(s), defined as strings, at run-time:

Execute [statement]

```
'Global variable x
Dim x

Execute "x = 2"

MsgBox x
'We need to use " as a escape character to specify a " inside a string
x = "Browser(""micClass:=Browser"")"

'x will get the browser object
Execute ("Set x = " & x)

MsgBox x.Exist(0)
```

Similarly we have an ExecuteGlobal Statement which executes the statement in global scope:

```
'Global variable x
Dim x

x = 4

Call Func1

Sub Func1()
 Dim x
 x = 3
 'Will give output as 3, local variable
```

```
Execute "Msgbox x"
'Will give output as 4, statement executed in global scope
ExecuteGlobal "Msgbox x",
End Sub
```

As the execute statement executes in the Local Scope the message box displays a value which is 3, while the ExecuteGlobal statement executes in the Global Scope and displays a value 4.

Eval function

The related Eval function is used to evaluate a statement:

```
'assigns a value 2 to x
Execute "x = 2"

'Compare x with 3. This will give False
Msgbox Eval("x = 3")
```

Problem 14-16. How can we declare and initialize a read only variable at run-time?

Sometime it's useful to declare a read-only initialized variable at run-time:

```
'define a read-only var at load time
Const URL1 ="http://www.noone.com"

x = "http://www.noone.com"

'define a read-only var/constant at run-time
Execute "Const URL2 = " & x
```

Optional arguments in VBScript

VBScript does not support optional parameters but there are some workarounds that can be used to achieve similar functionality:

- Method 1 - Optional arguments using Null/Empty values

- Method 2 - Optional arguments using Array members

- Method 3 - Optional arguments using an Array of (key, value) pairs

- Method 4 - Optional argument using an Array of (key:=value) pairs

- Method 5 - Optional arguments using an Array of Hybrid (key, value or key:=value) pairs

Using Null/Empty values

This method uses Null or Empty value for optional parameters.

```
'This method checks if its parameter is a Null or a Empty value.
Public Function IsMissing(ByVal Param)
  On error resume next
  'Check if the parameter is null or empty
  IsMissing = IsEmpty(Param) or IsNull(Param)

  'In case of error assume that it's a object and return false
  If err.Number <> 0 Then IsMissing = False
```

```
End Function

'Demonstrate Method 1 - Optional arguments using Null/Empty values
Public Function OptParameter_Method1 (ByVal Param1, ByVal Param2)
   If IsMissing(Param1) Then Param1 = "Tarun"
   If IsMissing(Param2) Then Param2 = "Lalwani"

   MsgBox Param1 & " " & Param2
End Function

'Usage:

Call OptParameter_Method1("Tarun", Null)
Call OptParameter_Method1("Tarun", "Lalwani")
Call OptParameter_Method1(Empty, "Lalwani")
```

Using an Array of values

This method defines an array as the input parameter and then uses one or more Array elements and the actual parameters

```
'Method 2 for optional arguments
Public Function OptParameter_Method2 (Arguments)
   'Take the values from arguments
   FirstName = Arguments(0)
   LastName = Arguments(1)

   If IsMissing(FirstName) Then FirstName = "Tarun"
   If IsMissing(LastName) Then LastName = "Lalwani"

   'Do processing on the data.

'Incase you want to implement the ByRef then Reassign
   'the values back to the array
   Arguments(0) = FirstName
   Arguments(1) = LastName

   Msgbox FirstName  & " " & LastName
End Function

'Usage:

Call OptParameter_Method2 (Array("Tarun",Null))
Call OptParameter_Method2 (Array(Null,Null))
```

The problem with this approach is that if the last parameter is missing we have to pass a Null value every time. We can improve that by expanding the array automatically in case there are missing parameters

```
'Method 2A for optional arguments
Public Function OptParameter_Method2A (Arguments)
   Const ParamCount = 2

   Dim Params
```

```
'Check if no array has been passed
If IsMissing(Arguments) Then
 ReDim Params(ParamCount - 1)
Else
  'In case Arguments is not an Array, then make it an Array
      If VarType(Arguments) < vbArray Then
    Arguments = Array(Arguments)
        End If

  Params = Arguments

      'Resize the arguments array to get the expected parameter length
      'Use preserve to prevent loss of other arguments
      ReDim Preserve Params(ParamCount - 1)
End If

  'Not repeating the code here
  Call OptParameter_Method2(Params)
End Function

'Usage:

Call OptParameter_Method2A (Null)
Call OptParameter_Method2A ("Tarun")
Call OptParameter_Method2A (Array(Null, "Lalwani"))
Call OptParameter_Method2A (Array("Tarun"))
```

Using an Array of (Key, Value) pairs

In this method we pass the arguments as a value pair, one as the name and another as its value. The number of arguments in this case needs to be even. We would create a dictionary from the array and use it as parameters. Let's first look at the parameter conversion from array to dictionary.

```
'Method 2A for optional arguments
Public Function OptParameter_Method2A (Arguments)
   Const ParamCount = 2

   Dim Params

   'Check if no array has been passed
   If IsMissing(Arguments) Then
    ReDim Params(ParamCount - 1)
   Else
     'In case Arguments is not an Array, then make it an Array
         If VarType(Arguments) < vbArray Then
       Arguments = Array(Arguments)
           End If

   Params = Arguments

       'Resize the arguments array to get the expected parameter length
```

```vbscript
            'Use preserve to prevent loss of other arguments
            ReDim Preserve Params(ParamCount - 1)
    End If

    'Not repeating the code here
    Call OptParameter_Method2(Params)
End Function

'Usage:

Call OptParameter_Method2A (Null)
Call OptParameter_Method2A ("Tarun")
Call OptParameter_Method2A (Array(Null, "Lalwani"))
Call OptParameter_Method2A (Array("Tarun"))
```

Now let's look at how to use the above techniques

```vbscript
'Method to demonstrate
Public Function OptParameter_Method3 (Arguments)
    Set Params = CreateObject("Scripting.Dictionary")

    GetArgumentsList_v1 Params, Arguments

    FirstName = GetParamValue(Params, "FirstName","Tarun")
    LastName = GetParamValue(Params, "LastName", "Lalwani")

    MsgBox FirstName & " " & LastName
End Function

'Usage:
Call OptParameter_Method3 (Null)
Call OptParameter_Method3 (Array("FirstName","Tarun","LastName","Lalwani"))
Call OptParameter_Method3 (Array("FirstName","Tarun"))
Call OptParameter_Method3 (Array("LastName","Lalwani"))
```

Using an Array of Key:=Value pairs

In this method function arguments are passed as key:=value pairs. The function which converts the passed values to a dictionary would change:

```vbscript
'This Function creates a dictionary from the array
Public Sub GetArgumentsList_v2(ArgListDict, Arguments)
    'Set the compare mode as text so that parameters
    'are in-case sensitive
    ArgListDict.CompareMode = vbTextCompare

    'If argument is missing then do not process
    If IsMissing(Arguments) Then Exit Sub

    Dim i, iCount
    iCount = UBound(Arguments)
    For i = LBound(Arguments) to iCount step 1
            valPos = InStr(Arguments(i), ":=")
            ParamName = Left (Arguments(i), valPos - 1)
            ParamValue = Mid (Arguments(i), valPos + 2)
```

```vbscript
                    ArgListDict.Add ParamName, ParamValue
        Next
    End Sub

    'Method to demonstrate
    Public Function OptParameter_Method4 (Arguments)
        Set Params = CreateObject("Scripting.Dictionary")

        GetArgumentsList_v2 Params, Arguments

        FirstName = GetParamValue(Params, "FirstName","Tarun")
        LastName = GetParamValue(Params, "LastName", "Lalwani")

        MsgBox FirstName & " " & LastName
    End Function

    'Usage:
    Call OptParameter_Method4 (Null)
    Call OptParameter_Method4 (Array("FirstName:=Tarun","LastName:=Lalwani"))
    Call OptParameter_Method4 (Array("FirstName:=Tarun"))
    Call OptParameter_Method4 (Array("LastName:=Lalwani"))
```

Arrays of Hybrid (Key, Value or Key:=Value) pairs

In this method we support passing function parameters using both (Key, Value) or Key:=Value pairs. The advantage of this method is the ability to pass arguments in any order and the ability to pass objects at the same time using (Key, Value) pairs.

```vbscript
    'This Function creates a dictionary from the array
    Public Sub GetArgumentsList_v3(ArgListDict, Arguments)
        'Set the compare mode as text so that parameters
        'are in-case sensitive
        ArgListDict.CompareMode = vbTextCompare

        'If argument is missing then do not process
        If IsMissing(Arguments) Then Exit Sub

        Dim i, iCount
        iCount = UBound(Arguments)
        For i = LBound(Arguments) to iCount step 1
                valPos = InStr(Arguments(i), ":=")

                If valPos = 0 Then
                        'It's a key,value pair
                        ParamName = Arguments(i)
                        'Move to the value
                        i = i + 1
                    ParamValue = Arguments(i)
                Else
                        'It's a Key:=Value pair
                        ParamName = Left (Arguments(i), valPos - 1)
                        ParamValue = Mid (Arguments(i), valPos + 2)
                End if
```

```
        ArgListDict.Add ParamName, ParamValue
    Next
End Sub

'Method to demonstrate
Public Function OptParameter_Method5 (Arguments)
    Set Params = CreateObject("Scripting.Dictionary")

    GetArgumentsList_v3 Params, Arguments

    FirstName = GetParamValue(Params, "FirstName","Tarun")
    LastName = GetParamValue(Params, "LastName", "Lalwani")

    MsgBox FirstName & " " & LastName
End Function

'Usage:
Call OptParameter_Method5 (Null)
Call OptParameter_Method5 (Array("FirstName:=Tarun","LastName:=Lalwani"))
Call OptParameter_Method5 (Array("FirstName:=Tarun"))
Call OptParameter_Method5 (Array("LastName:=Lalwani"))
```

Reader's Note

Chapter 15

Synchronization

Synchronization Points

When the application under test takes some time to respond to an action, QTP might execute the next step for which the application is not yet ready. In this situation QTP might throw an error. For example, if in the Step1 QTP selects a value from a list that will cause a button to be enabled after some processing, QTP's attempt to click the button before it gets enabled will result in QTP throwing an "Object is disabled" exception.

Synchronization Points are used to insert pause time or wait time before executing certain steps within a test. These points help avoid unnecessary errors due to the higher response time of the application under test. QTP provides three different types of Synchronization Points:

1st Method – Using the Sync method

```
'Select Option1
Browser("..").Page("..").WebList("List").Select "Option1"

'Wait for page to reload
Browser("..").Sync

'Click on the Next button now
Browser("..").Page("..").WebButton("Next").Click
```

But sometimes the Sync method may itself throw an error. In such cases the On Error resume next constructs should be used as shown below:

```
'Disable all error popups
On Error Resume Next
'Sync the browser and page objects
Browser("..").Sync
Browser("..").Page("..").Sync

'Enable error popups
On Error Goto 0
```

2nd Method – Using the Wait statement

```
'Select option1
Browser("..").Page("..").WebList("List").Select "Option1"

Wait 2 'Wait for 2 sec

'Click on the next button
Browser("..").Page("..").WebButton("Next").Click
```

3rd Method – WaitProperty method

```
'Select option 1
Browser("..").Page("..").WebList("List").Select "Option1"

'Wait for max 5 sec or until the button gets
'enabled, whichever is lesser
Browser("..").Page("..").WebButton("Next").WaitProperty("Enabled", True, 5000)

'Click the next button
Browser("..").Page("..").WebButton("Next").Click
```

In case the object does not exist before the operation starts we can also use the Exist method:

```
'Select option 1
Browser("..").Page("..").WebList("List").Select "Option1"

'Wait max 5 seconds for button to appear
bButton = Browser("..").Page("..").WebButton("Next").Exist(5)

'Check if button exits or not
If bButton Then
  'Click the next button
  Browser("..").Page("..").WebButton("Next").Click
Else
  'Process the error
End if
```

Checking Object Existence

Consider the following Login example:

```
'Set the user name and password
Browser().Page().WebEdit("uid").Set "Username"
Browser().Page().WebEdit("password").Set "password"

'Click on the login button
Browser().Page().WebButton("login").Click

'Check if login failed text exist
If Browser().Page().WebElement("innerText:=Login failed").Exist(5) Then
   Report.ReportEvent micFail, "Login", "Login failed"
Else
   Report.ReportEvent micPass, "Login", "Login Successful"
End if
```

Using the above code, users who specify a good login and password, which is normally the case, these users will waste 5 seconds waiting for a Login failure message that will not occur. In this example, a "Logout" link appears when the login is successful, so if we test for both conditions we can proceed as soon as either occurs:

```
'Set the username and pasword
Browser().Page().WebEdit("uid").Set "Username"
Browser().Page().WebEdit("password").Set "password"

'Click on login button
Browser().Page().WebButton("login").Click

'Check the existence of both objects
bLoginPass = Browser().Page().Link("text:=Logout").Exist(0)
bLoginFail = Browser().Page().WebElement("innerText:=Login failed").Exist(0)
i = 0

'Wait up to 5 seconds for a success or failure indication
While (Not bLoginPass or Not bLoginFail) and i < 5
   Wait 1
   i = i + 1
   bLoginPass = Browser().Page().Link("text:=Logout").Exist(0)
   bLoginFail = Browser().Page().WebElement("innerText:=Login failed").Exist(0)
Wend

'Check if login fialed
If bLoginFail Then
   Report.ReportEvent micFail, "Login", "Login failed"
'Check if login passed
ElseIf bLoginPass Then
   Report.ReportEvent micPass, "Login", "Login Successful"
Else
   Report.ReportEvent micFail, "Login", "Failed to determine login status"
End if
```

The above code might seem lengthy, but putting the code in a function and re-using it will reduce the time wasted during execution.

Browser Vs Page Sync

There is no documented difference between Sync on browser and a Page. Though these two seem to be different on what they wait for. Page sync will wait for the page to load which will work in cases where there are no frames inside the page. While a Browser Sync will wait for the page to load and also for all the frames inside the web page.

Events

There might be times when synchronization does not help. This might happen because of events not being fired. Let's look at an example of an HTML code

```
<HTML>
    <BODY>
        <INPUT name=txtName type=text size=10 onkeyup="cmdClick.
```

```
disabled=false">
        <INPUT name=cmdClick type=button DISABLED value="Click me">
    </BODY>
</HTML>
```

The page behaves in such a way that when a user presses any key in the text box the Click Me button gets enabled. Let's record typing something into the textbox:

```
'Set the value of WebEdit as Test
Browser("..").Page("..").WebEdit("..").Set "Test"
```

But when we re-run this code the Click Me button won't get enabled as shown in the next figure:

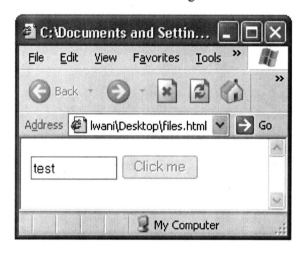

Figure 15-1. Button not enabled

When we run the above code in QTP, we observe that the text is set but the button does not get enabled. This happens because QTP has an event configuration which tells it to optionally record an event. Looking at the HTML source code we used above, we find that its onkeyup event needs to be triggered to enable the button. So we can use the QTP code below to cause this event to occur:

```
'Set the webedit as Test
Browser("..").Page("..").WebEdit("..").Set "Test"

'Fire the onkeyup event
Browser("..").Page("..").WebEdit("..").FireEvent "onkeyup"
```

If we don't know which event has been defined for the edit we can fire all of them:

```
'Fire all the events
Browser("..").Page("..").WebEdit("..").FireEvent "onkeydown"
Browser("..").Page("..").WebEdit("..").FireEvent "onkeyup"
Browser("..").Page("..").WebEdit("..").FireEvent "onkeypress"
```

When we use descriptive programming we always need to add the fire event ourselves. And in the situation where the code is added by QTP then it will only record the FireEvent statement based on the Web Event Recording Configuration. There are three possible profiles for this (Low, Medium & High). To change the configuration, go to *Tools→Web Event Recording Configuration...* and click the *Custom Settings...* button. Select the test object we want to modify as shown in the Figure 15-2

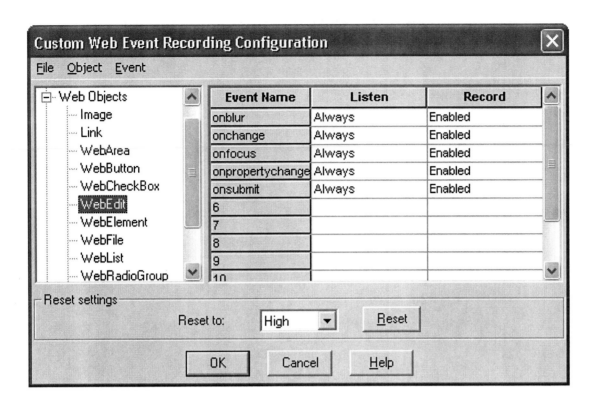

Figure 15-2. High WebEvent Configuration

Notice that even in the High configuration only onkeydown is supported. But in our example the onkeyup event must be fired, but QTP does not support recording this event. QTP only supports the following—all others need to be fired manually:

onchange, onblur, onfocus, onmousedown, onmouseup, onmouseover, onmouseout, onsubmit, onreset and onpropertychange.

Replay Options

By default QTP is configured to replay against web objects using browser events and that is why we had to explicitly use FireEvent in the above code. But we can configure QTP to replay events using the mouse. To change the replay type go to *Tools→Options...→Web(tab)→Advanced...(button)* and select the *ReplayType* radio button value as *Mouse*, as shown below:

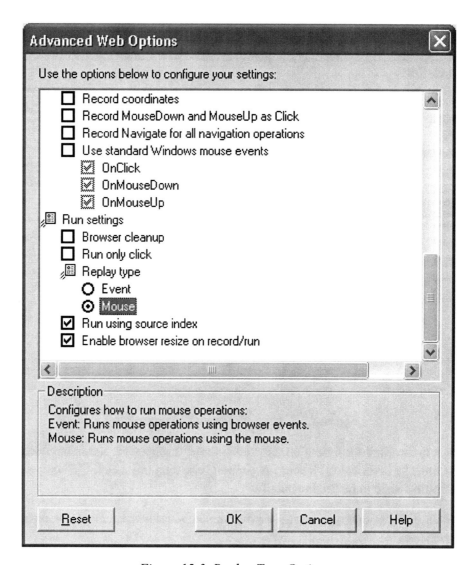

Figure 15-3. Replay Type Options

Or we also change the setting at run-time using the following statement:

```
'1 to replay using Browser events
'2 to replay using Mouse events
Setting.WebPackage("ReplayType") = 2
Browser("..").Page("..").WebEdit("..").Set "Test"
```

Reader's Note

Reader's Note

Chapter 16

Test Results

Test Results provides a summary of a QuickTest run session. The results are stored in an XML file format. QTP provides a Test Results viewer tool used to review and print these results. Test Results optionally contain image snapshots, based on QTP configuration settings. Figure 16-1 shows a typical test result summary:

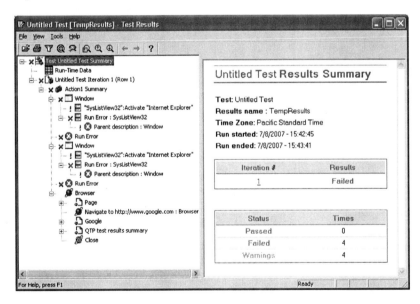

Figure 16-1. Test Results summary

The left hand pane provides summary information about each step performed during the test run. Icons to the left of each step provide the following information as well:

- ⊙ A Cross (X) icon denotes a failed step

- ⊙ An Exclamation (!) icon denotes a warning step

- ⊙ A Tick (✓) icon denotes a passed step

⊙ A step without any of these symbols denotes an information step

QTP assigns status to a step based on one of the follow situations:

⊙ Checkpoint: Checkpoint can cause a step to pass or fail

⊙ Smart Identification: If Smart identification is used to identify an object then that step is assigned the warning icon

⊙ Error: If a step encounters any error, it will be assigned the failed icon

⊙ Custom events: Custom events are used to directly assign a step an explicit status

Filtering Steps in a Report

It is possible to control what types of steps are written to the test results using the following statement:

```
Reporter.Filter = <Filter Value>
```

The <Filter Value> must use one of the following QTP built-in variables:

⊙ rfEnableAll – Report all steps. This is the default setting

⊙ rfEnableErrorsAndWarnings – Only report error (failed) and warning steps

⊙ rfEnableErrorsOnly – Only report error steps

⊙ rfDisableAll – Does not report any steps

The following code shows how to suppress a single checkpoint's pass/fail status:

```
'Store the old filter value
oldFilter = Reporter.Filter

'Disable reporting of all events
Reporter.Filter = rfDisableAll

Set oPg = Browser("Browser").Page("Page")
chkStatus = oPg.WebEdit("username").Check (Checkpoint("username"))

If chkStatus Then
  MsgBox "Passed"
Else
  MsgBox "Failed"
End If

'Restrore the old filter value
Reporter.Filter = oldFilter
```

Reporting Custom Steps

We can insert our own steps in the Test Results using the following statement:

```
Reporter.ReportEvent <EventStatus>, <ReportStepName>, <Details>
```

The <EventStatus> should use one of the following QTP built-in variables:

- ⊙ micPass – Reports a step with passed status

- ⊙ micFail – Reports a step with failed status

- ⊙ micWarning – Reports a step with warning status

- ⊙ micDone – Reports a step with no status

```
'Get the actual link href
actualLink = Browser("Browser").Page("Page").Link("Login").
GetROProperty("href")

If actualLink = "http://mywebsite.com/login.do" Then
   Reporter.ReportEvent micPass, "Validate Link - Login", "Correct Link"
Else
   Reporter.ReportEvent micFail, "Validate Login", "Wrong Link - " & actualLink
End if
```

While the <ReportStepName> and <Details> parameters are plain text strings, it is possible to embed HTML tags into these strings as follows:

```
'HTML text to be entered
sHTML = "&lt;<A target=_New href=""http://www.mywebsite.com"">Click Me</A>&gt;"

'Add to reporter
Reporter.ReportEvent micDone, "Link", sHTML
```

QTP also supports one more undocumented EventStatus, micInfo. Using micInfo creates a step with an "i" icon for the step. This is useful to report just information in the report, which we may want to visually segregate from the similar micDone entries.

Inserting Files in Test Results

Consider the following code:

```
'Create the html file path
'store it in a Test Results folder
sFile = Reporter.ReportPath & "\StepsToRecreate.html"

'Create the HTML file
Set FSO = CreateObject("Scripting.FileSystemObject")
Set file = FSO.CreateTextFile(sFile,True)
file.Write "<I><B>Step 1</B></I>. Launch www.mywebsite.com"
file.Write "<P><B>Step 2</B>. Click on the Login link"
file.Write "<P><B>Step 3</B>. Enter the username as tarun"
```

```
file.Write "<P><B>Step 4</B>. Enter password as tarun"
file.Write "<P><B>Step 5</B>. Click on the Login button"
file.Write "<P><B><I>Step 6</I></B>. Close the browser"
file.close

'Insert the above file as a IFRAME in the report
sHTML = "&lt;<IFRAME width=""100%"" height=250 src=""file:///" &
sFile & """></IFRAME>&gt;"
Reporter.ReportEvent micPass, "Steps To Recreate", sHTML

'Clean up
Set file = Nothing
Set FSO = Nothing
```

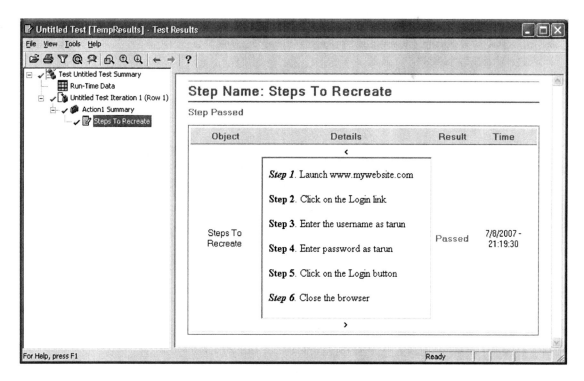

Running the above code will display the file as shown below:

Figure 16-2. Embedding File in test results

Inserting Snapshots in Test Results

This section describes various ways of inserting screen snapshots into the Test Results.

Method 1

Configure QTP to save a screen snapshot for every step. Go to *Tools→Options…→Run (Tab)* and set the option for *"Save step screen capture to results:"* **to** *"Always"* as shown in the Figure 16-3.

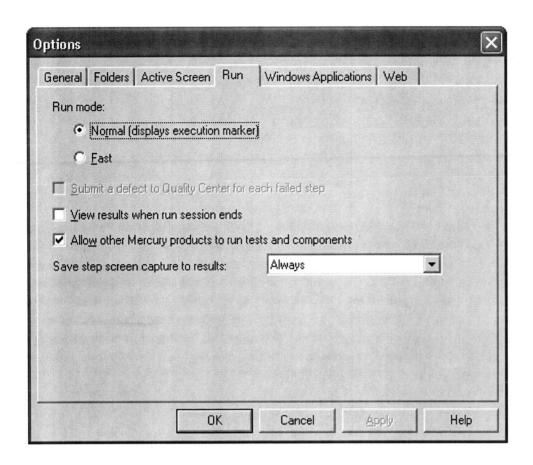

Figure 16-3. Settings for saving screenshots

This is a disk intensive option when the script contains even a modest number of steps, as each screenshot taken increases the size of the results folder.

Method 2

In this approach we use the SnapshotReportMode setting. This allows us to selectively determine when a snapshot is captured. The trick here is to use the Exist method on the object's whose snapshot needs to be captured:

```
'Save the old mode
oldMode = Setting("SnapshotReportMode")

Setting("SnapshotReportMode") = 0

'To capture a window use the below statment
x = Window("title:=Run").Exist(0)

'To capture a browser use the below statment
x = Browser("micclass:=Browser").Page("micclass:=Page").Exist(0)

'Restore the old mode
Setting("SnapshotReportMode") = oldMode
```

Method 3

This approach saves an explicit snapshot using the CaptureBitmap method in the Test Results folder. After adding the snapshot we also add an HTML image tag to the results to display the image.

```
'Create the html file path
'store it in report folder
currentTime = Replace(Replace(Replace(now(),":","-"),"/","-")," ","-")
sFile = Reporter.ReportPath & "\Snap_" & currentTime & ".png"
Desktop.CaptureBitmap sFile

'Insert the above file as a IFRAME in the report
sHTML = "&lt;<IMG width=""100%"" src=""file:///" & sFile & """></IMG>&gt;"
Reporter.ReportEvent micPass, "Snapshot", sHTML
```

 NOTE: Problem with using above approach is that we use absolute file path for the image. So when the test results folder is transferred to any other location, the above path will become invalid and the test results would become invalid. Unfortunately QTP does not provide any way of using Relative paths for such situation.

Converting XML Results to HTML

QTP creates Test Results in XML format in a proprietary folder structure that can't be viewed without the using QTP's Test Results viewer tool. But results can be converted into HTML format using XSLs. QTP provides three such XSLs which can be used to convert a XML file to HTML:

- PDetails.xsl

- PShort.xsl

- PSelection.xsl

We can apply the first two XSL using the ApplyXSL function created in Chapter "Working with XMLs". Using the PSelection.xsl is beyond the scope of this book.

Configuring QTP to generate HTML results

QTP has a Logger routine which sends events to all installed and enabled media. Each reporting library is called as Media and is a COM library. QTP by default provides the following media:

- Report – Creates the xml results ("Mercury.ReportLogger")

- Log - Creates HTML results ("Mercury.GeneralLogger")

- TD – Creates results in the Quality center or Test director project ("Mercury.TDReportLogger")

By default the HTML media is disabled. To activate the HTML results open *regedit.exe* and Navigate to *"HKEY_LOCAL_MACHINE\SOFTWARE\Mercury Interactive\QuickTest Professional\Logger\ Media\Log"* and change the "Active" value from 0 to 1. Now QTP will generate results in HTML format as well.

NOTE: QTP must be restarted after changing this setting.

We can create our own custom reporting media templates also. Refer to QTP Plus help for further information on this.

The QTP Reporter Object

The QTP Reporter object supports the following methods and properties:

- Filter
- ReportEvent
- ReportPath
- RunStatus (in QTP 9.2 and above)

Additionally the Reporter object also supports the following undocumented methods:

- GetContext
- GetParentId(Id)
- LogEvent(et, pDescription, ParentId)
- RestoreContext
- SetContext(EventId)
- SetRegistryRoot (Root)
- SetStatus (Id, Status)
- StoreContext
- UnStoreContext

The two methods from this list we are interested in are GetContext and LogEvent. The Context method defines the id of current node in the tree structure of the results.

```
LogEvent(et, pDescription, ParentId)
```

- et – Name of the event that occurred
- pDescription – Dictionary of parameters and their value for given event type
- ParentId – Context id of the parent id

The function returns the context id of a newly created node in the report. By using this return value in ParentId we can report nested events. Earlier we saw that we cannot use relative paths while reporting images to results.

But we can use relative paths when using these undocumented methods as described below:

```
'Capture the desktop to the Report folder in current test results path
Desktop.CaptureBitmap Reporter.ReportPath & "\DesktopImage.png", True

'Create a dictionary for event parameters
Set oEventDesc = CreateObject("Scripting.Dictionary")

'View Type to be use.
oEventDesc("ViewType") = "Sell.Explorer.2"

'Status of the event
oEventDesc("Status") = micPass

'HTML information about the step
oEventDesc("StepHtmlInfo") = "<h1>Test"

'Name of the node
oEventDesc("NodeName") = "Desktop Image"

'Relative path for the image. <Reporter.ReportPath>\Report
'is the current folder from where the relative paths would be resolved
oEventDesc("BottomFilePath") = "..\DesktopImage.png"
oEventDesc("ShowTopFile") = False

'Enable Filter when set to False will display the node even if the
'filters are set in report viewer
oEventDesc("EnableFilter") = False

'Icon details
oEventDesc("DllPAth")="C:\WINDOWS\system32\shell32.dll"
iconIndex = 23
oEventDesc("DllIconIndex") = iconIndex
oEventDesc("DllIconSelIndex") = iconIndex
oEventDesc("IconIndex") = iconIndex
oEventDesc("IconSelIndex") = iconIndex

'Report the event
newEventContext = Reporter.LogEvent ("Replay", oEventDesc, Reporter.
GetContext())

'Change the step information
oEventDesc("NodeName") = "Desktop Info"
oEventDesc("StepHtmlInfo") = "This desktop was captured at 1024 X 780"

oEventDesc("Status") = micGeneral

'Do not display file
oEventDesc.Remove "BottomFilePath"
oEventDesc("ShowTopFile") = True
'Create a nested event in the log by using the last context id
newEventContext = Reporter.LogEvent ("Replay", oEventDesc, newEventContext)
```

These techniques have the following advantages over the ReportEvent method:

⊙ Support for relative paths

⊙ Inserts HTML step information without having to use "<" and ">", etc. HTML tags.

The Test Results produced using the script above is shown in the Figure 16-4

Figure 16-4. Custom Test results

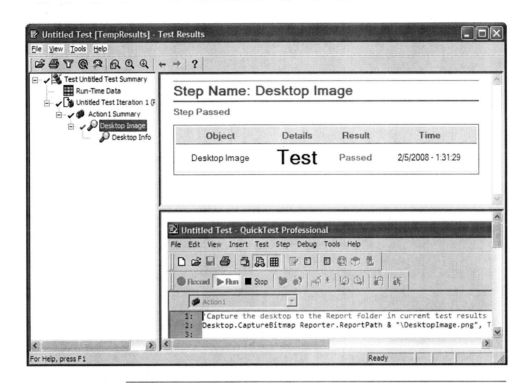

 NOTE: The images inserted using above method are also visible when results are viewed from Quality Center. This was considered a impossible task till QTP 10

Accessing Test Results at the end

QTP creates the results in the test results folder. We may want to access these results at the end of the test script to save them to another location or to send them through email. Let's say we want to copy the Results.xml file which is created in the Report folder. We can write the following code to perform this task in a QTP script:

```
'Report a pass event
Reporter.ReportEvent micPass, "Testing Report", "Testing Exporting of Report"

'Get the result directory
sResultDir = Environment("ResultDir")

'Copy the file to destination
Set fso = CreateObject("Scripting.FileSystemObject")
fso.CopyFile  sResultDir  & "\Report\Results.xml", "C:\Copy_Results.xml", True
Set fso = Nothing
```

When we run this code, it executes without error, but when we inspect "Copy_Results.xml" file the size is 0. This occurs because QTP does not save the Test Results to disk until the script has terminated. This means we can only export the results when QTP has finished script execution. But we can't execute the code to export the test results with QTP stopped. There are two possible workarounds for this problem.

Method 1

In this method we create an external VBS file. The source and destination location of the results is then passed to the external VBS file that we created. The script waits for QTP to finish execution and then copies the results to the specified destination. Here is what the VBS file looks like:

```
'C:\CopyResultsAtEnd.vbs
'Get the input arguments to the script
sSourceFile = WScript.Arguments.Item(0)
sDestinationFile = WScript.Arguments.Item(1)

'Get QTP Automation object
Set qtpApp = CreateObject ("QuickTest.Application")

'Check if QTP is running or not
While qtpApp.Test.IsRunning
  'If QTP is running then loop until it stops
Wend

'QTP has finished execution and the test results
'are available now
Set FSO = CreateObject ("Scripting.FileSystemObject")
FSO.CopyFile sSourceFile, sDestinationFile, True
Set FSO = Nothing
```

In QTP we use the following code to execute the above VBS in asynchronous mode:

```
'External Script which will wait for
'QTP to stop and then copy the results
'to our destination location
sReportScript = "C:\CopyResultsAtEnd.vbs"
sResultsFile = Environment("ResultDir") & "\Report\Results.xml"
sCopyToFile = "C:\Results_Copy.xml"

Set WShell = CreateObject("WScript.Shell")
'Pass the source and destination files as arguments
sCommand = "WScript" & DQ(sReportScript) & DQ(sResultsFile) & DQ(sCopyToFile)

'Run the above command in Async mode
'Execution will not wait for the command to finish
'and will move on to the next line
WShell.Run sCommand
Set WShell = Nothing

'Function to Double quote a string this is needed
'when passing parameters with spaces
Public Function DQ(strText)
    DQ = " """ & strText & """ "
End Function
```

NOTE: The above code should be put in a VBS File and associated with the test, so that the code only runs once during the test. Refer to the "Library Files" chapter on how to load a library only once

Method 2

This method is a never recommended compared to method 1 but it allows us to copy the results from QTP itself. As discussed in the earlier problems, we know that QTP sends an "EndTest" and "EndRepLog" to all the media. The media then finalize the report. So if we can send these events to the media from QTP itself this means we can finalize the results and then copy it from within the QTP script itself using the following code:

```vbs
'Create the event description
Set pDesc = CreateObject("Scripting.Dictionary")
pDesc.Add "ViewType", "Sell.Explorer.2"
pDesc.Add "Status", 2
pDesc.Add "StepInfo", ""
pDesc.Add "ArgumentsDispatch", Empty
pDesc.Add "ReturnLogStatus", 2
'Send the End Test event
Reporter.LogEvent "EndTest", pDesc, 0

'Send the EndRepLog event
pDesc.Remove "ArgumentsDispatch"
Reporter.LogEvent "EndRepLog", pDesc, 0

'Exports the results
sResultDir = Environment("ResultDir")
Set fso = CreateObject("Scripting.FileSystemObject")
fso.CopyFile  sResultDir & "\Report\Results.xml", "C:\Copy_Results.xml", True
Set fso = Nothing
```

NOTE: If the above code gets executed at every iteration then it will not create the complete test results. This should be run only on the last iteration of the test case

WARNING: This is not recommended, as it is an undocumented way of ending the test result.

Reader's Note

Chapter 17

Working with APIs

The Microsoft Windows Application Programming Interface (API) provides building blocks used by applications written for Windows. Windows APIs provide various functions to do operations like getting cursor coordinates, window handles, colors, etc. QTP supports calling these functions defined within the DLL file, but due to VBScript limitations only a limited set of APIs can effectively be used within QTP.

Additional details and information about APIs used in this chapter can be obtained from MSDN or the API Viewer tool that comes with Visual Studio.

Extern object

QTP provides an Extern utility object which is used to declare APIs and then call them,

Syntax

```
Extern.Declare (RetType, MethodName, LibName, Alias [, ArgType(s)])
```

For further details refer to the QTP user manual.

VB API Definition Syntax

```
Private Declare Function GetForegroundWindow Lib "user32.dll" () As Long
```

Looking at this API we need to determine parameters suitable for use with the QTP Declare method:

RetType = micLong (Return type of the function)

MethodName = "GetForegroundWindow" (we can use any name but it's a good practice to use the actual API name)

LibName = "user32.dll". In situations where we are not using a windows system DLL then we must specific a fully qualified filename, for example "C:\MyApp\Lib\mylib.dll"

Alias = "" or "GetForegroundWindow". Since the MethodName we provided is the same as the Alias name, we can leave the Alias name blank.

ArgType(s) = No arguments are needed in this example.

QTP API Definition

```
Extern.Declare micLong,"GetForegroundWindow","user32.dll","GetForegroundWindow"
```

Some examples are provided below to show how we can use APIs to solve commonly encountered problems.

Problem 17-1. How can we determine if the topmost window on the desktop is a browser window?

```
'API declaration for GetForeGroundWindow
extern.Declare micLong,"GetForegroundWindow","user32.dll","GetForegroundWindow"

'Get the handle of the top most window
hwnd = extern.GetForegroundWindow()

'Check if a browser with that window handle exists
isBrowser = Browser("hwnd:=" & hwnd).Exist()

If isBrowser then
    Msgbox "The top most window is a browser"
End if
```

Problem 17-2. How can we get the value of a Windows Environment variable? (Note that QTP environment variables differ from Windows environment variables).

```
'Variable declaration
Dim s_EnvValue

'Declare the API GetEnvironmentVariable
Extern.Declare micLong,"GetEnvironmentVariable","kernel32.dll","GetEnvironmentVariableA", _
                micString,micString+micByRef,micLong

'Get the environment variable "TEMP" value
Extern.GetEnvironmentVariable "TEMP",s_EnvValue,255 'This will get the path for
the temporary folder.
MsgBox s_EnvValue
```

Problem 17-3. How can we check (select) an item in a List box using a Windows API?

```
'Declare the API
Extern.Declare micLong,"SendMessage","user32.dll","SendMessageA",micLong,micLong,micLong,micLong
```

```
'List Box message to set a selection
Const LB_SETSEL = &H185


'Function to check the box at given index
Function CheckListBox(hwnd, index)
        extern.SendMessage hwnd, LB_SETSEL, True, index
end function


'Function to uncheck the box at given index
Function UnCheckListBox(hwnd, index)
        extern.SendMessage hwnd, LB_SETSEL, False, index
end function
```

Problem 17-4. How can we get the background color of a text box (helpful when a color for a mandatory field is different than an optional color)?

```
'Declare all the needed APIs
Extern.Declare micLong,"GetPixel","gdi32","GetPixel",micLong,micLong,micLong
Extern.Declare micLong,"GetWindowDC","user32","GetWindowDC",micLong
Extern.Declare micLong,"ReleaseDC","user32","ReleaseDC",micLong,micLong
Extern.Declare micLong,"GetDC","user32","GetDC",micLong
Extern.Declare micLong,"SetForegroundWindow","user32","SetForegroundWindow",mic
Long


Dim hDCSource
Dim hWndSource
Dim backColor
'Get the handle of the control
hWndSource = Window("Window").WinEdit("MandatoryField1").GetROProperty("hwnd")
'bring the window to foreground. This is important as GetPixel
'works only on visible pixels
extern.SetForegroundWindow hWndSource


'Get the devic context handle
hDCSource = Clng(Extern.GetDC(hWndSource))
'Get the background color of pixel 1,1 relative to the control.
backColor = Clng(Extern.GetPixel(hDCSource, Clng(1),Clng(1)))


MsgBox backColor
'Release the device context handle
Extern.ReleaseDC hWndSource, hDCSource
```

Problem 17-5. How can we simulate a keyboard event using the Windows APIs?

```
'API declarartion for keybd_event
extern.Declare micVoid,"keybd_event","user32" ,"keybd_event", _
                                micbyte,micbyte,miclong,miclong


'API declarartion for MapVirtualKey
extern.Declare micLong,"MapVirtualKey","user32","MapVirtualKeyA", _
                                micLong, micLong
```

```
Const KEYEVENTF_EXTENDEDKEY = &H1
Const KEYEVENTF_KEYUP = &H2
Const KEYEVENTF_KEYDOWN = &H0

Sub KeyDown(KeyAscii)
   keyCode = extern.MapVirtualKey(KeyAscii, 0)
   'Fire the key down event
   extern.keybd_event KeyAscii, keyCode, KEYEVENTF_KEYDOWN, 0
End Sub

Sub KeyUp(KeyAscii)
   keyCode = extern.MapVirtualKey(KeyAscii, 0)
   'Fire the key up event
   extern.keybd_event KeyAscii, keyCode, KEYEVENTF_KEYUP, 0
End Sub

Sub KeyPress(KeyAscii)
   KeyDown KeyAscii
   KeyUp KeyAscii
End Sub
```

Using the above code on a calculator window

```
'Declare Key Constants
Const vbKey1 = 49
Const vbKey2 = 50
Const vbKeyAdd = 107
Const vbKeyReturn = 13

SystemUtil.Run "calc.exe"
Window("title:=Calculator").Activate
Call KeyPress(vbKey1)
Call KeyPress(vbKeyAdd)
Call KeyPress(vbKey2)
Call KeyPress(vbKeyReturn)
```

Using the above code to simulate CTRL + ALT + S

```
'Declare key constants
Const vbKeyControl = 17
Const vbKeyAlt = 18
Const vbKeyS = 83

Call KeyDown(vbKeyControl)
Call KeyDown(vbKeyAlt)
Call KeyDown(vbKeyS)
Call KeyUp(vbKeyS)
Call KeyUp(vbKeyAlt)
Call KeyUp(vbKeyControl)
```

Problem 17-6. How can we prevent a PC from being locked by its screen saver?

Sometime it's necessary to run scripts unattended for long periods of time. This can be a problem when the screen saver policy causes the PC to become locked after a few minutes without keyboard or mouse activity. QTP will not execute a script while the PC is locked. We can avoid this situation by simulating keyboard or mouse events as follows:

```
'C:\PreventPCLock.vbs
Const micVoid = 0
Const micByte = 26
Const micLong = 3
Const KEYEVENTF_KEYUP = &H2

'Create the Extern Object
Set Extern = CreateObject("Mercury.ExternObj")
extern.Declare micVoid,"keybd_event","user32" ,"keybd_event" , _
        micByte,micbyte,miclong,micLong

Extern.Declare micVoid,"Sleep","kernel32","Sleep",micLong

While True
   extern.keybd_event 0, 0, KEYEVENTF_KEYDOWN, 0
   Extern.Sleep 20000
Wend
```

 NOTE: The above code may produce an error indicating that the specified module could not be found. This happens because information about the DLLs hosting these classes in registry is stored without the complete path. To overcome this issue the bin folder of the QTP installation should be added to windows PATH environment variable.

We can also add the QTP bin folder to windows PATH environment variable using the code below

```
'Function to add a folder to PATH
Public Function AddToSystemPath(ByVal Path)
  Set objWMIService = GetObject("winmgmts:\\.\root\cimv2")

  'Get the windows environment
  Set colItems = objWMIService.ExecQuery _
      ("Select * From Win32_Environment Where Name = 'Path'")

  For Each objItem in colItems
      'Add to PATH only if the path does not already exists
      If InStr(objItem.VariableValue, Path)= 0 Then
        'If path does not exist already then add it
        strPath = objItem.VariableValue & ";" & Path
        objItem.VariableValue = strPath
        objItem.Put_
      End If
```

```
      Next
   End Function
   AddToSystemPath "C:\Program Files\Mercury Interactive\QuickTest Professional\bin"
```

Sending a keyascii 0 to keybd_event causes a keyboard event but no key press. The above script can be run as a VBScript file.

Problem 17-7. How can we maximize a window or a browser?

```
'Declarations
Private Const SW_MAXIMIZE = 3
Extern.Declare micLong, "ShowWindow", "user32.dll", "ShowWindow", _
               micHwnd, micLong


'In case we want to maximize a window then handle
'of that window needs to be used.
hWndWindow = Browser("creationtime:=0").GetROProperty("hwnd")
'Maximize the window
Extern.ShowWindow hWndWindow, SW_MAXIMIZE
```

Problem 17-8. How can we download a file from a URL to disk?

```
'Declare Function URLDownloadToFile Lib "urlmon" Alias "URLDownloadToFileA"
'( ByVal pCaller As Long, ByVal szURL As String, ByVal szFileName As String,
'ByVal dwReserved As Long, ByVal lpfnCB As Long ) As Long
Extern.Declare micLong,"URLDownloadToFile","urlmon","URLDownloadToFileA", _
               micLong,micString,micString,micLong,micLong

sSourceURL = "http://mysite/logo.gif"
sTargetFile = "C:\logo.gif"

Extern.URLDownloadToFile 0, sSourceURL, sTargetFile, 0,0
```

QTP API Limitation

Since VBScript only supports variant data types it imposes restrictions when attempting to call APIs that use structures. This section discusses workarounds to these limitations.

API using COM Objects in VB6

We can execute the GetCursorPos API which uses a Point structure to obtain the current mouse coordinates. First we create a COM object in VB6 using the steps given below and then we use the just created COM object in QTP to execute the API.

Launch VB6 and create a blank "ActiveX DLL" project as shown in the Figure 17-1

Figure 17-1. ActiveX DLL Project

By default a class will be added to the project. Rename the project and class as appropriate. Here we arbitrarily name the project "WindowsAPI" and the class as "API".

Open the Visual Studio API Text Viewer and add the required API (GetCursorPos) and Structures (POINTAPI) as shown in the Figure 17-3

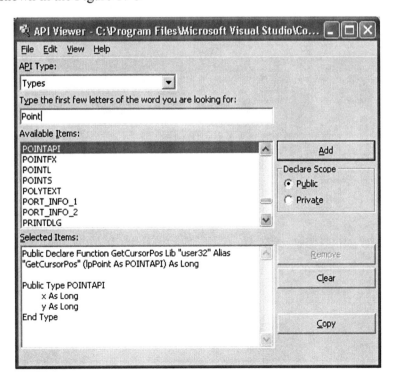

Figure 17-2. API Text Viewer

Copy these definitions into a module file.

```
'Declare the API
Public Declare Function GetCursorPos Lib "user32" Alias "GetCursorPos" _
               (lpPoint As POINTAPI) As Long

Public Type POINTAPI
        x As Long
        y As Long
End Type
```

Now we must create a function inside the class which executes the API and returns the result. We will pass X and Y arguments 'by reference' to this function. The function will now call the API and use the values returned in the structure to assign it to the X and Y parameters. The code below needs to be added to the class module (remember to keep the arguments as variant, otherwise a "Type Mismatch" exception is thrown when used in QTP):

```
'Mandate variable declaration
Option Explicit

Public Function GetCursorPosition _
     (ByRef x As Variant, ByRef y As Variant) _
     As Long

    Dim lpPoint As POINTAPI
    GetCursorPosition = GetCursorPos(lpPoint)
    x = lpPoint.x
    y = lpPoint.y
End Function
```

We could add functions for other APIs as well. Once done we need to create a DLL of the library. Go to the *File→Make WindowsAPI.dll* and save it to the desired location:

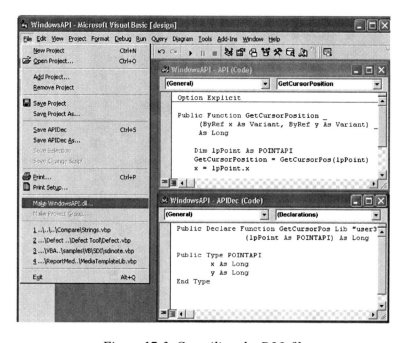

Figure 17-3. Compiling the DLL file

Once done the DLL must be registered on each PC where it will be used. Copy the DLL into a folder on the target PC and register it using the REGSVR32 utility, as shown next:

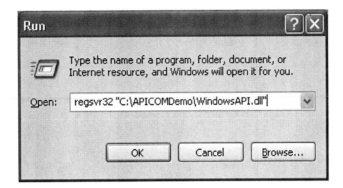

Figure 17-4. Registering the DLL

To access this new DLL in QTP we need to create its object. The ProgID that needs to be used with CreateObject would be "<ProjectName>.<ClassName>", as shown below:

```
'Create the COM object
Set winAPI = CreateObject("WindowsAPI.API")

Dim x,y
winAPI.GetCursorPosition x,y

Msgbox "(" & x & "," & y & ")"
```

This technique does have its limitations:

◉ The need to copy and register the DLL on each PC where the script will be executed. This often requires Administrator rights

◉ ActiveX objects sometimes present issues like "ActiveX component can't create object"

◉ VB6 or a similar tool, which often requires an additional license, is needed to create the custom COM library

Running API using Excel

This section presents a solution which is easy as compared to creating a custom COM library, because Microsoft Excel is widely used and it is available on most PCs. The solution is to embed the needed function(s) inside an Excel spreadsheet and execute it using Excel COM APIs.

Use the steps below to create an Excel spreadsheet wrapper containing the same functionality that we developed in the previous custom COM library example:

Create a new Excel spreadsheet and open the VBA editor by pressing ALT + F11 or by going to menu *Tools → Macro → Visual Basic Editor*

Add a module and then copy the following API declaration into that module:

```
'GetCursorPos API declaration
Public Declare Function GetCursorPos Lib "user32" Alias "GetCursorPos" _
            (lpPoint As POINTAPI) As Long
```

```
Public Type POINTAPI
        x As Long
        y As Long
End Type
```

Go to "ThisWorkbook" sheet and write the functions that we want to execute as shown in the Figure 17-5

```
'Mandate declaration of variables
Option Explicit

Public Function GetCursorPosition _
    (ByRef x As Variant, ByRef y As Variant) _
    As Long

    Dim lpPoint As POINTAPI
    GetCursorPosition = GetCursorPos(lpPoint)
    x = lpPoint.x
    y = lpPoint.y
End Function
```

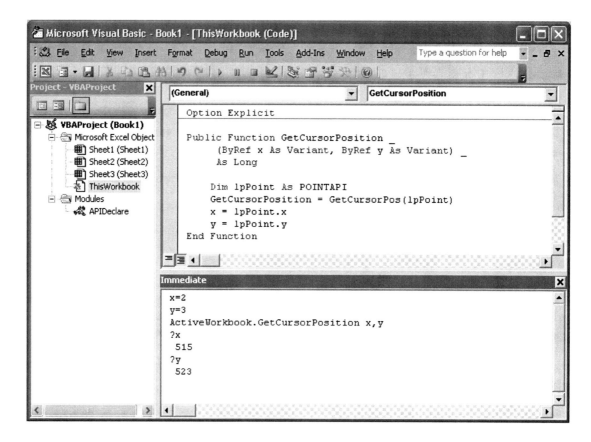

Figure 17-5. ThisWorkbook code

Save this sheet to a desired location—in this example we will use C:\APICode.xls.

Use the QTP code below to execute the function inside the just saved spread sheet:

```
'Open excel and the sheet containing the API Code
Set xlsApp = CreateObject("Excel.Application")
Set xlsWorkBook = xlsApp.WorkBooks.open("C:\APICode.xls")

'declare these variables as the need to be
'passed by reference
Dim x,y
'Run the function which is inside "ThisWorkBook"
xlsWorkBook.GetCursorPosition x,y
Msgbox "(" & x & "," & y & ")"

'Close the sheet and excel
xlsWorkBook.Close
xlsApp.quit
Set xlsWorkBook = Nothing
```

Advantages of using the spreadsheet approach:

⊙ The code can be added to the QTP test script's data table itself, which is always available on each PC where the test script is configured to be executed by QTP

⊙ There is no need to create a custom COM library

⊙ The code can be easily modified and there is no need to recompile as it is in the case of a custom COM library

 NOTE: Macros should not be saved in the Data table sheet (usually Default.xls found in the script directory), as these sheets are overwritten when test cases are saved.

Some QTP developers may see this 2nd approach as an unwanted dependency. So the next section describes a third approach that generates the needed macro at the run-time using VBE automation classes.

Dynamically generating an Excel Macro

Create the following text file and save it to a desired location:

```
'C:\MyCode.bas:
Attribute VB_NAME = "MyCode"
Option Explicit
Private Type POINTAPI
        x As Long
        y As Long
End Type
Private Declare Function GetCursorPos Lib "user32" Alias "GetCursorPos"
(lpPoint As POINTAPI) As Long
```

```
Public Function GetCursorPosition _
    (ByRef x As Variant, ByRef y As Variant) _
    As Long

    Dim lpPoint As POINTAPI
    GetCursorPosition = GetCursorPos(lpPoint)
    x = lpPoint.x
    y = lpPoint.y
End Function
```

 NOTE: We could also create the above file at run-time within QTP using the FileSystemObject.

```
'Create an excel automation object
Set xlsApp = CreateObject("Excel.Application")

'Add a new workbook
Set xlsWorkbook = xlsApp.Workbooks.Add

'Get the components
Set xlsVBComponents = xlsWorkbook.VBProject.VBComponents
'Import the code
xlsVBComponents.Import "C:\MyCode.Bas"
Dim x, y

'Run the Macro
xlsApp.Run "GetCursorPosition", x, y
Msgbox "X:="& x & ", y:=" & y
```

Note: The above code will error out if the Excel Macro security has the "Trust access to Visual Basic project" disabled. To change the settings go to *Tools→Macro→ Security...→Trusted Publishers (Tab)* and check the checkbox for "Trust access to Visual Basic project" as shown in the Figure 17-6

Figure 17-6. VBA Automation Security

We can change the security configuration using the registry as follows:

```
'Create the WSCript shell object
Set oShell = CreateObject("WScript.Shell")

'Enable Trust access
oShell.RegWrite "HKLM\SOFTWARE\Microsoft\Office\11.0\Excel\Security\AccessVBOM" _
        , 1,"REG_DWORD"

'Disable Trust access
oShell.RegDelete "HKLM\SOFTWARE\Microsoft\Office\11.0\Excel\Security\AccessVBOM"
```

 WARNING: We should always make sure that the key is deleted after this code is executed, so that the system is protected against any kind of threats when the option is enabled.

Now we import the module in the above code using:

```
'Get VB Components reference
Set xlVBComponents = xlWorkbook.VBProject.VBComponents
xlVBComponents.Import "C:\MyCode.Bas"
```

We can also use other ways to create the module:

Method 1:

```
'Create the module file
Const vbext_ct_StdModule = 1
Set oModule = xlWorkbook.VBProject.VBComponents.Add (vbext_ct_StdModule)
oModule.Name = "MyCode"
'Add code using file
oModule.CodeModule.AddFromFile "C:\MyCode.Bas"
```

Method 2:

```
'Get a refernce to ThisWorbook
Set oModule = xlsWorkbook.VBProject.VBComponents.Item ("ThisWorkbook")

'Create the code in a string
Dim newCode
newCode = "Public Sub TestThis(ByVal pParam as string)" + vbNewLine
newCode = newCode + "Msgbox pParam" + vbNewLine
newCode = newCode + "End Sub" + vbNewLine

'Add the code from a string
oModule.CodeModule.AddFromString newCode

'Access the function we just added
xlsWorkbook.TestThis "Tarun Lalwani"
```

 NOTE: In this we can use the TestThis function/method as a normal function accessed using the Workbook. In Method 1 we had used the Application object to run the code instead of the workbook object.

This technique solves the following issues:

◉ There is no QTP/VBScript limitation in terms of API usage and other availability of VBA supported functionality

◉ It opens a new path for advanced QTP automation frameworks

◉ This technique can also be used to run code specific to Excel inside Excel as it eliminates any external process communication and increases code performance

◉ This technique can be used to create generic functions with optional parameters as VBA support optional and ParamArray parameters

Working with Modal dialog boxes

QTP can't proceed in situations where it is waiting for a modal dialog box to close, Consider the following page of html code:

```
<HTML>
<BODY>
<P> Select the file
<INPUT type=file name=mod>
</BODY>
</HTML>
```

Now we attempt to execute the following QTP code, when the above page is open:

```
'Click using DOM
Browser("creationtime:=0").Page("micclass:=Page").WebFile("name:=mod").Object.
click

MsgBox "2"
```

QTP waits forever for the click event to complete and can't execute the MsgBox statement. A QTP Recovery scenario does not help because no error occurs while QTP waits indefinitely for the dialog to close. In this situation the dialog has to be closed either manually, or externally through another program, or the click has to be done using mouse events.

Let's look at some possible API solutions to this problem.

FindWindow

This API is used to get a Window handle for a specified Window.

FindWindowEx

This API is used to get a child object of a specified window. This will be used to get the handle of the button inside the message box.

PostMessage

This API is used to send a message to a specific window's message queue.

SetActiveWindow

This API activates the specified window and brings it to the top of the desktop.

Now we combine these APIs in the following code to close a non-QTP message box. This code finds the handle of the dialog with a specific title, then finds the handle of the child button to close the dialog and then sends a message to click that button:

```
'API declarations
Extern.Declare micLong,"FindWindow","user32.dll","FindWindowA", _
               micString,micString
Extern.Declare micLong,"FindWindowEx","user32.dll","FindWindowExA", _
               micLong,micLong,micString,micString
Extern.Declare micLong,"PostMessage","user32.dll","PostMessageA", _
               micLong,micLong,micLong,micRef+micLong
Extern.Declare micLong,"SetActiveWindow","user32.dll","SetActiveWindow", _
               micLong

'Constant for the Click event message for a button
Private Const BN_CLICK = 245

'Note the window and button name are case sensitive
sWindowName = "Test Window"
sWindowButton = "OK"

'Get the window handle from window caption/title
hwndWindow = Extern.FindWindow (vbNullString,sWindowName)

'If we find a non-zero handle
If hwndWindow Then
    'find the handle to the button inside the window
    hwndButton = Extern.FindWindowEx(hwndWindow,0,vbNullString,sWindowButton)

    If hwndButton Then
        Msgbox "Got the button, Activating the window and clicking the button"
        'Activate the window
        Extern.SetActiveWindow hwndWindow
        'Post the BN_CLICK message twice. We are doing it twice as
        'sometimes the first message is missed
        Extern.PostMessage hwndButton,BN_CLICK, 0, 0
        Extern.PostMessage hwndButton,BN_CLICK, 0, 0
    Else
      Msgbox "Cannot find the button"
    End If
Else
   Msgbox "Cannot find the window"
End If
```

We can test this code by creating a VBScript file that contains the following code:

```
'Display a modal dialog box using MsgBox
MsgBox "Kill me now?", vbOKOnly, "Test Window"
```

Run the VBScript and see that the message box is appearing. Now run the script we created in QTP and see that the message box disappears as QTP clicks on the button. But there are some limitations to this solution:

- It runs in QTP and hence we cannot do anything else while running the code

- If we are not sure when the window will appear then the above code can't be successfully used

- This code can't be used to close a QTP launched message box

To overcome these issues we need to write the code in VBS file and invoke it from QTP asynchronously using the WSH Shell object. It means that the script does not execute in the QTP environment and therefore the Extern object is not available. As it turns out the QTP Extern object is simply the "Mercury.ExtrenObj" COM object, so we can replicate this functionality in a VBScript, as long as the QTP is installed on the execution PC. Since this solution does not use the QTP environment so we need to declare all needed QTP constants in the script as follows:

```
'C:\AutoClick.vbs:
Const micLong = 3
Const micString = 8
Const micByRef = 32768

Set Extern = createObject("Mercury.ExternObj")

Extern.Declare micLong,"FindWindow","user32.dll","FindWindowA", _
               micString,micString
Extern.Declare micLong,"FindWindowEx","user32.dll","FindWindowExA", _
               micLong,micLong,micString,micString
Extern.Declare micLong,"PostMessage","user32.dll","PostMessageA", _
               micLong,micLong,micLong,micRef+micLong
Extern.Declare micLong,"SetActiveWindow","user32.dll","SetActiveWindow", _
               micLong

'Constant for the Click event message for a button
Private Const BN_CLICK = 245

'Note the window and button name are case sensitive
'Get the WindowName and Button Name from the arguments
'specifi
sWindowName = WScript.Arguments(0)
sWindowButton = WScript.Arguments(1)

'Run the Script until the window is clicked atleast once
While Not AutoClickButton(sWindowName,sWindowButton)
Wend

Set Extern = Nothing

Private Function AutoClickButton(ByVal sWindowName, ByVal sWindowButton)
  AutoClickButton = False

  'Get the window handle from window caption/title
  hwndWindow = Extern.FindWindow (vbNullString,sWindowName)
```

```
    If hwndWindow Then
     'find the handle to the button inside the window
     hwndButton = Extern.FindWindowEx(hwndWindow,0,vbNullString,sWindowButton)

     If hwndButton Then
            'Activate the window
            Extern.SetActiveWindow hwndWindow
            'Post the BN_CLICK message twice. We are doing it twice
            'as sometimes the first message is missed
            Extern.PostMessage hwndButton,BN_CLICK, 0, 0
            Extern.PostMessage hwndButton,BN_CLICK, 0, 0
            AutoClickButton = True
     End If
    End If
End Function
```

Now let's run the following QTP test script:

```
'Create the sheel object
Set WshShell = CreateObject("WScript.Shell")

'Enclose both strings in double quotes. This needs to be
'done because we want to pass the window name an
'argument to the script and just passing Test Window
'will make it as 2 arguments instead of just one "Test Window"
sWindowName = """" & "Test Window" & """"
sWindowButton = """" & "OK" & """"

Return = WshShell.Run("C:\AutoClick.vbs "& sWindowName & " " & sWindowButton,
1, False)
Set WshShell = Nothing

Msgbox "Kill me now?",vbOKOnly,"Test Window"
```

 NOTE: We won't explain how WScript works as that is beyond the scope of this book. Refer to a VBScript reference for more details about the Wscript object.

When we run the above code the message box get closed automatically. The script we created is only good for a single use as it quits if it's successful once. In case there are more than one message box we must make multiple calls using the following code:

```
'Initiate the auto click script
ret = WshShell.Run("C:\AutoClick.vbs "& sWindowName & " " & sWindowButton, 1,
False)
```

We can also utilize the same concept to work on the security dialogs that pop up when we use outlook to send emails.

Reader's Note

Chapter 18

QTP Automation
Object Model

QTP Automation Object Model (AOM)

QTP provides a COM interface which allows automating QTP itself. This can be used to write code that performs tasks like launch QTP, configure QTP, run a script etc. QTP provides a "QuickTest Automation Reference" that explains all objects, properties and methods supported by the QTP AOM.

Problem 18-1. How can we use AOM to run a QTP test case?

```
'Create an instance of the QTP application
Set qtpApp = CreateObject("QuickTest.Application")

'Launch QTP
qtpApp.Launch

'Make QTP visible
qtpApp.Visible = True

'Open a test
qtpApp.Open "C:\Tests\Sample Test", True

'Run the test
qtpApp.Test.Run

'When completed. close the script and terminate QTP
qtpApp.Close
Set qtpApp = Nothing
```

NOTE: We will use the qtpApp object in the remainder of this chapter.

Problem 18-2. How can we use AOM to change the starting and ending iterations for a test case?

```
'Open the test
qtpApp.Open "C:\Tests\Sampe Test", True

' Run for iterations 5 to 9
qtpApp.Test.Settings.Run.IterationMode = "rngIterations"
qtpApp.Test.Settings.Run.StartIteration = 5
qtpApp.Test.Settings.Run.EndIteration = 9
qtpApp.Test.Settings.Run.OnError = "Stop" ' Stop in case of any error

qtpApp.Test.Run

'Check the overall status of test case
MsgBox qtpApp.Test.LastRunResults.Status
qtpApp.Close
Set qtpApp = Nothing
```

Passing arguments to Test Cases

Just as parameters can be passed to Actions, we can also pass arguments to a test case. We specify test arguments using the *Test → Settings... → Parameters (Tab)* as shown in the Figure 18-1:

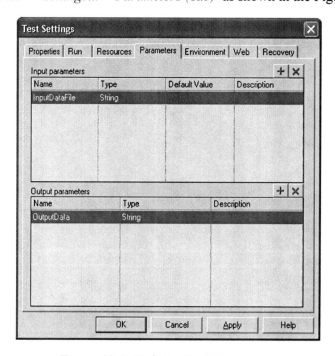

Figure 18-1. Defining Test Parameters

Using Test Arguments

We use test arguments by accessing the TestArgs collection. Here is the example using the just defined arguments

```
'Check for the test arguments
If TestArgs("InputDataFile") <> "" Then
    DataTable.Import TestArgs("InputDataFile")
End If

'...
'...

TestArgs("OutputData") = "This is the output"
```

> **NOTE:** The input and output arguments are displayed in the test results summary.

Passing Test Arguments

There are two ways of passing test arguments to a test case.

The first method is to specify it in the "Input Parameters" tab when we run the test case as show in the Figure 18-2.

Figure 18-2. Test Run Parameters

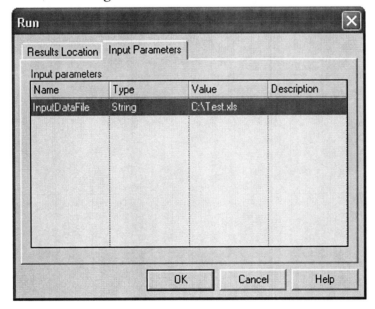

The second method is to use the QTP AOM and pass the arguments as show in the next example:

```
'Get the parameter collection
Set TestArgs = qtpApp.Test.ParameterDefinitions.GetParameters()
```

```
'Add the input arguments
TestArgs ("InputDataFile").Value = "C:\Test.xls"

'Run the test with arguments
qtpApp.Test.Run , ,TestArgs

'Check the output data
MsgBox TestArgs("OutputData").Value
```

Problem 18-3. How can we use AOM to launch QTP on a remote machine?

We can run QTP on any remote machine which we can connect to and on which QTP is installed, as by doing the following:

```
'Remote IP
Const remoteMachineIP = "127.2.3.4"

'Create QTP instance on the remote machine
Set qtpApp = CreateObject("QuickTest.Application", remoteMachineIP)
```

Any operation that we do now using the qtpApp object will be performed on the remote machine.

Note: Make sure the checkbox "Allow other mercury products…" is checked in the *Tools Options…* ⟶ *Run (Tab)* on the remote machine.

Reader's Note

Reader's Note

Chapter 19

HTML DOM

The HTML DOM is a platform and language independent Document Object Model for HTML documents. It defines a standard set of objects in a tree structure of elements which provide a standard way to access and manipulate HTML documents. All elements, along with their text and attributes, can be accessed and manipulated through the DOM tree.

The QTP Page Test Object's *Object* property provides access to the HTML DOM:

```
'Get the DOM document object
Set oDocument = Browser("...").Page("...").Object
```

When to use the HTML DOM

Sometimes a QTP Test Object fails to provide a property that is needed to solve a particular problem or implement a solution. Consider the following situations:

- QTP only provides access to radio buttons through its WebRadioGroup Test Object, rather than providing access to the individual radio button elements

- QTP provides no way to access web page style sheets

Using the HTML DOM is faster in terms of performance. Consider a web page where 500 text boxes need to be filled with same data. A QTP script using Descriptive Programming would look like:

```
'Loop through all 500 webedits
For i = 1 to 500
    Browser("...").Page("...").WebEdit("name:=txt_Box" & i).Set "data"
Next
```

The same script using the HTML DOM would look like:

```
'Loop through all web edits using DOM
For i = 1 to 500
  Browser("...").Page("...").object.all("txt_Box" & i).Set "data"
Next
```

The HTML DOM version will be substantially faster because there is no object recognition overhead needed to find and interact with each WebEdit object on the page.

Performance will also be improved when extracting values from a large WebTable using the HTML DOM for the same reason.

Sometimes QTP throws a general exception—for no obvious reason—while working with a web Test Object. Using the HTML DOM to interact with that object can provide a workaround in these situations.

When not to use the HTML DOM

- When QTP Test Object is doing the job fine and performance is not an issue

- Using the HTML DOM may make it difficult to maintain our script by other test engineers on the team who do not know the HTML DOM and its elements

HTML DOM Objects

HTML Node

Every TAG in the HTML source represents a node in the HTML DOM tree. Once a TAG is opened, all the tags following it become child nodes of the starting node. Each TAG can have a variety of attributes, some of which are predefined and some user-defined.

Consider the following HTML node:

```
<INPUT type="textbox" value="Name" name="txt_Name" myval="Test">
```

Here the pre-defined attributes are type, value and name. The myval attribute is user defined for the INPUT tag.

Consider the following HTML source code:

```
<html>
    <head>
        <script type="text/JScript">
            function ChangeColor()
            {
            document.body.bgColor="yellow"
            }
        </script>
    </head>
    <body onclick="ChangeColor()">Click on this document!</body>
</html>
```

Figure 19-1 shows the DOM tree structure for the above page

Figure 19-1. HTML DOM Tree

The Document Object

The Document object represents the entire document. It is the top most node in the DOM tree. The Document node doesn't have any sibling nodes as it's the root node.

It provides various collections for Links, Anchors, Scripts, Images etc., in the document. It also provides various functions that we can use to access an element using the name of the element

The HTML Element Object

The HTML Element object refers to any particular node in the DOM. Depending on the type of node the element refers to, it provides access to methods and properties related to that type of element. Every element object supports these properties - outerText, outerHtml, innerText, innerHtml, tagName etc.

The HTML Element Collection

The HTML Element Collection object is a collection of one or more elements. Consider the following HTML code:

```
<INPUT name="txt_Name" type="text">
<INPUT name="txt_Name" type="text">
```

We can access the above DOM objects using the following code:

```
'Get a DOM Element Collection by name
Set txt_Boxes = document.getElementsByName("txt_Name")

For i = 0 to txt_Boxes.Length - 1
  txt_Boxes.item(i).value = "Tarun"
  'The default property is item so it can skipped
  txt_Boxes(i).value = "Tarun"
Next
```

In QTP a script using this collection will look something like:

```
'This gives access to the browser COM
Set browserObj = Browser("").Object

'This gives access to the browser's document object
Set pageObj = Browser("").Page("").Object
```

```
Set txt_Boxes= browserObj.document.getElementsByName("txt_Name")
'OR
Set txt_Boxes= pageObj.getElementsByName("txt_Name")

For i = 0 to txt_Boxes.Length - 1
  txt_Boxes.item(i).value = "Tarun"
  txt_Boxes(i).value = "Tarun" 'The default property is item so it can skipped
Next
```

We will be using the Document object directly in the next several explanations, so the following code shows how to get the Document object using several different techniques:

```
'Method 1
Set Document = Browser("").Page("").Object

'Method 2
Set Document = Browser("").Object.document

'Method 3
Set Document = Browser("").Page("").Frame("").Object.document
```

Getting the Web page Element using the DOM

Consider the following HTML code:

```
<INPUT name="txt_Name" id="firstname" type="text" value="Tarun">
```

There are several ways to get this element and the following code shows most of them:

```
'Mainly used at the time of IE4. These are compatible
'with later versions of IE, but is not recommended
Set txt_Elem = Document.All("firstname")
Set txt_Elem = Document.All("txt_Name")

'Used with IE 5.0
Set txt_Elem = Document.getElementsById("firstname")

'Checking if the elements is present or not
If txt_Elem is Nothing then  Msgbox "Element Is not present"

'Getting the elements using getElementsByTagName method
'with the element Tag Name
Set txt_Elem = Document.getElementsByTagName("INPUT").item(0)
Set txt_Elem = Document.getElementsByTagName("INPUT").item("txt_Name")
Set txt_Elem = Document.getElementsByTagName("INPUT").item("firstname")

'Getting the elements using getElementsByName method
'with the name of the element
Set txt_Elem = Document.getElementsByName("txt_Name").item(0)
```

The last four lines will throw an exception if there is no element with and INPUT tag or with the name of "txt_Name". To avoid this we can first check the length of the collection returned by the getElementsByTagName or getElementsByName methods using the following code:

```
'Check the length of collection returned by getElementsByName
If Document.getElementsByName("txt_Name").length <> 0 then
  Set txt_Elem = Document.getElementsByName("txt_Name").item(0)
Else
  MsgBox "Element is not present"
End if
```

Other HTML Elements

Link/Button

Sample HTML source code is:

```
<A href="http://www.microsoft.com" id=mslinkid name=mssoft>Microsoft</A>
<INPUT type="button" id=mslinkid name=mssoft value="Click">
```

The various ways to click on this link or button are:

```
'Different ways of clicking on the link
document.Links("mslinkid").click
document.Links("mssoft").click
document.getElementById("mslinkid").click
document.getElementsByName("mssoft")(0).click
document.all("mslinkid").click
document.all("mssoft").click
```

Text Box

Sample HTML source code is:

```
<INPUT myprop=test name="name" id="firstname" type="text" value="initial">
```

The various ways of changing the value of the text box are:

```
'Various ways to set the value of a text box
document.getElementById("firstname").value = "Tarun"
document.getElementsByName("name")(0).value = "Tarun"

'If name and id is not available then use the
'below example code to change value
Set allElems= document.getElementsByTagName("INPUT")
For each elem in allElems
  if elem.myprop = "test" then
    elem.value = "Tarun"
    Exit For
  end if
Next
```

Combo or List Box

Combo and list boxes have a list of options that a user can select. Sample HTML source code is:

```
<SELECT size="1" name="demo_ComboBox">
    <option value="Actual Value 1">Displayed Value 1</option>
    <option value="Value 2" >Value 2</option>
    <option value="Value 3" >Value 4</option>
</SELECT>
```

The different methods of selecting the value in the Combo box or list box are:

```
'Get the combox box object by name
Set objCombo = document.getElementsByName("demo_ComboBox").item(0)

' Would give 3 in our case
numOptions = objCombo.Options.length

' "Actual Value 1" in our case
firstOptionValue = objCombo.Options(0).value

' "Displayed Value 1" in our case
firstOptionText = objCombo.Options(0).text

'To select one of the options use the below code
objCombo.Options(0).Selected = true
objCombo.value = "Actual Value 1"
```

Checkbox

Sample HTML Source code is:

```
<input type="checkbox" name="demo_CheckBox">
```

The following code shows how to evaluate a checkbox:

```
'Get the check box object by name
Set objChkBox = document.getElementsByName("demo_CheckBox").item(0)

'Check the checkbox
objChkBox.Checked = True
```

Radio Button

Radio buttons offer a user a list of choices, from which only one can be selected. To group all related radio buttons the elements are given the same name. Sample HTML source code is:

```
<input type="radio" name="Sex" value="male" checked="checked" />
<input type="radio" name="Sex" value="female" />
```

To select a radio button, we need to assign the appropriate value to its object:

```
'Get the radio button by name
Set objRadio = document.getElementsByName("Sex").item(1)

'Will select female
objRadio.checked = True

Set objRadio = document.getElementsByName("Sex").item(0)
'Will select male
objRadio.checked = True

'Will select female even if we point to the male object node
objRadio.value = "female"
```

HTML Table

```
<table id="myTable" border="1">
    <tr>
        <td>Row1 cell1</td>
        <td>Row1 cell2</td>
    </tr>
    <tr>
        <td>Row2 cell1</td>
        <td>Row2 cell2</td>
    </tr>
</table>
```

The Table object provides two collections:

◉ cells provide an access to all the cells present in the table

◉ rows provide an access to all the rows present in the table. Rows also provide a 'cells' collection to access a specific cell present in a row

```
'To access the 1st row and 1st column cell, use the following code
Set objTable = document.getElementById("myTable")

objTable.rows(0).cells(0).outerText
objTable.cells(0).outerText

'To access the 2nd row and 1st column cell, use the following code
objTable.rows(1).cells(0).outerText

'Index 2 comes from 0,1 index given for 1st row
'and 2 for the first cell in 2nd row.
objTable.cells(2).outerText

'will give total # of rows in the table
objTable.rows.length

'will give total # of cells in the table
objTable.cells.length

'will give total # of cells in the 1st row of the table
objTable.rows(0).cells.length
```

We have now discussed the most common DOM elements and will now look into some other uses for the DOM.

Converting a DOM object to QTP Test Object

The HTML DOM sourceIndex property is the index value of an object in the DOM tree and can be used to get its corresponding QTP Test Object. The following code shows various techniques for getting a DOM sourceIndex:

```
'Getting the sourceIndex
'using the QTP Objects + DOM
srcIndex = Browser("").Page("").WebEdit("").Object.sourceIndex

'Using QTP only
srcIndex = Browser("").Page("").WebEdit("").GetROProperty("attribute/
sourceIndex")

'Using QTP only
srcIndex = Browser("").Page("").WebEdit("").GetROProperty("source_Index")

'Using DOM only
Set oText = document.getElementsByName("txt_name")(0)
srcIndex = oText.sourceIndex
```

Once we have the sourceIndex and know what type of object we are working with we can then use the following code:

```
'Get the webedit using source index
Browser("").Page("").WebEdit("source_Index:=" & srcIndex).Set "Test"
Browser("").Page("").WebEdit("sourceIndex:=" & srcIndex).Set "Test"
```

 NOTE: There is a difference in the names in DOM and QTP. The DOM uses sourceIndex while QTP uses source_Index. But we can access objects using the either technique by using the code above.

Checking Appearance using Style Sheets

QTP Test Objects do not provide any method for accessing the style sheets in an HTML element. But this can be done using the currentStyle and Style objects of every element.

Checking Visibility of a Object on a Page

Certain pages hide HTML elements using their style sheets. Using the QTP Exist method on these elements always returns a True value. Consider the following style sheet fragment:

```
<style>
    .visi1 { visibility:"visible" }
    .visi2 { visibility:"hidden" }
    .disp1 { display:"block" }
    .disp2 { display:"none" }
</style>
```

And the following HTML source code:

```
<DIV class=disp2 id=checkHidden>
    <P>DHTML using DISPLAY</P>
</DIV>
```

Notice the class for the element is disp2 and as per the styleSheet the disp2 has display set to 'none'. There are different ways to check for this situation.

Technique 1

```
'Get the page object
Set oPg = Browser("micClass:=Browser").Page("micClass:=Page")


'We neet to know that the class of the potentially hidden object is disp2
If oPg.WebElement("html id:=checkHidden").GetROProperty("class") = "disp2" then
    Msgbox "The object is hidden using style disp2"
Else
    Msgbox "The object is visible"
End if
```

Technique 2

This technique uses the DOM to get the class value:

```
'Get the page object
Set oPg = Browser("micClass:=Browser").Page("micClass:=Page")


'Get the object's DOM class
If oPg.WebElement("html id:=checkHidden").object.className = "disp2" then
    Msgbox "The object is hidden using style disp2"
Else
    Msgbox "The object is visible"
End if
```

Technique 3

This technique directly checks for the sytleSheet properties using the DOM:

```
'Get the page object
Set oPg = Browser("micclass:=Browser").Page("micclass:=Page")


'Check the display property of the currentStyle
If oPg.WebElement("html id:=HideMe2").object.currentStyle.display = "none" then
    Msgbox "The object is hidden using style display none"
Else
    Msgbox "The object is visible"
End if
```

 NOTE: The currentStyle object can be used to validate many things like font name, font size etc... using this object can also make an automated test case to validate the CSS specifications of Application under Test AUT. Here are the few examples:
currentStyle.backgroundColor
currentStyle.fontFamily
currentStyle.fontSize
currentStyle.textAlign
For more details refer to msdn.microsoft.com for currentStyle object

Selecting a Radio button by Text

Radio buttons in HTML are only associated with value properties and not with the text appearing with them. Consider the following HTML source code:

Case 1

```
<INPUT type=radio name=addressType value="hm"> Home Address
<INPUT type=radio name=addressType value="ofc"> Office Address
```

So, the QTP code to select a radio button in this grouping would be:

```
'Select the radio button option
Browser("").Page("").WebRadioGroup("addressType").Select "hm"
Browser("").Page("").WebRadioGroup("addressType").Select "ofc"
```

Now if we want to select a radio button using its associated text, e.g. "Home Address" or "Office Address", we can use the DOM, which provides the getAdjacentText method to obtain text adjacent to an element. In this situation it will be the radio button element which is used to get the reference text. But this might not always be the case. Consider the following HTML code:

Case 2

```
<TABLE>
    <TR>
        <TD>
            <INPUT type=radio name=addressType value="hm">
        </TD>
        <TD>
            Home Address
        </TD>
    </TR>
    <TR>
        <TD>
            <INPUT type=radio name=addressType value="ofc">
        </TD>
        <TD>
            Office Address
        </TD>
    </TR>
</TABLE>
```

In the above HTML, the Home Address text is not next to the radio element but is inside a TD element. In this situation, we need a path to the reference object from the radio button, which would be *Parent node (with TD tag) → Next node (with TD tag).* Now we need a function to get a reference object for a given object and path. The following function can be used to do that:

```
'Path is to be seperated by colon. The keyword that can be used
'for navigation are
'parent - for a parent node. To reach a to a parent with specific
'tag use the pipe as parent|TD
'next/right - to navigate to a next node
'previous/left - to navigate to a previous node
'child/children - navigate to the 1st child node or the specified child
'node
```

```
Public Function GetDOMObjectByPath(ByVal DOMObject, ByVal Path)
  'Split the path based on ; as the delimiter
  Path = Split(LCase(Path), ";")
   Set GetDOMObjectByPath = DOMObject
   'Loop through all the navigation keywords
  For i = LBound(Path) To UBound(Path)
    If Path(i) <> "" Then

        'Check if any tag was specified using a |
      If InStr(Path(i), "|") Then
        'If yes then get the tag
        sTag = UCase(Split(Path(i), "|")(1))

         'Get the navigation keyword
        Path(i) = Split(Path(i), "|")(0)
      Else
        'No Tag specified
        sTag = ""
      End If

       'Check the navigation keyword
      Select Case Path(i)
        Case "parent"
          'Loop until we get the first parent node
          'or the one with tag specified (in case any)
          Do
            Set GetDOMObjectByPath = GetDOMObjectByPath.parentNode
          Loop Until (sTag = "") Or _
                (GetDOMObjectByPath Is Nothing) Or _
                (GetDOMObjectByPath.tagName = sTag)
        Case "next", "right"
          'Loop until we get the next node
          'or the one with tag specified (in case any)
          Do
            Set GetDOMObjectByPath = GetDOMObjectByPath.nextSibling
          Loop Until (sTag = "") Or _
                (GetDOMObjectByPath Is Nothing) Or _
                (GetDOMObjectByPath.tagName = sTag)
        Case "previous", "left"
          'Loop until we get the previous node
          'or the one with tag specified (in case any)
          Do
            Set GetDOMObjectByPath = GetDOMObjectByPath.previousSibling
          Loop Until (sTag = "") Or _
                (GetDOMObjectByPath Is Nothing) Or _
                (GetDOMObjectByPath.tagName = sTag)
        Case "child", "children"
          'Check if the current node has ant childrens or not
          If GetDOMObjectByPath.childnodes.Length = 0 Then
            Set GetDOMObjectByPath = Nothing
            Exit Function
```

```
                        Else
                        If sTag<> "" Then
                            'If there was tag sepcified then get the first child with
                            'the given tag
                            If GetDOMObjectByPath.getElementsByTagName(sTag).Length <> 0 Then
                                Set GetDOMObjectByPath = GetDOMObjectByPath.getElementsByTagNam
e(sTag).Item(0)
                            Else
                                'No such tag present
                                Set GetDOMObjectByPath = Nothing
                                Exit Function
                            End If
                        Else
                            'No tag specified retrun the first child node
                            Set GetDOMObjectByPath = GetDOMObjectByPath.childNodes.Item(0)
                        End If
                    End If
                End Select
            End If
        Next
End Function
```

We can now use this function in the following QTP code:

```
'Get the DOM document
Set Document = Browser().Page().Object

Set firstRadio = document.getElementsByName("addressType")(0)

'1st method to get the reference TD tag
Set oRefObject = GetDOMObjectByPath(firstRadio, "parent;next"

'2nd method to get the reference TD tag
Set oRefObject = GetDOMObjectByPath(firstRadio, "parent|TD;next|TD"
```

Once we have the reference object we need to the location of the Text. It can be the outerText/ innerText of the object or text on the left or right of the tag. The getAdjacentText takes a string parameter with 4 possible values "afterEnd", "afterBegin", "beforeBegin" and "beforeEnd". To select the radio button we can use the below function

```
'objWbRGP - the Radio button object
'Text - Text to be searched
'Index - In case of multiple matches
'Path - Path to be used to get the reference object
'TextLocation - Location of the text from the reference object
Public Function SelectRadioByTextIndex(objWbRGP, Text, Index, Path,
TextLocation)
    'RegEx object to test regulat expressions
    Dim RegEx: Set RegEx = New RegExp

    'Mathc the pattern with the whole string
    RegEx.Global = True
```

```
'Pattern to be matched
RegEx.Pattern = Text
'Ignore the case
RegEx.IgnoreCase = True

'Get the name of the radio button from the RO property
radioName = objWbRGP.GetROProperty("name")

'Get all the DOM  radio buttons with the name
Set allRadios = objWbRGP.object.document.getElementsByName(radioName)

'Current count of matched
Dim iMatches: iMatches = -1

'Loop throw all of the the radio buttons
For Each oRadio In allRadios
  'Get the reference object from the radio button using
  'the specified path
  Set oReferenceObject = GetDOMObjectByPath(oRadio, Path)

  'Check the text location
  If IsNull(TextLocation) Or IsEmpty(TextLocation) Or TextLocation = "" Then
    TextLocation = "after"
  Else
    TextLocation = LCase(TextLocation)
  End If

  'Get the text of the reference node text
  nodeText = oReferenceObject.outerText

  'Check the text location and get the text
  Select Case TextLocation
    Case "after" ,"next", "right", "afterend"
      RefText = oReferenceObject.getAdjacentText("afterEnd")
    Case "before", "left", "beforebegin"
      RefText = oReferenceObject.getAdjacentText("beforeBegin")
    Case "beforeend"
      RefText = oReferenceObject.getAdjacentText("beforeEnd")
    Case "afterbegin"
      RefText = oReferenceObject.getAdjacentText("afterBegin")
  End Select

  'Check if it matches the node text or the adjacent text
  If RegEx.Test(nodeText) Or RegEx.Test(RefText) Then
    'Increase the matches index
    iMatches = iMatches + 1

    'Check if the match index is equal to the
    'current match index
    If iMatches = Index Then
      'Check the radio button
```

```
             oRadio.checked = 1

          'Return its value
          SelectRadioByTextIndex = oRadio.Value
          Exit Function
       End If
     End If
  Next

  'Return -1 for no macthes found
  SelectRadioByTextIndex = -1
End Function

'Register the method
RegisterUserFunc "WebRadioGroup","SelectRadioByTextIndex",
"SelectRadioByTextIndex"
```

Reader's Note

Reader's Note

Chapter 20

Working with Web Tables

Web pages often use Web Tables to present formatted information. Often the table's data is dynamically extracted from the backend databases and represented to the user. Content and the size of the tables change according to the data fetched from the backend; this dynamic nature makes it difficult to work with these tables. Therefore it is important to understand how to work with these tables in QTP. A web table is simply a two dimension grid composed of spreadsheet-like rows and columns. In this chapter we will walk through different ways of identifying the WebTable object and also the objects inside them.

Web Tables

Consider the following web table HTML syntax shown below in Table 20-1:

```
<TABLE border="1">
    <TR>
        <TD>COLUMN 1</TD>
        <TD>COLUMN 2</TD>
        <TD>COLUMN 3</TD>
    </TR>
    <TR>
        <TD>100</TD>
        <TD>200</TD>
        <TD>300</TD>
    </TR>
    <TR>
        <TD>400</TD>
        <TD>500</TD>
        <TD>600</TD>
    </TR>
</TABLE>
```

Each TR tag represents a row and each TD tag represents an individual cell within its parent row. QTP identifies this syntax and structure as a WebTable object and provides several methods to work with this type of table, the most important of which are summarized below:

⊙ RowCount – returns the number of rows in a selected WebTable

⊙ ColumnCount – returns the number of columns in a selected row

⊙ GetCellData – returns the data contained in a selected cell

⊙ ChildItem – returns the type of test object residing in a selected cell. For example this function allows us to find and then get access to a WebTable nested within another WebTable

⊙ ChildItemCount - returns the number of specified test objects, of a specified object type, present in the selected cell. For example, it returns the number of WebEdit objects located in a cell

Table 20-1. Sample Table

Column 1	Column 2	Column 3
100	200	300
400	500	600

Next we use these functions to evaluate the contents of the above WebTable:

```
'Get the web table object reference
Set objTbl = Browser("..").Page("..").WebTable("..")

'Displays 3, the number of rows in the table
MsgBox objTbl.RowCount

'Displays 3, the number of columns in the 1st row
MsgBox objTbl.ColumnCount(1)

'Displays 200, the data value in the 2nd column in the 2nd row
MsgBox objTbl.GetCellData (2,2)

'Displays 0 because there are no WebEdit objects present in the
'cell located in the 2nd column of the 2nd row
MsgBox objTbl.ChildItemCount(2,2,"WebEdit")
```

Accessing the WebTable

The biggest problem faced by QTP automation engineers is to gain a reference to a specific table. Many pages contain web tables which are dynamically generated, so the properties used to identify the WebTable should be chosen in such a way that the table can be consistently identified for one test run to the next one. This section discusses different methods for identifying and accessing web tables reliably.

Using Index

This method can be used when we know the web page is static in nature, or that the table's position, relative to other WebTable's on the page, is static. QTP can be used to access a table using an Index when other properties like name or html id are not available. The Index property should never be used when a web page is dynamic in nature. Below is an example of using the Index property to access a page's third web table:

```
Set objTbl = Browser("..").Page("..").WebTable("Index:=3")
```

Using Name or HTML ID

The most effective method for accessing a WebTable is to use its name or HTML ID. Unfortunately developers rarely name tables, but doing so really eases the job of an automation engineer and makes it possible to write much more robust scripts.

```
'Accessing a table object using its Name property
Set objTbl = Browser("..").Page("..").WebTable("Name:= TableName")

'Accessing a table object using its HTML ID
Set objTbl = Browser("..").Page("..").WebTable("html id:= TableID")
```

Using innerText/outerText

This method can be used when we know a table's row heading text will be constant:

Table 20-2. Table Caption Text Goes Here

Attribute	Value	Description
Align	left center right	Aligns the table. Deprecated. Use styles instead.
Bgcolor	rgb(x,x,x) #xxxxxx Colorname	Specifies the background color of the table. Deprecated. Use styles instead.

Referring to Table 20-2, notice that the heading row will always have the words "Attribute", "Value" and "Description". Therefore we can use the regular expression, "Attribute.*Value.*Description.*", to search for and then access the web table based on its outerText property, which is the text displayed for a DOM object on the HTML page.

```
'Access a table object using its outerText with a regular expression
Set objTbl = Browser("..").Page("..").WebTable("outerText:=
Attribute.*Value.*Description.*")

' Access a table object using its innerText with a regular expression
Set objTbl = Browser("..").Page("..").WebTable("innerText:=
Attribute.*Value.*Description.*")
```

But this approach might not be successful at all times, for the reasons described in the next few examples:

Case 1

```
<TABLE><TR>
    <TABLE><TR>
        <TABLE>
            <TR>
                <TD>Attribute</TD>
                <TD>Value</TD>
                <TD>Description</TD>
            </TR>
            <TR>
                <TD>align</TD>
                <TD>left</TD>
                <TD>Alignment of the element</TD>
            </TR>
        </TABLE>
    </TR></TABLE>
</TR></TABLE>
```

In this case the table we need to access is nested inside another table. So if we use the following code:

```
'Access the table object using innerText with a regular expression
Set objTbl = Browser("..").Page("..").WebTable("innerText:=
Attribute.*Value.*Description.*")
```

It won't work, as there are three Table tags which have the same innerText property. So we have to use the index property to get a desired match. The index would be 2 in our case (which is the 3nd table). But in case we have more tables then we would need to handle this situation at run-time. The code below shows how to do this:

```
'Create a Description of the object
Set oTableDesc = Description.Create

'Set the identifiers for the table
oTableDesc ("innerText").Value = "Attribute.*Value.*Description.*"
oTableDesc ("innerText").RegularExpression = True

'Get all matching tables
Set allTables = Browser("..").Page("..").ChildObjects(oTableDesc)

'Get the count of all tables
iCount = allTables.Count

If iCount <> 0 Then
  'Get the last table matching our description
  Set table2use = allTables.item(iCount - 1)
Else
  MsgBox "Could not find the table"
End if
```

Case 2

This case is bit more challenging than Case 1. Consider the next table:

```
<TABLE><TR>
    <TABLE><TR>
        <TD>Attribute</TD>
        <TD>Value</TD>
        <TD>Description</TD>
    </TR></TABLE>
    <TABLE><TR>
        <TD>align</TD>
        <TD>left</TD>
        <TD>Alignment of the element</TD>
    </TR></TABLE>
</TR></TABLE>
```

The fixed header row is just above the table containing the data. We can locate the header table using the techniques used in Case 1 but getting the next table is a bit tricky. We need to get the index of the table relative to the entire page. For example, if the header table we are looking for is recognized as WebTable("Index:=19") then the table containing the data will be WebTable("Index:=20"). In this situation we need to use the DOM to get all the TABLE elements and then compare the sourceIndex with our header table to get its index. The code below shows how we can do this:

```
'Function to find index identifier of QTP
'WebTable test object
Function GetQTPTableIndex(TableObj)
  'Convert the table to a DOM object, doing
  'this allows working of DOM as well as
  'QTP test objects
  On Error Resume Next
  TableObj = TableObj.Object
  On Error Goto 0

  'Get the source index of web table
  'this would be used later to search
  'the table using DOM
  srcIndex = TableObj.sourceIndex

  'Get the page document object using the table object
  Set domDocument = TableObj.document.documentElement

  'Get all the elements having the TABLE tag
  Set allTables= domDocument.getElementsByTagName("TABLE")

  i = 0
  'Loop through each of the tables

  For each table in allTables
     'compare the source index of this table
     'with the QTP test object table
```

```
    If table.sourceIndex = srcIndex Then
      'It's a match. Return this index
      'it is the same index QTP will use to identify
      'a table with just the index property
      GetQTPTableIndex = i

      Exit Function
    End If

    'Increment the table index
    i = i + 1
  Next
End Function
```

The code we will use to work on the case #2 table is given below:

```
'Get the index of header table
headerTableIndex = GetQTPTableIndex(table2use)

'Index of the table containing data is +1 from the header
dataTableIndex = headerTableIndex + 1

'Get the table using the index
oWebDataTable = Browser("..").Page("..").WebTable("index:=" & dataTableIndex)
```

Using OR

This method is not always perfect but can be used in situations where it's difficult to apply the methods discussed in the previous section.

To add a WebTable to the Object Repository (OR), open the OR and click on Add Objects and then click in one of the cells in the target WebTable. After clicking in the web table's cell we see an object hierarchy window similar to the one shown in the Figure 20-1

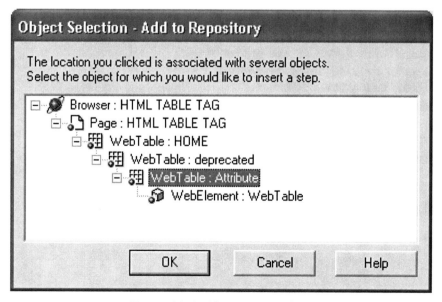

Figure 20-1. Object Hierarchy

We should now be able to add the last WebTable, that appears in the hierarchy, to the OR. In the OR we will see the properties QTP used to recognize this new WebTable object, similar to that shown in the Figure 20-2

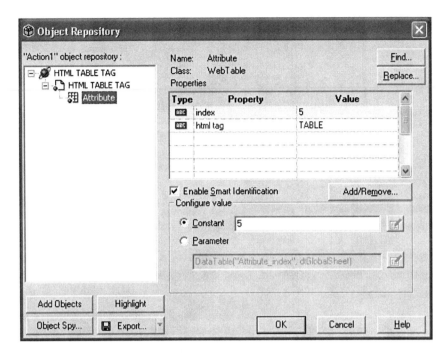

Figure 20-2. WebTable in Object Repository

Notice that QTP used the Index property, which might not be reliable on a page composed of dynamic content. But we can change this in the OR by clicking on the "Add/Remove..." button and selecting the "outerText" property, or any other unique and appropriate property as shown in the Figure 20-3

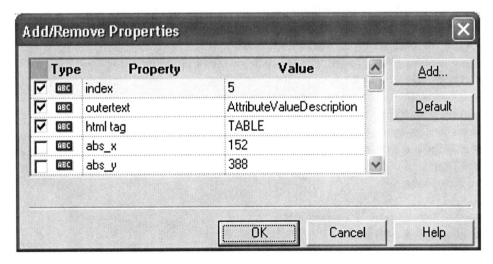

Figure 20-3. Adding the outerText property

The outerText property has the value for the whole WebTable (including the data as well), so we need to use a regular expression. We do this by clicking on the "configure value options" button for the outerText property and then changing the value to an appropriate regular expression. Lastly select the "RegularExpression" checkbox as shown in the Figure 20-4

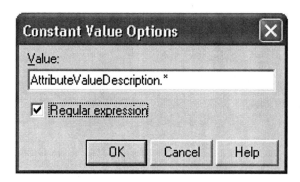

Figure 20-4. outerText Regular Expression value

Now the only thing left to do is to configure the Index value. Change the index value to 0 and execute the code below in QTP to:

```
'Get the no. of rows in the table
MsgBox Browser("..").Page("..").WebTable("..").RowCount
```

If the displayed row count is incorrect then increment the index value by 1 and execute the code again, until the correct row count is displayed. Once the index calibration is completed we can use the table reference in our scripts.

 NOTE: We should run off Smart Identification for this WebTable, as it may lead to incorrect web table selection at runtime.

Using an object inside the table

This method is useful when we have a known object which resides inside the target table. This technique uses the DOM to reference the object's parent table tag. Consider the code below:

```
'Function to get parent node on element
Function GetParentOfElement(ByVal pObject,ByVal pParentTagName)
  On error resume next
  'In case a QTP Test object is passed, convert it
  'to the DOM Object. This allows using the
  'function on both DOM and QTP Test Objects
  Set pObject = pObject.Object
  Err.Clear
  On Error Goto 0

  'Search for object's parent node
  Set oParent = pObject

  'Seacrh for the node with specified Tag Name
  Do
    Set oParent = oParent.parentNode
  'if oParent == Nothing then we didn't find any parent object
  'with the specified tag
  Loop While Not (oParent is Nothing) And oParent.tagName <> pParentTagName
```

```
        'Return the object found, else return Nothing if a tag is not found
        Set GetParentOfElement = oParent
End Function
```

In the next example we access a table by first referencing a known Image object inside the target table:

```
'Locate the Image object inside the table
Set oImg = Browser("..").Page("..").Image("..")

'Get the DOM TABLE object from the element
'present inside the table
Set oDOMTable = GetParentOfElement(oImg, "TABLE")

'Get the index of the table
Set iTableIndex = GetQTPTableIndex(oDOMTable)

'Get the QTP Test object for the given table
Set oQTPWebTable = Browser("..").Page("..").WebTable("index:=" & iTableIndex)
```

Getting the location of an object inside the table

The above technique can also be used to locate the exact position of an object inside the table:

```
'Function to get the Table and location of an object inside the
'table.
Public Function GetTableFromElement(ByVal oElement, ByRef Row, ByRef Col)
    'Values to be returned if nothing is found
    Set GetTableFromElement = Nothing
    Row = 0
    Col = 0

    'Convert the QTP TO object to a DOM object
    on error resume next
    Set oElement = oElement.Object
    On error goto 0

    'Check if the current element is a cell of the table
    'then we don't need to look for the parent cell
    If oElement.tagName = "TD" Then
        'Assign the cell DOM object to Col
        Set Col = oElement
    Else
        'Get the cell from object
        Set Col = GetParentOfElement (oElement, "TD")
        If Col is Nothing Then
            Col= 0
            Exit Function
        End If
    End If

    'Get the row of the object
    Set Row = GetParentOfElement (Col, "TR")
```

```
'Get the table object
Set GetTableFromElement = GetParentOfElement (Row, "TABLE")

'Get the row and column index from the dom objects
'Add 1 to both of them as DOM indexes as 0 based
'while QTP Web Table indexes are 1 based.
Row = Row.rowIndex + 1
Col = Col.cellIndex + 1
End Function
```

 NOTE: The above method returns the DOM table object and not its QTP test object.

Usage:

```
'Define the variable to pass by reference
Dim Row, Col

Set oLink = Browser("..").Page("..").Link("text:=Add to Cart","index:=0")
Set oDOMTable = GetTableFromElement (oLink ,Row, Col)

'Method 1 of getting the webTable
Set iTableIndex = GetQTPTableIndex(oDOMTable)
Set oQTPWebTable = Browser("..").Page("..").WebTable("index:=" & iTableIndex)

'Method 2 of getting the webTable
srcIndex = oDOMTable.sourceIndex
Set oWebTable = Browser("..").Page("..").WebTable("source_Index:=" & srcIndex)

'Get the data in first column of the found row
Msgbox oWebTable (Row, 1)
```

The above method is quite useful in cases where there is an array of controls (like checkboxes) which might be present inside a WebTable. When we use the ChildObjects function on a Page object it does not provide the elements present inside a WebTable. But we can use the DOM to get the element collection and then get the WebTable. Consider the table show in the Figure 20-5:

Figure 20-5. Objects in different tables

Let's assume that the checkbox name is "product". As the above figure indicates, these products can exist in different tables. Here is an example on how to handle this situation:

```
'Get the the object with name as product
Set oChkProd = Browser("..").object.document.getElementsByName("product")

iCount = oChkProd.length - 1

'Loop through all the object with name is product
For i = 0 to iCount

  'Get the table, row and  col where the checkbox exist
  Set oTable = GetTableFromElement (oChkProd.Item (i) ,Row, Col)

  'Get the QTP web table object for the table
  Set oWebTable = Browser("").Page("").WebTable("source_Index:=" & oTable.
sourceIndex)

  'Search the product we want to add. The name of
  'the product is present in the first column of the table
  If  oWebTable.GetCellData(Row, 1) = "Product 3" Then
    oChkProd.Item(i).checked  = True
    Exit For
  End if
Next
```

Clicking inside a WebTable

There are no built-in functions provided by the QTP WebTable object to click a cell but there are several ways, as described below, to achieve this needed action.

Method 1

```
'Get the table's DOM object
Set oDOMTable = Browser("").Page("").WebTable("").object

'To click on 1,1 we can use
Row = 1
Col = 1
oDOMTable.rows(Row - 1).Cells(Col - 1).Click
```

Method 2

We can use the QTP click method by getting the WebElement object for a table cell and then click it:

```
'Get the DOM table object
Set oDOMTable = Browser("").Page("").WebTable("").object

Row = 1
Col = 1

'Get the source index of the table
sIndex  = oDOMTable.rows(Row - 1).Cells(Col - 1).sourceIndex

'Click on the WebElement using it's source index
Brower("").Page("").WebElement("source_Index:=" & sIndex).Click
```

Method 3

This method uses the concept of object identification hierarchy. Each Row is a child object of a Table and each cell is a child of its table row. So to click (1, 1) we can use the following code:

```
'Get the WebTable test object
Set oWebTable = Browser("").Page("").WebTable("")

Row = 1
Col = 1

'Get the Row WebElement of the object
Set oRow = oWebTable.WebElement("html tag:=TR","index:=" & (Row-1))

'Get the Cell WebElement of the object from the row element
Set oCell = oRow.WebElement("html tag:=TD","index:=" & (Col -1))

'Click on the cell
oCell.Click
```

Method 4

This method can be used when we want to click an object located inside a table cell:

```
'Get the WebTable test object
Set oWebTable = Browser("").Page("").WebTable("")

Row = 1
Col = 1

'Get the number of WebEdits present in specified
'Row, Col.
iEditCount = oWebTable.ChildItemCount(Row, Col, "Link")

If iEditCount = 0 Then
  MsgBox "No WebEdit present in 1, 1"
Else
  'Get the 1st WebEdit present in 1, 1
```

```
Set oWebEdit = oWebTable.ChildItem(Row, Col, "Link", 0)

   'Set the value
   oWebEdit.Set "This is 1st WebEdit in 1, 1"
End if
```

Asynchronous Table loading

Some pages use asynchronous data loading, where all the objects on the pages are loaded and the data is then populated in chunks. In this situation the page is loading data asynchronously, so using ".Exist" or ".Sync" or "WaitProperty" on one of the objects of the web page can't be used to determine when data loading is complete.

In the next example, we have an object reference to a WebTable being updated with data asynchronously. The trick here is to evaluate the RowCount of the WebTable after a specified interval—when the count stabilizes data updating is presumed to be complete. Consider the code below:

```
'Reference the table being asynchronously loaded
Set objTbl = Browser("..").Page("..").WebTable("..")

oldRowCount = 0

'Stop when the row count is stable for 2 iterations
While (oldRowCount <> objTbl.RowCount)
     'Get the new row count
     oldRowCount = objTbl.RowCount

     'Wait for 3 seconds and try again
     Wait 3
Wend
```

The above mentioned code gets and evaluates the web table's row count every 3 seconds. Data loading is presumed to be complete when the row count is the same for two iterations of the loop.

Exporting WebTable to a DataTable

The next function reads the contents of a WebTable and exports that data to a DataTable:

```
'Function to export webtable to datatable
Public Function ExportWebTable2Sheet(webTableObj, sheetName, hasHeaderRow)
   'Create the output sheet
   Set dtSheet = DataTable.AddSheet (sheetName)

   Dim i,j,rows, cols, start

   'Get the rows in the table
   rows = webTableObj.RowCount

   'Get the columns in the first row
   cols = webTableObj.ColumnCount(1)
```

```
        'If 1st Row is the Haeder row then add that
        'as the Parameters name in exported sheet
        If hasHeaderRow Then
          For i = 1 to cols
            dtSheet.AddParameter webTableObj.GetCellData(1,i), ""
          Next
          ''Header row means that 1st row does not contain
          'data and needs to be ignored.
          start = 2
        Else
          'If no hearder row then add then default Col1,Col2, Col3 ....as headings
          For i = 1 to cols
            dtSheet.AddParameter "Col" & i , ""
          Next
          'No header row means all rows need to be read
          start = 1
        End If

        'Export the data to the created data table
        For i = start  to rows
          dtSheet.SetCurrentRow i - start + 1
          cols = webTableObj.ColumnCount(i)
          For j = 1 to cols
            dtSheet.GetParameter(j).value = webTableObj.GetCellData(i,j)
          Next
        Next
      End Function
```

Usage:

```
    ExportWebTable2Sheet  Browser("..").Page("..").WebTable(".."), "Export", False
```

Extending WebTable functionality

QTP 8.x does not provide any Find method to locate a text string in a table. But we can extend these by creating new methods. There are various parts were the functionality can be extended and we would be discussing them one by one. I would be using the functions we created earlier in this chapter

Getting a QTP Table from a element

The GetTableFromElement we created earlier returns the DOM Table object, so let's create another function which will return mapping QTP WebTable test object instead of DOM table object.

```
    'Get the QTP WebTable from a specified object
    Public Function GetWebTableFromElement(ByVal pObject)
      Dim oTable, oParent

      'Get the parent table, a DOM object
      Set oTable = GetParentOfElement (pObject.Object, "TABLE")

      'Get QTP test object parent of supplied object
      Set oParent = pObject.GetTOProperty("parent")
```

```
   If oTable is Nothing Then
      Set GetWebTableFromElement = Nothing
   Else
      'Return the table using the source index
      Set GetWebTableFromElement = oParent.WebTable("source_Index:=" & oTable.
sourceIndex)
   End If
End Function
```

Finding a cell in a Table

Each cell in a Table is a TD tag element. Use the following code in situations where we need to find a cell by using its text value:

```
'get an object reference to the webtable
Set objTable = Browser("..").Page("..").WebTable("..")

'Next define regular expression to find the text we want to locate
text2Find = "This is in cell \(4,5\)"

'Find the first cell containing the search text
Set cellFound = objTable.WebElement("html tag:=TD","text:=" & text2Find)

'Confirm that the cell exits
If cellFound.Exist(0) Then
   'Get the DOM table and location of the cell
   Set oFoundTable = GetTableFromElement (cellFound, Row, Col)
Else
   'Nothing found
   Set oFoundTable = Nothing
   Row = 0
   Col = 0
End If
```

We can determine if the table we found is the original table or a child of that table:

```
If oFoundTable.sourceIndex = objTable.object.sourceIndex Then
   MsgBox "Text found in the same table"
Else
   MsgBox "Text found in a child table"
End If
```

In case we don't find a match using the above method, we can loop through the entire table and see if a matching row can be located. In case there are multiple matching rows then we can use a matchIndex:

```
'Function to search a text within in a Table
'objTable - QTP WebTable Test Object on which search needs to be done
'SearchText - Text to be searched
'matchIndex - Used in case of multiple matches. 0 based value
'Row - a ByRef value which is use to return the value of the Row found
'We can pass initial values to this variable
```

```
'0 - search in all the rows
'+ve - Search starting from the specified rows
'-ve - Search in specified rows only
'Col - a ByRef value which is use to return the value of the Column found
'We can pass initial values to this variable
'0 - search in all the columns
'+ve - Search starting from the specified Column
'-ve - Search in specified Column only

'Return Value - True/False depending on if the search text is found

Function FindTextBySearch(ByVal objTable, byVal SearchText, ByVal matchIndex,
ByRef Row, ByRef Col)
  iRowCount = objTable.RowCount
  curIndex =0

  SearchText = Trim(LCase(SearchText))

  'Return vakue in case a row is found
  FindTextBySearch = False

  If Row = 0 Then
    'We need to search in all the rows
    startRowSearch = 1
    endRowSearch = iRowCount
  ElseIf Row < 0 Then
    'We need to search just in specified row only
    startRowSearch = Abs(Row)
    endRowSearch = Abs(Row)
  Else
    'A positive row # indicates to search starting from
    'specified row till the end
    startRowSearch = Row
    endRowSearch = iRowCount
  End If

  'Loop through all the cells
  For i = startRowSearch To endRowSearch
    iCellCount = objTable.ColumnCount(i)

    If Col = 0 Then
      'We need to search in all the rows
      startColSearch = 1
      endColSearch = iCellCount
    ElseIf Col < 0 Then
      'We need to search just in specified column only
      startColSearch = Abs(Col)
      endColSearch = Abs(Col)
    Else
      'A positive row # indicates to search starting from
      'specified row till the end
      startColSearch = Col
```

```
          endColSearch = iCellCount
      End If


      For j = startColSearch To endColSearch
        CellText = LCase(Trim(objTable.GetCellData(i, j)))
        If CellText = SearchText Then
          If curIndex = matchIndex Then
            'If current index is the one we are lookig for then
            'stop looking further
            Row = i
            Col = j

            FindTextBySearch = True
            Exit Function
          Else
            'Increase the current matching index by 1
            curIndex  = curIndex + 1
          End If
        End If
      Next
    Next

    'Could not find the found
    Row = 0
    Col = 0
End Function
```

Examples:

```
'Various search examples
SearchText = "California"
Set objTable = Browser("..").Page("..").WebTable("..")

'Search in all rows and columns
Row = 0
Col = 0

If FindTextBySearch(objTable, SearchText, 0, Row, Col) Then
  MsgBox "Cell Found - (" & Row & ", " & Col & ")"
Else
  MsgBox "Cell Found"
End If

'Search in Column 2 only
Row = 0
Col = -2
Call FindTextBySearch(objTable, SearchText, 0, Row, Col)

'Search in Column 2 only and starting from row 2 to the end
Row = 2
```

```
Col = -2
Call FindTextBySearch(objTable, SearchText, 0, Row, Col)


'Search in all Columns in row 2
Row = -2
Col = 0
Call FindTextBySearch(objTable, SearchText, 0, Row, Col)

iMatch = 0
'Find all the matching text in a column 2 of a table
While FindTextBySearch(objTable, SearchText, 0, Row, -2)
  MsgBox "Found in Row - " & Row
  iMatch = iMatch + 1
  'Search from the next row
  Row = Row + 1
Wend

MsgBox "Total Matches found - " & iMatch
```

Reader's Note

Reader's Note

Chapter 21

Working with XML

XML is a markup language for documents containing structured information. XML is used to implement many solutions, such as defining program settings, providing input to or receiving output from a system using a well known protocol. QTP provides a built-in utility object which allows parsing and manipulating files containing XML. While QTP has a good set of functions to manipulate XML, those function are not documented in the QTP user manual—but online Help provides adequate information to use them effectively. The remainder of this chapter is intended to provide the missing overview, as well as to explore some of the more useful QTP functions for working with XML.

Sample XML

```
<Environment>
    <Variable>
        <name>601A4</name>
        <value type="savings" bank="abc">602126609042</value>
    </Variable>
    <Variable>
        <name>631A5</name>
        <value type="checking" bank="def">602126609043</value>
    </Variable>
</Environment>
```

The key elements of the above XML are discussed below.

Root node

The first node in an XML file is called the root node. A valid XML file can have only one root node. In our example, the "**<Environment>**" node is the root node. Note that this, and all other fully formed nodes, are terminated by matching the "**</Environment>**" tag.

Child nodes

Child nodes are the children of an enclosing parent node. In our example the "<Variable>" node is a child node of the "<Environment>" parent node; while the "<name>" and "<value>" nodes are children of the "<Variable>" node. This parent/child hierarchy is what gives structure to XML syntax/ files.

Node values

Node value is the value assigned to a given node. A node may only have a value assignment if it does not have any child nodes. Here the first "<name>" node has a value assignment of "601A4" and <value> node has a value assignment of "602126609042".

Attributes

A node can have attributes. If we look at the first "<value>" node which is *<value type="savings" bank="abc">* here "type" and "bank" are attributes and "savings" and "abc" are their attribute values respectively.

QTP XML Objects

QTP provides a rich set of utility XML objects, the most important of which are described next.

- ◉ XMLUtil - This is the object which is used to create or read an XML file. Like HTML, XML also has a document object model (DOM). But this object provides a much smaller set functions as compared to the HTML DOM. The XML DOM is beyond the scope of this chapter

- ◉ XMLAttribute - Provides access to the name and value of attributes of a specified node

- ◉ XMLAttributesColl - Provides a collection of attributes

- ◉ XMLItemColl - Provides a collection of XML Items. XML Items are used for CDATASection and comments in the XML

- ◉ XMLElementsColl - Provides a collection of XML elements

- ◉ XMLData - Represent an XML Block. XML Data contains the complete XML file loaded using XMLUtil or from WebXML test object

- ◉ XMLElement - Represent an XML Element. An XML element can have attributes, a value, and/or one or more children, all of XMLElement type

Rather than attempt to define each and every function supported by each of these objects, we use the more common ones in the examples in the remainder of this chapter. For details on all the methods and properties supported by these objects refer to the QTP Help.

Reading and Modifying XML

Problem 21-1. How can we copy an XML file and save it to another XML file?

```
'Method 1:
'Create an empty XMLData object
Set xmlDocument = XMLUtil.CreateXML
```

```
'Initialize the object with XML from a file
xmlDocument.LoadFile "c:\source.xml"

'save it to a specified destination file
xmlDocument.SaveFile "c:\destination.xml"
Set xmlDocument = Nothing

'Method 2
'Create an XMLData object with file data in a single step
Set xmlDocument = XMLUtil.CreateXMLfromFile ("C:\source.xml")
xmlDocument.SaveFile "c:\destination.xml"
Set xmlDocument = Nothing
```

Problem 21-2. How can we get an entire **XML** file into a string and then save it to another **XML** file using that string?

```
'Create and initialize and XMLData object, the write to a String
Set xmlDocument = XMLUtil.CreateXMLfromFile ("C:\source.xml")
sXML = xmlDocument.ToString

'Create a 2nd XMLData object using the String as the initializer
set xmlDoc2 = Document.CreateXML(sXML)
xmlDoc2.SaveFile "c:\destination.xml"
Set xmlDocument = Nothing
Set xmlDoc2 = Nothing
```

Problem 21-3. How can we create the following **XML** code at run-time in QTP, and then save it to an **XML** file?

```
<Environment>
    <Variable>
        <Name>FirstName</Name>
        <Value>Tarun</Value>
    </Variable>
    <Variable>
        <Name>LastName</Name>
        <Value>Lalwani</Value>
    </Variable>
</Environment>
```

The code given below will create the specified XML at run-time:

```
' Create an empty XMLData object
Set xmlDoc=XMLUtil.CreateXML
'Create a document with Environment as the root node
xmlDoc.CreateDocument "Environment"
'Get the root nod element.
'The data type returned would be of type XMLElement
Set xmlRoot = xmlDoc.GetRootElement()

'Add a new variable node
```

```
Set newNode = xmlRoot.AddChildElementByName("Variable","")

'Add the name and value child nodes
newNode.AddChildElementByName "Name","FirstName"
newNode.AddChildElementByName "Value","Tarun"

'Add a new variable node
Set newNode = xmlRoot.AddChildElementByName("Variable","")

'Add the name and value child nodes
newNode.AddChildElementByName "Name","LastName"
newNode.AddChildElementByName "Value","Lalwani"
xmlDoc.SaveFile "c:\destination.xml"

Set newNode = Nothing
Set xmlRoot = Nothing
Set xmlDoc = Nothing
```

Problem 21-4. How can we load environment variables from multiple XML files?

QTP's Environment.LoadFromFile has a disadvantage, that is, it does not allow loading multiple environment files. But we can overcome this shortcoming by creating our own function to read and create environment files.

```
'Function to add environment files at run-time
'Overwrite flag allows overwriting variables which
'already exist in the environment
Public Function AddENVFromFile(ByVal FileName, ByVal Overwrite)
    On error resume next
    Dim xmlDoc, xmlRoot, xmlElement
    Dim sName, sValue
    'Load the xml file
    Set xmlDoc = XMLUtil.CreateXMLFromFile (FileName)
    Set xmlRoot = xmlDoc.GetRootElement()
    'Get all the variables node
    Set xmlValues = xmlRoot.ChildElementsByPath("Variable")
    'Loop through all variable nodes
    For i= 1 to xmlValues.Count
            Set xmlElement = xmlValues.Item(i)
            sName = xmlElement.ChildElementsByPath("Name").item(1).value
            sValue = xmlElement.ChildElementsByPath("Value").item(1).value
            'Check if the environment already exist
            If IsEnvExist(sName) Then
                    If Overwrite Then Environment(sName) = sValue
            Else
                    Environment(sName) = sValue
            End If
    Next
End Function

'Function to check if environment exist r not
'we need to creat this function Environment object doesn't
'provide any methods to check if an variable exists or not
```

```
Public Function IsEnvExist(ByVal varname)
   IsEnvExist = True
   On error resume next
   Dim envVal
   envVal = Environment(varname)
   'In case there was an error that means the environment does not exist
   If err.number<>0 Then
        IsEnvExist = False
   End If
   On error goto 0
End Function
```

Usage:

```
'Add all the environment varaiables and allow overwrite
AddENVFromFile "C:\Env_All.xml", True

'Add environment files for test environment and allow overwrite
AddENVFromFile "C:\Env_Test.xml", True
```

Now this will add a variable in both the XMLs and will overwrite any existing ones

 NOTE: These XMLs should not contain any environment variable which was loaded from any XML using LoadFromFile or any Environment variable associated with the test as QTP loads them in the read only mode.

Working with Multiple environments of an Application

The above AddENVFromFile function is very useful when we want to create test cases for different environments. Consider the folder structure shown below:

Figure 21-1. Environment folder structure

Each folder can have its own Config.xml and the Common folder will have variables which are shared by all the scripts. Dev and Test can override shared variables that are unique to the Dev or Test environments and the script can select an environment as follows:

```
'Load the common configuration
AddENVFromFile "..\..\Common\Config.xml"

'Load config specific to our environment
AddENVFromFile "..\Config.xml"
```

Problem 21-5. How can we modify the contents of an XML file?

Consider the next XML file:

```
<Environment>
    <Variable>
        <Name>FirstName</Name>
        <Value>Tarun</Value>
    </Variable>
    <Variable>
        <Name>LastName</Name>
        <Value>Lalwani</Value>
    </Variable>
</Environment>
```

Now consider the next QTP code that can be used to modify the above XML definitions:

```
'Create the XML document object
Set xmlDoc = XMLUtil.CreateXML ()

strXML = "<Environment>" & _
        "<Variable><Name>FirstName</Name> <Value>Tarun</Value> </Variable>" & _
        "<Variable><Name>LastName</Name> <Value>Lalwani</Value> </Variable>" & _
        "</Environment>"
xmlDoc.Load strXML

Set xmlRoot = xmlDoc.GetRootElement()

UpdateEnvFileValue xmlRoot, "FirstName", "New First Name"
UpdateEnvFileValue xmlRoot, "LastName", "New Last Name"

msgbox xmlDoc.toString()

Public Function UpdateEnvFileValue(ByVal xmlRoot, ByVal varNam, ByVal varVal)

'Get all the variable in the environment
Set xmlCol = xmlRoot.ChildElementsByPath ("/Environment/Variable")
For i =1 to xmlCol.count

    'Look for the Name child from current node
    If xmlCol.item(i).ChildElementsByPath ("./Name").item(1).Value = varNam Then

        'Set the value for Value node
        xmlCol.item(i).ChildElementsByPath ("./Value").item(1).SetValue varVal
        Exit Function
    End if
Next
End Function
```

The ChildElementsByPath method allows using relative paths for an XML node. We use the same concept in the above code and enumerate all the variable nodes. The path that is passed to ChildElementsByPath methods is XPath. More information on XPath can be found at *http://www. w3schools.com/xpath/*. To validate a unique name in the XML we use "\\<NodeName>" as the XPath and validate its value. It is very helpful to have knowledge of XPath when creating XML validation functions

Exporting XML to a DataTable

Problem 21-6. How can we export a part of XML to a DataTable?

Like the previous problem we use the ChildElementsByPath method to get an array of nodes. We use the same concept and export values from each child of the nodes in the array to the DataTable.

```
'Function to export XML to Data Table
Public Function ExportXML2Table(ByVal oDataTable, ByVal envFile, ByVal keyNode)

'Get all the variable in the environment
Set xmlDoc = XMLUtil.CreateXMLFromFile (envFile)
Set xmlRoot = xmlDoc.GetRootElement()
'
Set xmlCols = xmlRoot.ChildElementsByPath (keyNode)

If xmlCols.Count<> 0 Then
   On error resume next
   Set xmlCol = xmlCols.item(1)
   iCount = xmlCol.ChildElements().Count

   'First loop through all the elements and creat the data table parameters
   For i = 1 to iCount
        oDataTable.AddParameter xmlCol.ChildElements.item(i).ElementName(), ""
   Next

   'Now loop through all the nodes
   For i =1 to xmlCols.count
        Set xmlCol = xmlCols.item(i)
        iCount = xmlCol.ChildElements().Count

        'Loop through direct childrens
        For j = 1 to iCount
             sParamName = xmlCol.ChildElements.item(i).ElementName()
             sParamValue = xmlCol.ChildElements.item(i).Value()
             oDataTable.GetParameter(sParamName).Value = sParamValue
        Next
        oDataTable.SetCurrentRow i + 1
   Next
   On error goto 0
End If
End Function
```

Usage:
```
'Export the Environment varaibles from environment XML to Data table
ExportXML2Table DataTable.GlobalSheet, "C:\ENV.xml", "/Environment/Variable"
```

NOTE: We can also use XMLUtil in an external VBScript by using the following QTP COM object:
Set XMLUtil = CreateObject("Mercury.XMLUtil")

Problem 21-7. How can we extract XML from a URL or Web browser?

To extract XML from a URL, or one displayed in the web browser, we must get the document object of that XML. Here is an example of using the QTP WebXML test object to do this:

```
'URL of the XML
sURL = "http://mywebsite/set.xml"

'open internet explorer with the xml URL
SystemUtil.Run "iexplore.exe", sURL
Browser("creationtime:=0").Sync

'Get XML document.
Set xmlDoc = Browser("creationtime:=0").WebXML("micClass:=WebXML").GetData()

'Save the document locally
xmlDoc.SaveFile "C:\Test.xml"
```

Comparing XML

Problem 21-8. How can we compare two XML documents for equality?

The QTP XMLData object provides a method to compare two XML documents:

```
'Load both XMLs and
Set xmlDoc1 = XMLUtil.CreateXMLFromFile ("C:\File1.xml")
Set xmlDoc2 = XMLUtil.CreateXMLFromFile ("C:\File2.xml")
'Use the compare method of the XML to check if they are equivalent
isEqual = xmlDoc1.Compare (xmlDoc2, xmlResults)
'If return value of compare method is 1 that mean the files are equal
If isEqual = 1 Then
   Msgbox "The documents match"
Else
   Msgbox "The documents don't match"
End if
```

Problem 21-9. How can we compare two xml file with different ordering of nodes?

Consider the following XML files:

File1.xml
```
<Environment>
    <Variable>
        <Name>FirstName</Name>
        <Value>Tarun</Value>
```

```
    </Variable>
  </Environment>
```

File2.xml

```
  <Environment>
    <Variable>
      <Value>Tarun</Value>
      <Name>FirstName</Name>
    </Variable>
  </Environment>
```

These two XML files won't compare for equality because of their node ordering differences. The same issue exists for XML checkpoints created through QTP. A workaround is to sort the XML file using XSL (XML StyleSheet):

```
<?xml version="1.0" encoding="UTF-8"?>
<xsl:stylesheet version="1.0" xmlns:xsl="http://www.w3.org/1999/XSL/Transform">
  <xsl:output method="xml" indent="yes"/>
  <xsl:template match="@* |*">
    <xsl:copy>
      <xsl:apply-templates select="@* |*">
       <xsl:sort order="ascending" data-type="text" select="local-name()"/>
       <xsl:sort order="ascending" data-type="text" select="descendant-or-
self::node()"/>
       <xsl:sort order="ascending" data-type="text" select="@name"/>
      </xsl:apply-templates>
    <xsl:value-of select="text()"/>
    </xsl:copy>
  </xsl:template>
</xsl:stylesheet>
```

To use this workaround we need to use Microsoft XML Version 2.0 lib "MSXML.DOMDocument" document object and apply the above XSL to our XML

Here is the function for the same:

```
'Function to Apply a XSL to XML and save the output as a file
Public Function ApplyXSL(ByVal inputXML, ByVal inputXSL, ByVal outputFile)


  'This should always work. Bu there are different version of XML Lib
  'that we can use. Chnage the Lib name as per the library available on
  'the system
  sXMLLib = "MSXML.DOMDocument"
  'Load the XML document
  Set xmlDoc = CreateObject(sXMLLib)
  'Load the XSL sytlesheet
  Set xslDoc = CreateObject(sXMLLib)


  xmlDoc.async = False
  xslDoc.async = False
  'Load the XSL file
  xslDoc.load inputXSL
```

```
    'Load the XML file
    xmlDoc.load inputXML

    'Apply the XSL stylesheet and get the tranformed text
    outputText = xmlDoc.transformNode(xslDoc.documentElement)

    'Write the text to a file
    Set FSO = CreateObject("Scripting.FileSystemObject")
    Set outFile = FSO.CreateTextFile(outputFile,True)
    outFile.Write outputText
    outFile.Close

    'Cleanup all objects
    Set outFile = Nothing
    Set FSO = Nothing
    Set xmlDoc = Nothing
    Set xslDoc = Nothing
    Set xmlResults = Nothing
End Function
```

Reader's Note

Reader's Note

Chapter 22

Working with Databases

QTP does not provide any built-in support for databases. But since it uses VBScript as its scripting language, we can use that tool's support (ADODB) to interact with databases. Explaining ADODB is beyond the scope of this book, but this chapter provides examples that give a general idea on how to use ADODB to perform common database operations.

ADODB has 4 primary objects we can use to interact with databases:

- ADODB.Connection – Useed to connect to a database instance

- ADODB.Recordset – Used to retrieve data from a database

- ADODB.Command – Used to execute a DB command, for example an SQL query or to run a stored procedure

- ADODB.Fields – Used to retrieve a particular column from a record set

Connecting to a Database

The following code shows how to connect to a database:

```
'variable for database connection
Dim adoCon

'Create the Connection object
Set adoCon = CreateObject("ADODB.Connection")
'connection string for the database
conStr = "DSN=DSNname;UID=user;PWD=password;DATABASE=mydatabasename"
adoCon.Open conStr
'...
'do database operations
```

```
'...
'close the database connection
adoCon.close
'Destroy the connection object
set adoCon = Nothing
```

Building Connection Strings

A connection string is one of the most important properties used by ADODB to connect to a database. Different databases often require different types of connection strings. There are two methods to construct a connection string. The first method is to get the string from the database documentation which may not always be readily available. The second method is to use a connection string builder Wizard.

Connection Wizard

Use the following steps to create an empty Microsoft Data Access service's Data Link file and then use its Wizard to create a connections string as described in this section.

Create a blank file with name "mycon.udl" and double click on that file to open the Data Link Properties dialog. Then select the Provider tab as shown here:

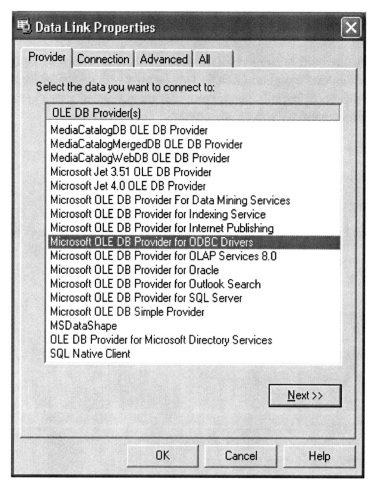

Figure 22-1 . Data Link Provider tab

After selecting a provider, click the *Next >>* button and move to the *Connection Tab*. After filling in the details on Connection tab, click on the *Test Connection* button to ensure that the connection is working as shown in the Figure 22-2Figure 22-2

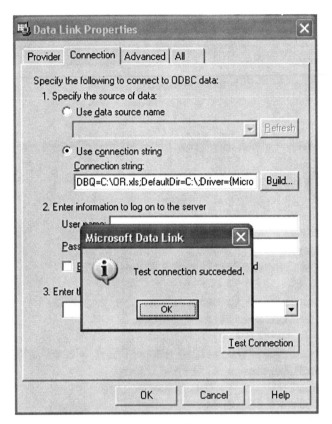

Figure 22-2. Testing the Connection

We can also configure more options in the Advanced tab and All tab like Read only mode or write only or access database user name or password etc...

Now when the myCon.udl file is opened in Notepad we will see the connection string just used to connect to the database as shown next:

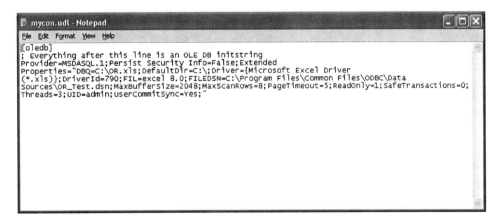

Figure 22-43. Connection String

We can now copy the above connection string into our QTP code to connect to the DB.

 NOTE: In all the upcoming examples we will be assuming that we already have an adoCon object present which is connected to a DB instance

Problem 22-1. How can we execute a query to access all records?

There are various methods of doing this using ADODB.

Method 1

This method uses the Recordset object to execute the query and extract the results:

```
'Variable to get recordset result
Dim adoRecordSet

'Create the recordset. A recordset can store results
'of a database query
Set adoRecordSet = CreateObject("ADODB.Recordset")

'Set the active connection to be used for the recordset
Set adoRecordSet.ActiveConnection = adoCon

'Cursor location can take two values adUseClient = 3 or adUseServer = 2.
adoRecordSet.CursorLocation = 3 'adUseClient
adoRecordSet.CursorType = 2 'adOpenDynamic

strSQL = "Select Val1, Val2 from Table2"
adoRecordSet.Source = strSQL

'Run the SQL query
adoRecordSet.Open

'Loop till we are not at the end of the record
While not adoRecordSet.eof()

 'Access the values of the fields. We can either use the name
 'of the column in the query or use the index
 Msgbox "Val1: " & adoRecordSet.Fields("Val1").value
 Msgbox "Val2: " & adoRecordSet.Fields("Val2").value

 'Move on to the next record
 adoRecordSet.MoveNext
Wend

'Close the recordset. Recordset should always be closed
'else we won't be able to make any further queries
adoRecordSet.Close

set adoRecordSet = Nothing
```

Method 2

This method uses the Command object to get the Recordset:

```
'Variable declaration
Dim adoRecordSet, adoCommand

'Create the command object
Set adoCommand = CreateObject("ADODB.Command")

strSQL = "Select Val1, Val2 from Table2"
adoCommand.CommandSource = strSQL
adoCommand.CommandType = 1 'adCmdText

'Run the query through the command object and get the recordset
Set adoRecordSet = adoCommand.Execute

'.....Loop through the records in adoRecordSet
```

Method 3

This method uses the connection object directly to get the Recordset.

```
'Variable declaration
Dim adoRecordSet
strSQL = "Select Val1, Val2 from Table2"

Set adoRecordSet = adoCon.Execute (strSQL)
```

 NOTE: adoRecordset.Close should not be used in case of UPDATE or DELETE queries as when these queries are execute the Recordset is not open and closing a closed Recordset will throw an error.

Checking the State of a Connection or Recordset

```
'Constant declaration for database state
Const adStateOpen = 1
Const adStateFetching = 8
Const adStateExecuting = 4
Const adStateConnecting = 2
Const adStateClosed = 0

Select Case adoCon.State 'or adoRecordSet.State in case of a recordset object
 Case adStateOpen
   Msgbox "Open"
 Case adStateFetching
   Msgbox "Fetching"
 Case adStateExecuting
   Msgbox "Executing"
 Case  adStateConnecting
   Msgbox "Connecting"
 Case  adStateClosed
   Msgbox "Closed"
End Select
```

> **Problem 22-2. How can we determine the number of rows altered by an update or a delete query?**

This is useful in situations where we need to determine if the last query altered any rows. For example, if we ran a syntactically correct update query which didn't alter any rows for any reason:

```
'Delete query
strSQL = "DELETE from Table1 where Val1 in (2,3,4)"

dim rowsAffected

'Execute the query through the connection
'and get the affected rows
adoCon.Execute strSQL, rowsAffected

If rowsAffected = 0 then
    Msgbox "No rows were deleted"
Else
    Msgbox rowsAffected & " row(s) were deleted"
End if
```

Exporting the Results of a Query to Data Table

We can export the Fields collection of a Recordset to a QTP data table. One issue that we might want to avoid is the spaces in the column name of the data table. To do that we should replace each space character in the column name from a query with an "_" character:

```
'First create a data table to export the data
'create a output sheet
Set outSheet = DataTable.AddSheet ("Output")
Dim adoRecordSet

strSQL = "Select * from Table1"
Set adoRecordSet = adoCon.Execute (strSQL)

Dim fld
'Loop through each field and get the name
'to create the data table parameters
For each fld in adoRecordSet.Fields
   outSheet.AddParameter Replace(fld.name," ","_")
Next

'Loop through all the rows of the query
While adoRecordSet.eof()
   'Loop through all the columns of the row
   For each fld in adoRecordSet.Fields
   outSheet.GetParameter(Replace(fld.name," ","_")).value = fld.value
   Next

   'Move on to the next record
   adoRecordSet.MoveNext
Wend
Set adoRecordSet = Nothing
```

NOTE: The query should not result in any field which cannot be handled normally like BLOB/CLOB etc...

Executing a Stored DB procedure

Stored procedures can be executed using the Command object. Care must be taken to properly define the required input and output parameters of the stored procedure. Consider the following stored procedure:

```
'1. Stored Procedure Name : Authentication
'2. Purpose : To Check Whether Given Person is Authorised or not
'3. Parameters
'   a) Input :
'      EMPID    - INPUT (number(5,0)) - Employee ID
'      Password - INPUT (varchar(10) - Password
'      PROJCODE - INPUT (varchar(10)) - Project Code to Login into
'   b) Output - N/A
'4. Return Value(s): number
' 0 - Succesfully Authenticated
' 1 - Invalid Password
' 2 - Employee Not Associated to Given Project
' 3 - Some Error Unable To Authenticate

'Needed constants
Const adVarChar = 200
Const adInteger = 3
Const adParamInput = 1
Const adParamInputOutput = 3
Const adParamOutput = 2
Const adParamReturnValue = 4

s_UserID = 37362
s_Password = "Test"
s_ProjID = "Project 1"

'create the command object
Set adoCommand = CreateObject("ADODB.Command")
With adoCommand
  .ActiveConnection = adoCon

  .CommandTimeout = 30
  .CommandType = 4 'adCmdStoredProc

  'Name of the stored procedure
  .CommandText = "Authentication"

  'Add all the Parameters to the Command Object
  'In case of a return value from the function that return value parameter
  'should be added before adding any other parameter
```

```
Set adoPrm =.CreateParameter("retvalue", adInteger, adParamReturnValue, 5)
.Parameters.Append adoPrm

Set adoPrm =.CreateParameter("empid", adInteger, adParamInput, 5, s_UserID)
.Parameters.Append adoPrm

Set adoPrm =.CreateParameter("password", adVarChar, adParamInput, 50, s_
Password)
.Parameters.Append adoPrm

Set adoPrm =.CreateParameter("projid", adVarChar, adParamInput, 50, s_ProjID)
.Parameters.Append adoPrm

'Execute the Stored Procedure
adoCmd.Execute

'Check the Return Value and Raise Error if Neccesary
Select Case adoCmd.Parameters("retvalue").Value
  Case 0
    MsgBox "Succesfully Authenticated"
  Case 1
    MsgBox "Invalid Password"
  Case 2
    Msgbox "Employee Not Associated to Given Project"
  Case Else
    Msgbox "Some Error Unable To Authenticate"
End Select
End With

Set adoCommand = Nothing
```

To learn more about ADODB visit the follow links:

http://www.w3schools.com/ado/

*http://msdn.microsoft.com/library/default.asp?url=/library/en-us/ado270/htm/mdmscsection1_ado.
asp*

Reader's Note

Reader's Note

Chapter 23

Working with Microsoft Excel

Like most of the Microsoft Office products, Excel provides methods for automating Excel through its COM interface. This chapter only presents various sample codes that shows demonstrate how to open and manipulate an Excel spreadsheet with QTP. To explore Excel's automation capabilities in greater depth refer to one of the many VBA/Macro Programming for Excel books available in the Market.

The Excel Automation Object Model

The next diagram shows the part of the Excel Object model we will use in this chapter:

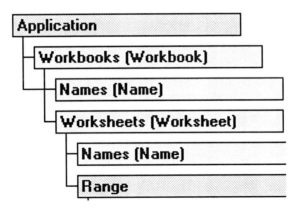

Figure 23-1. Excel Object Model

⊙ Application – The main object which references the Excel application itself

⊙ Workbooks – This object references a collection of currently opened Excel workbooks (i.e. spreadsheet files)

⊙ Workbook – This object references a single open Excel workbook

⊙ Worksheets – This object references a collection of sheets in a selected open workbook

⊙ Worksheet – This object references a single sheet in a selected open workbook

Problem 23-1. How can we invoke and terminate an instance of Excel?

```
'Variable to store excel application object
Dim xlApp

'Create a new instance of the Excel application.
'By default the application starts in invisible mode, which helps
'in performing startup & initialization operations in the background.
Set xlApp = CreateObject ("Excel.Application")

'Make the application visible
xlApp.Visible = True

Msgbox "The Excel application has been invoked"

'Terminate the Excel instance just started
xlApp.Quit

'Destroy the reference of the object
Set xlApp = Nothing
```

Problem 23-2. How can we create a new excel sheet and then save it?

```
'Excel object declarartion
Dim xlApp
Dim xlWorkbook
Dim xlWorkSheet

Set xlApp = CreateObject ("Excel.Application")

'Add a new workbook. The add method returns an object referencing the
'just created workbook, and can be used to interact with the workbook.
Set xlWorkbook = xlApp.Workbooks.Add

'Add a new worksheet. This add method returns an object references the
'just created added worksheet.
Set xlWorkSheet = xlWorkbook.WorkSheets.Add

'Update the A1 or 1,1 cell with some text
xlWorkSheet.Cells(1,1) = "Text in Row 1 and Column 1"
'The above statement can also be written as xlWorkSheet.Cells(1,"A") = "..."
```

```
'Save the new workbook. The SaveAs method is used because thw workbook has
'never been saved. In situations where we open and the re-save an
'existing workbook, the Save method should be used.
xlWorkBook.SaveAs "C:\NewBook.xls"

'Close the workbook and terminate our instance of Excel
xlWorkBook.Close
xlApp.Quit

'Lastly, destroy all of our object references
Set xlWorkSheet = Nothing
Set xlWorkBook = Nothing
Set xlApp = Nothing
```

NOTE: We won't use complete code in the remaining examples for the sake of brevity. Most notably we will assume Excel invocation and termination, creation of basic objects, etc.

Problem 23-3. How can we determine if an Excel file exists, and if not, how to create one?

First, we check if the file already exists using the FileSystemObject:

```
'Source file
sSourceFile = "C:\Source.xls"

Set fso = CreateObject("Scripting.FileSystemObject")

'Check if the file already exist
bFileExist = fso.FileExists(sSourceFile)

If bFileExist then
    'If the file exist open it
    Set xlWorkBook = xlApp.Workbooks.Open (sSourceFile)
Else
    'If the file does not exist create a new one
    Set xlWorkBook = xlApp.Workbooks.Add
End If

'...
'...
'Check if opened a new file
If bFileExist Then
    'Use the Save method in case
    xlWorkBook.Save
Else
    'Use the SaveAs method as the file has never been saved
    xlWorkBook.SaveAs sSourceFile
End if
```

Problem 23-4. How can we access all non-blank row values in a specific column?

There are two methods to do this. The first method is to loop through each cell in a selected column and stop when a blank value is encountered. The second method is to get the count of all non-blank values in the selected column.

Method 1:

```
'counter for row
I = 1

While xlWorkSheet.Cells (I, 1) <> ""
   Msgbox xlWorkSheet.Cells (I, 1)
   I = I + 1
Wend
```

Method 2:

```
'Use Evaluate function to determne how many rows have non-blank values
iRowCount = xlWorkSheet.Evaluate ("COUNTA(A:A)")

'In the above statement, A:A specifies all rows in column A, while
'1:1 would mean 1st row and A1:A100 would mean 1st to 100th row of column A.

For I = 1 to iRowCount
    Msgbox xlWorkSheet.Cells (I, 1)
Next
```

Problem 23-5. How can we search for a text string and then update another cell's value in that row?

Consider the spreadsheet shown in the Figure 23-2Figure 23-2

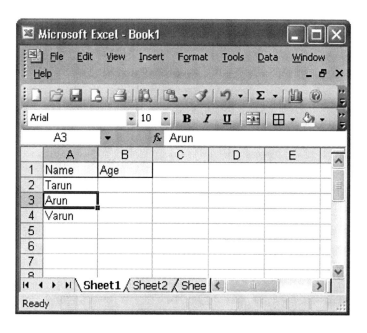

Figure 23-2. Spreadsheet to be updated

For example, let's say we want to update the Age for Tarun. Here is how we could do that:

```
'Find the text "Tarun" in column A
objFind = xlWorkSheet.Range ("A:A").Find ("Tarun")

If obFind is Nothing then
   MsgBox "Text not found"
Else
    iRowNum = objFind.Row
    'Update the age
    xlWorkSheet.Cells (iRowNum, 2) = 16
End if
```

Problem 23-6. How can we use an Excel sheet as a QTP output Data Table?

Consider the spreadsheet shown in the Figure 23-4Figure 23-3

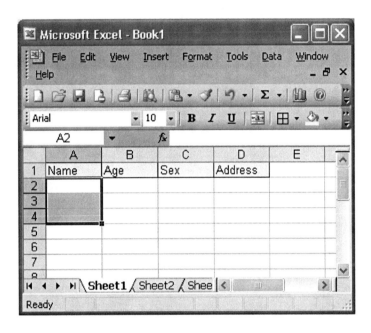

Figure 23-43. Excel sheet as output data table

Let's assume that we have opened the above file and now want to populate the data for various rows. But we are not sure about the ordering of the columns i.e. Name could be defined as column 1, column 2 or any other column. What we need to do first is to evaluate the first row's column titles and then create a Dictionary entry for each column title with its related column number.

```
'variable to store column dictionary index
Dim oCols

'Create a Dictionary object to store the index of each column
Set oCols = CreateObject ("Scripting.Dictionary")

'Make it case in-sensitive
oCols.CompareMode = vbTextCompare
iColumn = 1
```

```
'Loop through all the columns in the first row
While xlWorkSheet.Cells ( 1, iColumn) <> ""
        'Add the column's title text as the Key and the column index as the Value
        oCols.Add xlWorkSheet.Cells (1, iColumn), iColumn
        iColumn = iColumn + 1
Wend


'...
'...


'Update the sheet for 2 rows
'We started the loop from 2nd row as the
'1st row now is the header row and contains the column names.
For iRow = 2 to 3
        xlWorkSheet.Cells (iRow, iCols("Name")) = "Name : " & iRow
        xlWorkSheet.Cells (iRow, iCols("Age")) = iRow + 10
Next
```

Problem 23-7. How can we allow a user to select a file to be opened?

```
'Create the excel object application
Set xlsApp = CreateObject("Excel.Application")

sExcelFileName = xlsApp.GetOpenFilename("Excel Files, *.xls",,"Select the Excel File")

If sExcelFileName = False Then
   MsgBox "No File Selected"
Else
   MsgBox sExcelFileName
End If


xlsApp.Quit

Set xlsApp = Nothing
```

Converting VBA to VBScript

In Excel we can record macros which generate Visual Basic for Application (VBA) code.

Macro Recording

Excel provides the ability to record macros which are used to automate various actions in the application. This capability, built into Excel, can be used to determine what code needs to be written in QTP to implement a desired operation. This section describes how to perform a macro recording and then convert those steps in QTP VBScript code.

After opening Excel with a new blank worksheet, go to *Tools Macro Record new Macro...* and press *Ok* to start recording a macro.

Enter some values for Name, Age and Sex in the second row and then select all the cells and add borders also. Select the header row and give it some background color.

Press the stop button to stop recording

Press ALT + F11 to open the VBA editor. Browse to the Module file that contains the recorded macro.

Here is the macro that Excel generated:

```vba
'Recorded macro
Sub Macro1()
'
' Macro1 Macro
' Macro recorded 7/1/2007 by Tarun_Lalwani
'
'
    ActiveCell.FormulaR1C1 = "Tarun"
    Range("B2").Select
    ActiveCell.FormulaR1C1 = "16"
    Range("C2").Select
    ActiveCell.FormulaR1C1 = "Male"
    Range("D2").Select
    ActiveCell.FormulaR1C1 = "N/A"
    Range("A2:D2").Select
    Selection.Borders(xlDiagonalDown).LineStyle = xlNone
    Selection.Borders(xlDiagonalUp).LineStyle = xlNone
    With Selection.Borders(xlEdgeLeft)
        .LineStyle = xlContinuous
        .Weight = xlThin
        .ColorIndex = xlAutomatic
    End With
    With Selection.Borders(xlEdgeTop)
        .LineStyle = xlContinuous
        .Weight = xlThin
        .ColorIndex = xlAutomatic
    End With
    With Selection.Borders(xlEdgeBottom)
        .LineStyle = xlContinuous
        .Weight = xlThin
        .ColorIndex = xlAutomatic
    End With
    With Selection.Borders(xlEdgeRight)
        .LineStyle = xlContinuous
        .Weight = xlThin
        .ColorIndex = xlAutomatic
    End With
    With Selection.Borders(xlInsideVertical)
        .LineStyle = xlContinuous
        .Weight = xlThin
        .ColorIndex = xlAutomatic
    End With
    With Selection.Borders(xlInsideHorizontal)
        .LineStyle = xlContinuous
        .Weight = xlThin
        .ColorIndex = xlAutomatic
    End With
    With Selection.Interiorz
.ColorIndex = 35
```

```
        .Pattern = xlSolid
    End With
End Sub
```

To accomplish the same thing using VBScript in QTP we need to filter out things that we don't want to do, as well as convert VBA to the VBScript.

Consider this line of VBA code:

```
'Select range A2:D2
Range("A2:D2").Select
```

Since VBA code always executes within Excel we don't need to specify a WorkSheet object. But the equivalent QTP code using VBScript needs to explicitly reference a worksheet object, as in:

```
'Select range A2:D2
xlWorkSheet.Range("A2:D2").Select
```

Let's convert the following VBA code so that it will work in QTP with VBScript:

```
'Select range A1:D1
Range("A1:D1").Select

With Selection.Interior
    .ColorIndex = 35
    .Pattern = xlSolid
End With
```

The above code uses a constant, xlSolid, defined in Excel but not available in QTP. Therefore we need to define it ourselves. But in order to do that, we need to determine the constant's integer value. There are two ways to achieve this.

Method 1

In the VBA Editor view press CTRL + G to launch the immediate window pane.

Type "?xlSolid" inside the window and press Enter to display the constant's value:

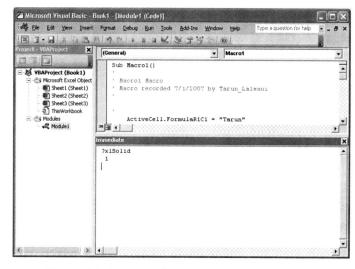

Figure 23-64. Immediate window pane in Excel

The window will display the value of the constant which we can now use in a QTP script:

```
'Constant declaration
Const xlSolid = 1
```

Method 2

In the VBA editor view, press F2 key to launch the object browser. Type xlSolid to search for the constant as shown here:

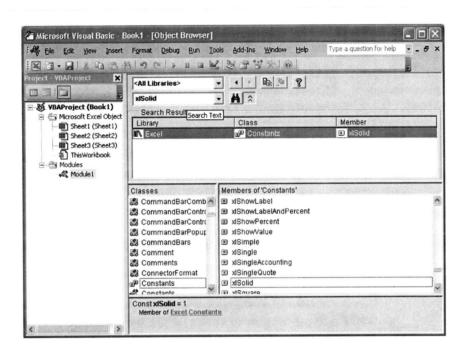

Figure 23-75. Excel Object Browser

We can avoid the Select and With Selection objects in the last VBA code fragment by directly referring to the object we want to set in the VBScript code. So the VBA code can be converted as below:

```
'Constant declaration
Const xlSolid = 1

xlWorkSheet.Range("A2:D2").Interior.ColorIndex = 35
xlWorkSheet.Range("A2:D2").Interior.Pattern = xlSolid
```

The VBA to VBScript conversions gets easier when we more fully understand the objects that we need to work with and where those objects resided in the Excel object model.

 NOTE: We can use the Excel object browser to look at the various methods that are supported by the different types of object.

If we were to observe the macro recorded VBA code for saving a new file to a specific location, it would appear something like this:

```
'Save workbook as
ActiveWorkbook.SaveAs Filename:="C:\SheetExample.xls", FileFormat:=xlNormal _
        , Password:="", WriteResPassword:="", ReadOnlyRecommended:=False, _
        CreateBackup:=False
```

Notice that VBA supports passing parameters without regard to the position order using "ParamName:=ParamValue" syntax. But VBScripts does not support this type of parameter passing. So we need to make sure that all function parameters are passed in the order specified in the function's definition. Use the Object browser to review a selected function's definition. For example the SaveAs function definition is:

```
'SaveAs function syntax
Sub SaveAs([Filename], [FileFormat], [Password], [WriteResPassword],
[ReadOnlyRecommended], [CreateBackup], [AccessMode As XlSaveAsAccessMode
= xlNoChange], [ConflictResolution], [AddToMru], [TextCodepage],
[TextVisualLayout], [Local])
```

This VBA statement would be converted to a VBScript statement using the following simplified syntax, since all but the first parameter can normally use the default values:

```
'Save the workbook
xlWorkBook.SaveAs "C:\SheetExample.xls"
```

But in a case where we want to define a password for the sheet we would use this syntax:

```
'Save workbook and add Password protection
xlWorkBook.SaveAs "C:\SheetExample.xls", , "Password"
```

 NOTE: We didn't provide a value for the 2nd parameter, so it will use its default value.

Problem 23-8. How can we access an Excel spreadsheet embedded in Internet Explorer?

Internet Explorer and Explore can render many different types of documents. It could be a local folder, shared folder, ftp folder, web URL, word document etc. What both of these applications mainly do is to render a document object. And the document object differs based on the type of the URL being referenced.

For a browser displaying a web page, we can use the following statement to access the document object:

```
'Document object
Set objDoc = Browser("CreationTime:=0").object.document
```

But when the browser is displaying an embedded document then the above statement will cause QTP to throw a "General run error" exception. To access the embedded document object we need to use IE's COM interface. The following function provides an access to IE's COM interface through its window's handle:

```
'Function to get IE Object from window handle
Function GetIEObjectFromhWnd(ByVal hWnd)
    Dim objShell
```

```
Dim objShellWindows
'Create a shell application object
Set objShell = CreateObject("Shell.Application")

'Get the collection of all open explorer windows
Set objShellWindows = objShell.Windows

'Set the object to Nothing in case the code below can't find any IEs
Set GetIEObjectFromhWnd = Nothing

'Check if collection object is available
If (Not objShellWindows Is Nothing) Then
        Dim objEnumItems

        'Check each explorer window and compare with the hWnd
        For Each objEnumItems In objShellWindows
            If objEnumItems.hwnd = hWnd then
                'Return the object in case hWnd matches
                Set GetIEObjectFromhWnd = objEnumItems
                Exit For
            End if
        Next
End If

Set objShellWindows = Nothing
Set objShell = Nothing
End Function
```

We can now use the function given above to get the COM interface of the IE window which is displaying a spreadsheet:

```
'Get browser handle
hWnd = Browser("CreationTime:=0").GetROProperty("hwnd")

'Get IE COM interface object
Set ieBrowser = GetIEObjectFromhWnd(hWnd)

'Get document object for the IE window
Set objDocument = ieBrowser.document
```

But if we don't know what this document object actually contains, then how do we determine its object type? We have to just add the next statement and then run the code to review its output:

```
'This will give WorkBook
MsgBox TypeName(objDocument)
```

 NOTE: An embedded Excel sheet needs to be open in a browser, in order to get the above output.

Using the TypeName function we can determine that the document is a workbook object of the Excel application. Thereafter we can access all workbook properties and methods:

```
'Get the workbook from document object
Set objWorkbook = objDocument
Set objSheet1 = objWorkbook.Sheets(1)

objSheet1.Cells(1,1) = "Tarun Lalwani"

Msgbox objSheet1.Cells(1,1)
```

The above code is now able to operate against the embedded spreadsheet. The same technique can be used to evaluate and manipulate other embedded documents such as Microsoft Word documents, Microsoft PowerPoint presentations and many more.

Performance Enhancements

Each QTP call to an Excel object has its cost because it is an out-of-process communication. Consider the QTP code below:

```
'Store the current timer
X = Timer

'Write to 1000 rows and 7 cols, 1 cell at a time
For i = 1 To 1000
   For j = 1 To 7
         xlWorksheet.Cells(i,j) = i*j
   Next
Next

'Display the timer taken for the loop to execute
Msgbox Timer - X
```

The above code took 27 seconds on the author's PC. The performance problem with this code is that we make 7000 calls, each accessing a single spreadsheet cell. So if we can reduce the number of calls we can improve runtime performance. Consider the next improvement:

```
'Record the current timer
x = Timer

Dim iArray
ReDim iArray(6)
For i = 1 To 1000
   'create all column values for the next row
   For j = 1 To 7
         iArray(j-1) = i * j
   Next
   'Write all the cells in the next row with new values
   xlWorksheet.Range("A" & i & ":G" & i) = iArray
Next

'Display the time taken by the loop
MsgBox Timer - x
```

The above code executed in 4 seconds on the same PC. This improved function now updates the sheet row by row, which saves substantial time over writing each cell individually.

Finally a further performance improvement can be achieved by writing the spreadsheet a column at a time, which reduces the QTP to Excel object calls to 7. The only difference would be that we need to transpose the array before assigning it to the range, using the following function:

```
'Function to get the column name from column Index
Function GetColumnName(ByVal Index)
    GetColumnName = Chr(Asc("A") + (Index - 1) Mod 26)
    Index = (Index - 1) \ 26
    If Index <> 0 Then GetColumnName = Chr(Asc("A") + (Index - 1) Mod 26) +
GetColumnName
End Function

'Record the current timer
x = Timer

Dim iArray
ReDim iArray(1000)

'Loop for columns first
For i = 1 To 7
   'Loop for rows
   For j = 1 To 1000
        iArray(j-1) = i * j
   Next
   'Get the column name
   sColName = GetColumnName(i)

   xlWorksheet.Range(sColName  & "1:" & sColName & j) = xlApp.Transpose(iArray)
Next

'Display the time taken by the loop
MsgBox Timer - x
```

This 2nd improvement took only 0.21 seconds to execute. Still not fast enough? Well we can make one final performance improvement by using a 2 dimensional array and assigning it to the Excel spreadsheet in a single access, as in:

```
'Record the current timer
x = Timer
Dim iArray
ReDim iArray(999, 6)

'Populate the 2-D array
For i = 1 To 1000
    For j = 1 To 7
        iArray(i - 1, j - 1) = i * j
    Next
Next
'Assign it to the range
```

```
xlsWorksheet.Range(GetColumnName(1) & "1:" & GetColumnName(j-1) & (i-1)) =
iArray

'Display he time taken by the loop
MsgBox Timer - x
```

This third and final improvement took 0.04 seconds to execute, which is approximately 590 times faster than the cell by cell code we initially started with.

NOTE: We should always try to minimize calls to any external COM component as it involves data marshalling from windows and this type of overhead seriously impacts the performance.

Reading data from excel in one go

```
'Variable to store data as array
Dim iArray

'Get the range which has data
iArray = xlWorkSheet.UsedRange

'Get the dimension size of the array
rowCount = UBound(iArray,1)
colCount = UBound(iArray,2)

'Loop through the array
For i = LBound(iArray, 1) to rowCount
   For j = LBound(iArray, 2) to colCount
         'Process iArray(i, j)
   Next
Next
```

Reader's Note

Reader's Note

Chapter 24

Working with
Microsoft Outlook

Microsoft Outlook is one of the most commonly used desktop email tools. Outlook can be used to send and receive emails from a computer. Outlook operations can be automated using COM, and therefore, by QTP as well. In this chapter we show how to use Outlook to send and receive email messages.

Outlook Object model

Figure 24-1 shows objects from the Outlook object model that will be used in this chapter:

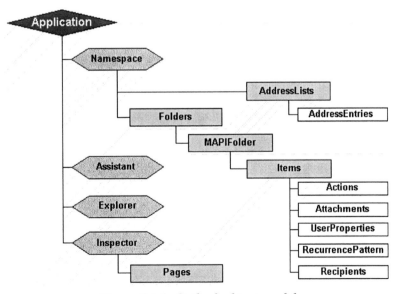

Figure 24-1. Outlook object model

Below is a list of the objects we will discuss in this chapter.

The Application object is the top level object and is used to create an instance of Outlook. The most commonly used child objects of the Application object are:

- ◉ Namespace – Outlook uses only a single namespace, "MAPI"

- ◉ Folders – Is a collection of folders under the namespace (Mail folders, Public Folders, PST)

- ◉ Items – Is a collection of outlook items (contacts, emails, calendar, appointment etc.)

- ◉ Attachments – Is a collection of attachments present in an item

- ◉ MAPIFolder – Is the sub folders present inside the MAPI folders

Launching the Outlook Application

The first step required to work with the Outlook application is to create its COM object using the following code:

```
'Create the Outlook application object
Set olApp = CreateObject("Outlook.Application")
```

Once the Application object is created we need to get its Namespace object. The only namespace that Outlook supports is MAPI:

```
'Get the MAPI name space
Set olMAPI = olApp.GetNamespace("MAPI")
```

 NOTE: We will use the just created olApp and olMAPI objects in the remainder of this chapter without any further comment.

Logging in to the Namespace

Syntax for the Namespace Logon method is:

```
'Syntax for Logon function
<namespace>.Logon(Profile, Password, ShowDialog, NewSession)
```

We do not need to log on when Outlook is already launched or when Outlook logs on to the default profile automatically:

```
'Logon in to the namespace
olMAPI.Logon ,,False, True

'Log out of the namespace
olMAPI.Logoff
```

Enumerating the top level folder

The Namespace object provides the Folders collection for the top level folder. We can enumerate all the folders using the following code:

```
'Enumerate all top level folders
For Each topFolder In olMAPI.Folders
  WScript.Echo topFolder.Name
Next
```

```
'The above code produces the below output on my machine
'Public Folders
'Mailbox - Tarun Lalwani
'Tarun Lalwani
```

We can also access these folder using their name or their index. So to access the "Public Folders" we can also use:

```
'Various ways To access the first folder (Public Folders)
Set oFirstFolder = olMapi.Folders.GetFirst
Set oFirstFolder = olMapi.Folders.Item(1)
Set oFirstFolder = olMapi.Folders.Item("Public Folders")
```

All these statements return an object of type MAPIFolder. MAPIFolder objects provide a Folders collection of their sub-folders. So we can create a function to get a folder from its path using the following function:

```
'Function to get a folder by its Path. Each folder is to be
'seperated by a \ and the function also supports
'using relative paths by using . and .. in the paths
Public Function GetSubFolderByPath(FromFolder, Path)
    arrFolders = Split(Trim(Path), "\")
    Set CurrentFolder = FromFolder


    On Error Resume Next
    For Each sFolderName In arrFolders
        If sFolderName <> "" Then
            Select Case sFolderName
                Case "."
                    'Do not do anything we are at current
                    'folder and remain on that only
                Case ".."
                    'Get the parent folder
                    Set CurrentFolder = CurrentFolder.Parent
                Case Else
                    Set CurrentFolder = CurrentFolder.Folders(sFolderName)
                    'In case the folder does not exist we will get an error

                    If Err.Number Then
                        Set CurrentFolder = Nothing
                        Exit For
                    End If
            End Select
        End If
    Next


    'Return the folder
    Set GetSubFolderByPath = CurrentFolder
End Function


'Usage
Set oFolder = GetSubFolderByPath(olMAPI, "\\Mailbox - Tarun Lalwani\Inbox")
```

```
'Prints "Inbox"
Print oFolder.Name

'Get sub folder from folder. Here we specify .. to get
'parent first which will be "Mailbox - Tarun Lalwani" and
'"Sent Items" folder from that folder
Set oFolder = GetSubFolderByPath(oFolder,"..\Sent Items")

'Prints "Sent Items"
Print oFolder.Name
```

Getting a Folder interactively from a user

We can then use the Namespace object's PickFolder method to present a dialog and get a folder selection from a user with the following code:

```
'Get the folder from user
Set oFolder = olMAPI.PickFolder()

'If the user presses the Cancel button then the function returns Nothing
If oFolder Is Nothing Then
  MsgBox "User pressed the Cancel button"
Else
  MsgBox "User selected the " & oFolder.FolderPath & " folder"
End If
```

The code will show a dialog as shown in Error! Reference source not found.

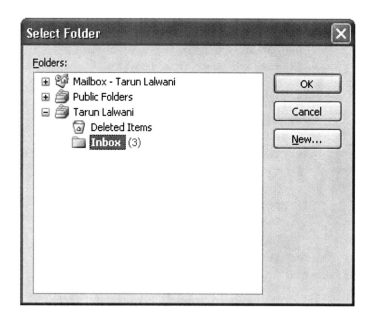

Figure 24-2. Select folder dialog

Getting the default folders

We can get the default folders using the following code:

```
'Constants for default folders
Const olFolderDeletedItems = 3
Const olFolderOutbox = 4
```

```
Const olFolderSentMail = 5
Const olFolderInbox = 6
Const olFolderCalendar = 9
Const olFolderContacts = 10
Const olFolderJournal = 11
Const olFolderNotes = 12
Const olFolderTasks = 13
Const olFolderDrafts = 16
Const olPublicFoldersAllPublicFolders = 18
Const olFolderConflicts = 19
Const olFolderSyncIssues = 20
Const olFolderLocalFailures = 21
Const olFolderServerFailures = 22
Const olFolderJunk = 23

'Get a deafult folder
Set oFolder = olMAPI.GetDefaultFolder(olFolderInbox)

'Prints "\\Mailbox - Tarun Lalwani\Inbox" on my machine
Print oFolder.FolderPath
```

Reading e-mail Messages

We can access e-mail messages inside a folder using the folder's Items collection as shown in the following code:

```
'Define the folder constant
Const olFolderInbox = 6

'Get the inbox folder
Set oFolder = olMAPI.GetDefaultFolder(olFolderInbox)

'Get all the items in the folder
Set allEmails = oFolder.Items

unreadCount = 0

'Read all the unread emails
For Each email In oFolder.Items
  If email.Unread = True Then
    unreadCount = unreadCount + 1
  End If
Next

'Display the unread email count
msgbox unreadCount
```

The above code displays the number of unread e-mail messages in the Inbox folder. This code loops through each message in the folder, so the code will take proportionally more time as the message count increases. But the Items collection provides a restrict method which can be used to filter emails based on various parameters, as shown in the following code:

```
'Get all the items in the folder
Set allEmails = oFolder.Items
```

```
'Restrict the collection to unread emails
Set unreadEmails = allEmails.Restrict("[Unread] = True")

'Display the count of unread emails
Msgbox unreadEmails.Count
```

We can use multiple restriction parameters as show in the following code:

```
'Restrict the collection to unread emails which have a name in the CC field
Set unreadEmails = allEmails.Restrict("[Unread] = True And [CC] <> ''")

'Restrict the collection to unread emails which have a specific subject
Set unreadEmails = allEmails.Restrict("[Unread] = True And [Subject] = 'Your
Order Confirmation'")

'Restrict the collection to unread emails from a specific sender
Set unreadEmails = allEmails.Restrict("[Unread] = True And [From]='Tarun Lalwani'")

'Restrict the collection to unread emails NOT from a specific sender
Set unreadEmails = allEmails.Restrict("[Unread] = True And NOT [From]='Tarun Lalwani'")
```

The Restrict method supports OR, AND, NOT operators. But there is no LIKE operator which means we cannot filter based on regular expression syntax. In such cases the filter should be set to limit the emails collection to a minimum and then loop through the selected messages to get just those we are looking for. The Unread flag is commonly used to limit the collection and in case the email is not required again it can then be marked as Read using the following code:

```
'Restrict the collection to unread emails NOT from 'Tarun Lalwani'
Set unreadEmails = allEmails.Restrict("[Unread] = True And NOT [From]='Tarun Lalwani'")

For Each email In unreadEmails
  email.UnRead = False
Next
```

Accessing e-mail Message Properties

Once we have an e-mail message we can access its various properties. Some of these properties are shown in the Table 24-1

Table 24-1. Email properties

Property	Description
Attachments	Collection of attachments in the email
Body BodyFormat	Text of the email body
	Format of the email text (Rich text, HTML and plain text)
CC	CC of the email

Property	Description
ConversationIndex	Index of the mail in conversation
ConversationTopic	Subject of the conversation (Without the Re:, Fw: etc...)
HTMLBody	HTML text of the body
ItemProperties	Collection of all the properties associated with the email
Parent	Get the parent folder in which the email exist
Recipients	Collection of all the recipient in the email
SenderEmailAddress	Email address of the sender
SenderEmailType	Sender's Email address type. eg – SMTP
SenderName	Name of the sender
Size	Size of the email
Subject	Subject of the email address
To	Display name of addresses in TO list
UnRead	Tells whether email is unread or not

Downloading attachments

An e-mail message's attachments can be downloaded by accessing its Attachments collection, using the following code:

```
'Get the email object from a folder
Set email = oFolder.items(1)

'Download all the attachments to "C:\Test" folder
For Each attachment In email.Attachments
  email.SaveAsFile "C:\Test\" & attachment.FileName
Next
```

Sending an E-mail Message

To send e-mail messages using Outlook we need to first create the message and then fill in all the details associated with the message and then send it using the following code:

```
'Item type constants
Const olMailItem = 0
Const olAppointmentItem = 1
Const olContactItem = 2
Const olTaskItem = 3
Const olJournalItem = 4
Const olNoteItem = 5
Const olPostItem = 6
Const olDistributionListItem = 7

'Create a new e-mail message item
Set newMail = olApp.CreateItem(olMailItem)

'Populate one or more of the email address fields
newMail.To = "toemail@website.com"
```

```
newMail.CC = "ccemail@website.com"
newMail.BCC = "bccemail@website.com"

'Edit in the message's subject and body information
newMail.Subject = "Test Subject"
newMail.Body = "Body of the email"

'Send the email
newMail.Send
```

Outlook Security Dialogs

When we attempt to execute the above code to send the e-mail message, a security modal dialog is presented as shown below. This is a security feature of Outlook. QTP code will be blocked from further execution until either Yes or No is clicked by a user or another program.

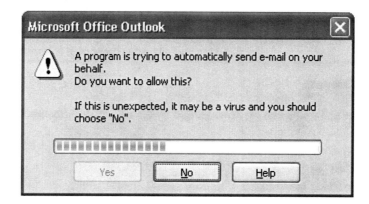

Figure 24-3. Security Dialog while sending email

There are several ways to deal with this security dialog.

Method 1

ClickYes is a third party tool available at *http://www.contextmagic.com/*. This tool automatically clicks yes on outlook security dialogs.

Method 2

Use a third party library which works with low level MAPI APIs and works around the limitation of Outlook security patch. One such library is Outlook Redemption available at *http://www.dimastr.com/*

Method 3

Send the email through the Outlook UI. When we create an email using the code above, it is created in a hidden window. But Outlook does not raise the security popup when a user clicks on the Send button in its own UI. So we need to display the email and then use QTP to click on the Send button just as a real user would. So the QTP code will change as follows:

```
'Set the subject and body of the email
newMail.Subject = "Test Subject"
newMail.Body = "Body of the email saJgsjhagsj"
```

```
'Display the email
newMail.Display

'Get the caption of the window
emailCaption = newMail.GetInspector().Caption

'Create a description
Set oMailWindow = Description.Create
oMailWindow("title").Value = emailCaption
oMailWindow("title").RegularExpression = False

'Send the ALT + S key to send the mail
Window(oMailWindow).Type micAltDwn + "s" + micAltUp

sTitle = "title:=.*Spelling.*"
'Check if a spelling check window is present
If Window(oMailWindow).Window(sTitle).Exist(2) Then
  Window(oMailWindow).Window(sTitle).Close
End If

sTitle = "title:=Microsoft Office Outlook"
'Check if a spelling cancelled dialog is present
If Window(oMailWindow).Window(sTitle).Exist(2) Then
  Window(oMailWindow).Window(sTitle).WinButton("text:=&Yes").Click
End If
```

Method 4

The Outlook security dialog blocks QTP execution, therefore the QTP Recovery Scenario can't be used to dismiss the dialog. The workaround to such a situation is to use an external VBScript to do the email work and then use QTP code or a Recovery Scenario to dismiss the security dialog.

Method 5

Use the approach of "Working with Modal Dialog boxes" as discussed in the "Working with APIs" chapter.

Method 6

We can use the CDO or CDONTS library to send the emails. The method is pretty similar to the one used with Outlook with the only difference being the additional code needed to specify the configuration:

```
'Constants declaration
'Send message using the local SMTP service pickup directory.
Const cdoSendUsingPickup = 1

'Send the message using the network (SMTP over the network).
Const cdoSendUsingPort = 2

'Do not authenticate
Const cdoAnonymous = 0
```

```
'basic (clear-text) authentication
Const cdoBasic = 1
'NTLM
Const cdoNTLM = 2

'Create a CDO email messages
Set newMail = CreateObject("CDO.Message")

'Configure the email network settings
With newMail.Configuration.Fields.
.Item("http://schemas.microsoft.com/cdo/configuration/sendusing") = cdoSendUsingPort

  'Name or IP of Remote SMTP Server
.Item("http://schemas.microsoft.com/cdo/configuration/smtpserver") = "smtp.mycompany.com"

  'Type of authentication, NONE, Basic (Base64 encoded), NTLM
.Item("http://schemas.microsoft.com/cdo/configuration/smtpauthenticate") = cdoBasic

  'Your UserID on the SMTP server
.Item("http://schemas.microsoft.com/cdo/configuration/sendusername") = "MyUserName"

  'Your password on the SMTP server
.Item("http://schemas.microsoft.com/cdo/configuration/sendpassword") = "MyPassword"

  'Server port (typically 25)
.Item("http://schemas.microsoft.com/cdo/configuration/smtpserverport") = 25

  'Use SSL for the connection (False or True)
.Item ("http://schemas.microsoft.com/cdo/configuration/smtpusessl") = True

  .Update
End with

'Set the mail properties
With newMail
  .To ="toemail@email.com"
  .subject = "Test Email"
  .HTMLBODY ="This is a test email"

  'Use display name as well
  .From= """My Name"" mystmpemail@email.com"
  .AddAttachment "C:\Test.txt"

  'Send the email
  .send
End with
Set newMail = nothing
```

Getting addresses from e-mail messages

To get email addresses from the messages, we access the Recipients collections. The following function shows how to get the addresses present in the To and CC collections.

```
'Function to get TO and CC list addresses from email object
Public Function GetAddressesFromMail(oMail, ByRef sTo, ByRef sCC)
    sTo = ""
    sCC = ""

    'Enumerate all recipientss in the email
    For Each oRecip In item.Recipients
        'Is the recipient in TO list
        If oRecip.Type = olTo Then
            sTo = sTo & oRecip.Address & ";"
        'Is the recipient in CC list
        ElseIf oRecip.Type = olCC Then
            sCC = sCC & oRecip.Address
        End If
    Next
End Function
```

To get the sender's email address in Outlook version 2003 or higher we can use the following code:

```
'Get sender's email address
sFrom = item.SenderEmailAddress
```

But in Outlook versions prior to 2003 there is no such property. But we can use the Outlook Redemption library or CDO to obtain the address. Each email item in Outlook is assigned a 48 character ID. These IDs can be use to get an email. So the trick here is to get the ID from the Outlook email object and then get the email in CDO object using the retrieved IDs. We can get the ID of the email and then get that email in CDO using the following code:

```
'Get the ID of the email
itemID = oMail.EntryID

'Create the CDO MAPI session object
Set oMAPI = CreateObject("MAPI.Session")

'Logon to the Outlook profile
oMAPI.Logon "Outlook",, False,True

'Get the email from the ID
Set oCDOMail = oMAPI.GetMessage(itemID)

'Get the sender's address
senderEmailAddress = oCDOMail.Sender.address

'Logoff the session
oMAPI.Logoff
```

Extended Email Address

When getting addresses from an Exchange Server Contacts, the address can be in an extended format.

For example:

```
network/postoffice/user
/c=US/p=mycompany/o=Finance/ou=Purchasing/s=Furthur/g=Joe
```

To get the SMTP email address we would need to use CDO again, using the following code:

```
'Define Property constants
Const PR_ADDRTYPE = &H3002001E
Const PR_SMTP_ADDRESS = &H39FE001E

'Get the SMTP address from th address object
Public Function GetSMTPAddress(oAddressObject)
   If oAddressObject.Fields(PR_ADDRTYPE) = "EX" Then
         GetSMTPAddress = oAddressObject.Fields(PR_SMTP_ADDRESS)
   Else
         GetSMTPAddress = oAddressObject.Address
   End If
End Function

'Get senders SMTP address
senderEmailAddress = GetSMTPAddress(oCDOMail.Sender)

'Enumerate each address
For Each oRecip In oCDOMail.Recipients

   'Get the ID of the address
   addressID = oRecip.ID

   'Get the address entry object as Recipient object does
   'not support Field collection to get the SMTP address
   Set oAddressEntry = oMAPI.GetAddressEntry(addressID)

   emailAddress = GetSMTPAddress(oAddressEntry)
Next
```

The above function uses the AddressEntry type object to get the SMTP addressees.

 NOTE: The technique described above will cause few security dialogs to popup.

Clicking links inside an e-mail message

Outlook Email messages support three different formats: Plain text, RTF and HTML. To click a link inside a message we need a method to get the link. Outlook can use different editors to display email – HTML, Word etc. Whatever the format of the email may be, the Outlook object model allows us to get it as HTML content. So we can actually get the email's HTML content and then write that onto an IE browser. This will display the email as a page inside the browser and then we can use the normal QTP code to click the link. The following code shows how this is done:

```
'Get the email body in HTML format
HTMLText = email.HTMLBody

'Launch a browser
SystemUtil.Run "iexplore.exe"

'Wait for browser to launch
Wait 5

'Write the text on to the browser
Browser("creationtime:=0").object.document.write HTMLText

Set allLinks = Browser("creationtime:=0").object.document.links

'Get all the links
For Each oLink In allLinks
    MsgBox oLink.href
Next
```

Launching QTP using an email trigger

When remote activation of a QTP script is required we can host code in Outlook and create various commands to perform this task. Outlook rules support running a VBA script when the conditions of a rule are met.

The first step is to create a function which is called when the conditions of a rule are satisfied. The function should have the following prototype:

```
'Function prototype
Public Sub Rule_Function1(Item as Outlook.MailItem)

End Sub
```

Open outlook and press ALT + F11 to launch the VBA macro editor. Create a new module and add a new function with the prototype shown earlier in the Figure 24-5

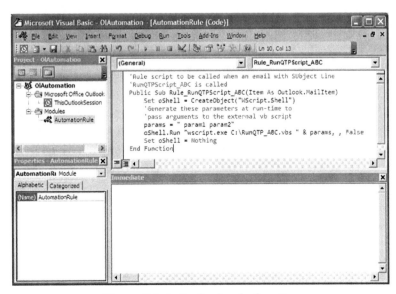

Figure 24-4. Outlook rule function

Now go to *Tools Rules & Alerts ...* and Click on the New Rule.,. button. Configure the rule as needed. Check the checkbox for 'run a script' and select the function Rule_RunQTPScript_ABC as shown in the Figure 24-7

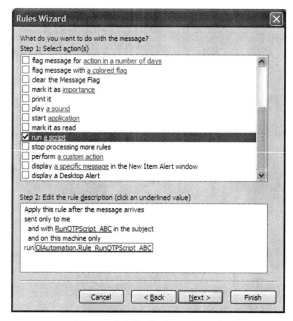

Figure 24-5. Rules wizard

Once the rule is triggered the VA function will be called. But we don't want to block Outlook to by running a QTP script directly from the VBA function. So the best method is to add the majority of the QTP activation codes in a VBScript file and then execute the VBScript file asynchronously as shown in the following code:

```
'Rule script to be called when an email with SUbject Line
'RunQTPScript_ABC is called
Public Sub Rule_RunQTPScript_ABC(Item as Outlook.MailItem)
    Set oShell = CreateObject("WScript.Shell")
    'Generate these parameters at run-time to
    'pass arguments to the external vb script
    Params = " param1 param2"
    oShell.Run "wscript.exe C:\RunQTP_ABC.vbs " & params,,False
    Set oShell = Nothing
End Function
```

The above code will run the same script again in case where the multiple emails are received. In cases where QTP might not be available to execute the request from a new email trigger, code should be added to create a request queue. This technique provides a very simple mechanism to execute QTP scripts on a remote PC using the email mechanism described above.

Reader's Note

Reader's Note

Chapter 25

Working with Microsoft Word

Microsoft word is widely used to present documents ranging for Books, Brochures, Reports etc. Like most of the Microsoft Office products, Word provides methods for automating Word through its COM interface. This chapter only presents the sample various code examples that shows demonstrate how to open and manipulate a Word document with QTP. To explore Word's automation capabilities in greater depth refer to one of the many VBA/Macro programming for Word books available in the market.

Word Automation Object Model

Figure 25-1 shows a high level picture of few basic objects in word object model

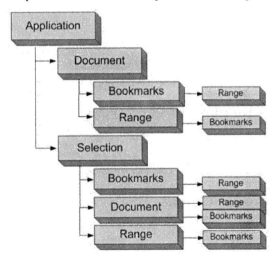

Figure 25-1. Word Automation Object Model: Basic Overview

- ⊙ **Application:** Represents the Microsoft Office Word application

- ⊙ **Documents:** A collection of all the Document objects that are currently open in Word

- ⊙ **Document:** Represents a document. The Document object is a member of the Documents collection

- ⊙ **Range:** Represents a contiguous area in a document. Each Range object is defined by a starting and ending character position

- ⊙ **Selection:** Represents the current selection in a window or pane. A selection represents either a selected (or highlighted) area in the document, or it represents the insertion point if nothing in the document is selected. There can be only one Selection object per document window pane, and only one Selection object in the entire application can be active

Problem 25-1. How to instantiate and terminate a word application?

```
'Create the word application object
Set oWordApp = CreateObject("Word.Application")

'Make the word application visible
oWordApp.Visible = True

MsgBox "Word Application instantiated! Click Ok to terminate word"

'Quit the word application
oWordApp.Quit

'Destroy the object reference
Set oWordApp = Nothing
```

Problem 25-2. How to get reference to an already open word application?

```
'Create the word application object
Set oWordApp = GetObject(,"Word.Application")

'Make the word application visible
oWordApp.Visible = True

'Check the name of currently open word document
MsgBox oWordApp.ActiveDocument.Name
```

Problem 25-3. How to enumerate all the open word documents?

```
'Create the word application object
Set oWordApp = GetObject(,"Word.Application")

'Make the word application visible
oWordApp.Visible = True

Dim oDoc

'Loop through all open documents in word
```

```
For Each oDoc In oWordApp.Documents
   'Print the file name and file path for each document
   MsgBox "Name: " & oDoc.Name & ", Path: " & oDoc.Path
Next
```

Problem 25-4. How to open and save a new document in word?

```
'Create the word application object
Set oWordApp = CreateObject("Word.Application")

'Make the word application visible
oWordApp.Visible = True

'Add a new document
Set oWordDoc = oWordApp.Documents.Add

'Since it is a unsaved document we cannot use Save method
'need to use SaveAs for the first time
oWordDoc.SaveAs "C:\Test.doc"

'Close the word document
oWordDoc.Close

'Quit word application
oWordApp.Quit

'Destroy object references
Set oWordDoc = Nothing
Set oWordApp = Nothing
```

Problem 25-5. How to get reference toan already existing word document?

There are two way of accomplishing this task

Method 1

This method uses GetObject function to get reference to the existing word file

```
'Get the reference to existing word file using GetObject
Set oWordDoc = GetObject("C:\Test.doc")

'Since we have got the refernce to the document directly
'we need to derive the application document from this
'document object to get refernce to the word application object
Set oWordApp = oWordDoc.Application

'Make the word application visible
oWordApp.Visible = True
```

Method 2

This method uses the Open method of the Documents collection to open the word document

```
'Create the word application
Set oWordApp = CreateObject("Word.Application")
```

```
'Make the word application visible
oWordApp.Visible = True

'Open a existing document
Set oWordDoc = oWordApp.Documents.Open ("C:\Test.doc")
```

Problem 25-6. How to open a word document in the read only mode?

```
'Create the word application object
Set oWordApp = CreateObject("Word.Application")

'Make the word application visible
oWordApp.Visible = True

'Function Open(ByVal FileName, [ByVal ConfirmConversions],
'[ByVal ReadOnly], [ByVal AddToRecentFiles], [ByVal PasswordDocument],
'[ByVal PasswordTemplate], [ByVal Revert], [ByVal WritePasswordDocument],
'[ByVal WritePasswordTemplate], [ByVal Format], [ByVal Encoding],
'[ByVal Visible], [ByVal OpenAndRepair], [ByVal DocumentDirection],
'[ByVal NoEncodingDialog], [ByVal XMLTransform]) As Document

'Create a new document
Set oWordDoc = oWordApp.Documents.Open("C:\Test.doc",,True)
```

 NOTE: In further examples we won't be creating the oWordApp and oWordDoc objects and would consider them to be available from one of the previous examples

Problem 25-7. How to print an open word document?

```
'Print the word document
oWordDoc.PrintOut
```

Problem 25-8. How to insert text into a word document from a pre-defined style?

```
'Select the whole word document
oWordDoc.Range.Select

'Get the selection object from the application object
Set oWordSel = oWordApp.Selection

With oWordSel
    'Type some text with style as /Heading 1/
    .Style = "Heading 1"
    .TypeText "This is Heading 1"
    .TypeParagraph

    'Type some text with style as /Heading 2/
    .Style = "Heading 2"
    .TypeText "This is Heading 2"
```

```
    .TypeParagraph
End With
```

Problem 25-9. How to insert an image in a word document and scale its size by 50%?

```
'Select the whole word document
oWordDoc.Range.Select

'Get the selection object from the application object
Set oWordSel = oWordApp.Selection

With oWordSel

    'Function AddPicture(ByVal FileName As String, [ByVal LinkToFile],
    '[ByVal SaveWithDocument], [ByVal Range]) As InlineShape

    'Insert the image and get the object reference to the inserted image
    Set oImg = .InlineShapes.AddPicture ("C:\DesktopImage.bmp", False, True)

    'Scale the image to 50% of the existing size
    oImg.Width = oImg.Width * 0.50
    oImg.Height = oImg.Height * 0.50

    'Center allignment of the paragraph
    Const wdAlignParagraphCenter = 1

    'Allign the image in the center of the page
    oImg.Range.ParagraphFormat.Alignment = wdAlignParagraphCenter

    'Type a small caption below the image
    .TypeParagraph
    .TypeText "This is the desktop capture scaled to 50%"
    .TypeParagraph
End With
```

Problem 25-10. How to find and replace some text in a word document?

```
'Select the whole word document
oWordDoc.Range.Select

'Get the selection object from the application object
Set oWordSel = oWordApp.Selection

With oWordSel
    .TypeText "Author name for this document is: %AUTHOR_NAME%"
    .TypeParagraph

    'Find the %AUTHOR_NAME% document in the word file and replace
    'the same with the actual value

    'Need to take the range from whole document since current selection
```

```
'does not have the typed text
With oWordDoc.Range.Find
        .Text = "%AUTHOR_NAME%"
        '.MatchCase = False
        '.MatchWholeWord = True

        .Replacement.Text = "Tarun Lalwani"

        Const wdReplaceAll = 2
        Const wdReplaceNone = 0
        Const wdReplaceOne = 1

        'Function Execute([FindText], [MatchCase], [MatchWholeWord],
        '[MatchWildcards], [MatchSoundsLike], [MatchAllWordForms],
        '[Forward], [Wrap], [Format], [ReplaceWith], [Replace],
        '[MatchKashida], [MatchDiacritics], [MatchAlefHamza], [MatchControl])
        As Boolean

        'Set the value of Replace as wdReplaceAll, rest all to parameters to
        take'default values
        .Execute ,,,,,,,,,,wdReplaceAll
    End with
End With
```

One can create a template document with all configurable/updatable values to be written between some special characters (%% in the above example). The document can be updated by the QTP test by replacing the parameterized values with the actual values and then the document can saved to a different location using the SaveAs method of the Document object.

 NOTE: It is advisable to either keep such a template document as read only or open the document in a read only format

Problem 25-11. How to insert a table into a word document?

```
'Select the whole word document
oWordDoc.Range.Select

'Get the selection object from the application object
Set oWordSel = oWordApp.Selection

With oWordSel
    'Add a new table and get the object reference to the newly added
    'table. Table size: 5 rows X 3 columns
    Set oNewTable = .Tables.Add(.range,5,3)

    'Set the font and style for the table
    oNewTable.Range.Font.Size = 8
    oNewTable.Range.Style = "Medium Grid 3"
```

```
i = 1

'Add the header rows
oNewTable.Cell(i, 1).Range.Text = "i"
oNewTable.Cell(i, 2).Range.Text = "i * 2"
oNewTable.Cell(i, 3).Range.Text = "i * 3"

'Fill the data for rest of the rows
For i = 2 To 5
        oNewTable.Cell(i, 1).Range.Text = i -1
        oNewTable.Cell(i, 2).Range.Text = (i - 1) * 2
        oNewTable.Cell(i, 3).Range.Text = (i - 1) * 3
Next

'Add one more row to the table
oNewTable.Rows.Add

'Add the details to the last row
i = oNewTable.Rows.Count
oNewTable.Cell(i, 1).Range.Text = i -1
oNewTable.Cell(i, 2).Range.Text = (i - 1) * 2
oNewTable.Cell(i, 3).Range.Text = (i - 1) * 3

End With
```

Problem 25-12. How to change the font for the text being written in a word document?

```
'Select the whole word document
oWordDoc.Range.Select

'Get the selection object from the application object
Set oWordSel = oWordApp.Selection

With oWordSel
    'Change the font to verdana (8)
    .Font.Name = "Verdana"
    .Font.Size = 8

    .TypeText "This is in verdana 8 point size"
    .TypeParagraph

    'Change the font to Arial (10)
    .Font.Name = "Arial"
    .Font.Size = 10

    .TypeText "This is in Arial 10 point size"
    .TypeParagraph
End With
```

Problem 25-13. How to preserve the text already present in a word document while writing?

All the examples that we discussed before this would overwrite any text that is already present in the document. This happens because of the following line in our code

```
'Select the whole word document
oWordDoc.Range.Select
```

So any type operation on the Selection object will delete all the text that existed in the document. To avoid such a situation we can move to the end of the document after selecting the range object. This can be done using following lines of code

```
'Select the whole word document
oWordDoc.Range.Select

'Get the selection object from the application object
Set oWordSel = oWordApp.Selection

With oWordSel
   Const wdStory = 6
   Const wdMove = 0

   'Move to the end of the document
   .EndKey wdStory , wdMove

   .TypeText "This is in text"
   .TypeParagraph
End With
```

Reader's Note

Reader's Note

Chapter 26

Working with Microsoft Internet Explorer

High percentage of people in the world today uses Internet Explorer (IE) as their Web Browser. Because of this high percentage, many Web applications are tested on the popular IE browser. In QTP we usually interact with and control an IE window using the Browser test object. But we can also use the IE COM Interface to work with IE. IE can run as a standalone browser or as an embedded browser within an application. QTP interacts with IE browser using the Browser and the Page Test Object. IE also supports COM based Automation, which allows automating IE without the need of QTP. In this chapter we will explore on how to work with the IE COM APIs, automation of web pages using the HTML DOM and changing configuration of IE through the system registry.

Launching Internet Explorer (IE)

Internet explorer can be launched as an application or by using its COM library. Let's see how both of these techniques can be used.

Method 1

```
'Launch IE as an application using a QTP method
SystemUtil.Run "iexplore.exe"

'Launch IE using the WScript shell
Set oShell = CreateObject("WScript.Shell")
oShell.Run "iexplore.exe"
```

Method 2

```
'Create IE application COM object
```

```
Set oIEApp = CreateObject("InternetExplorer.Application")

'By default the APP is not visible, so make it visible
oIEApp.Visible = True

'Navigate to a web site
oIEApp.Navigate2 "http://www.mywebsite.com"
```

When we launch IE using the 2nd method, we can use the IE Window's handle to reference the browser as a QTP Test object using the following code:

```
'Get the handle of the IE window
iehWnd = oIEApp.HWND

'Close the Browser using QTP test object
Browser("hwnd:=" & iehWnd).Close
```

IE COM Methods and Properties

The IE Application COM interface provides many useful methods and properties. We list just a few of the more common ones in Table 26-1 and Table 26-2

Table 26-1. IE COM Methods

Method Name	Description
Navigate2	Navigates to a specified URL. URL could be any http, https, ftp link or a local/network folder location.
Stop	Aborts the navigation.
Refresh	Refreshes the present URL
Quit	Closes the browser. Closing a browser while it is navigating to some URL is not recommended.
GoBack	Navigates one page back
GoHome	Navigates to home page
GoForward	Navigates one page forward
GoSearch	Opens the search page

Table 26-2. IE COM Properties

Property Name	Type	Description
Left	Long	Left position of the window
Top	Long	Top position of the window
Width	Long	Width of the window
Height	Long	Height of the window
AddressBar	Boolean	Controls whether address bar is shown
FullScreen	Boolean	Maximizes window and turns off statusbar, toolbar, menubar, and titlebar.
LocationName	String	Gets the short (UI-friendly) name of the URL/file currently viewed.

Property Name	Type	Description
LocationURL	String	Gets the full URL/path currently viewed.
Path	String	Returns the path to the application.
Resizable	Boolean	Controls whether the window is resizable
Silent	Boolean	Controls if any dialog boxes can be shown
Type	String	Returns the type of the contained document object.
Visible	Boolean	Determines whether the application is visible or hidden.
Busy	Boolean	Query to see if something is still in progress.
ReadyState	Long	Can have any of the following values· » READYSTATE_UNINITIALIZED: The default initialization state.· » READYSTATE_LOADING: The object is currently loading its properties.· » READYSTATE_LOADED: The object has been initialized.· » READYSTATE_INTERACTIVE: The object is interactive, but not all of its data is available.· » READYSTATE_COMPLETE: The object has received all of its data.

NOTE: Table 26-1 and Table 26-2 don't give a complete list of method and properties provided by the IE COM interface

Page Synchronization

We can use the IE COM object's Busy property to determine if IE is busy loading a page. The following example explains how we can wait for page to load

```
'Create an IE Application
Set IE = CreateObject("InternetExplorer.Application")
IE.Visible = True

'Browse to a website
IE.Navigate2 "http://www.mywebsite.com"

'Sync, wait for the page to load
Do
   DoEvents
Loop while IE.Busy = True

MsgBox "Page Loaded"
```

WARNING: This method might not work properly when the page has frames

Enumerating all IE Windows

We can enumerate all open IE windows using the windows shell application. The shell application provides a collection of all open explorer windows (Microsoft explorer + Internet explorer). The following function enumerates all open windows and returns a dictionary collection containing all IE windows:

```
'Function to enumerate all open IE windows
Function EnumerateIE()
  'This is needed in case an IE window is closed
  'while this function is executing
  On Error Resume Next

  'Create a dictionary for returning the collection of open IE
  'windows
  Set EnumerateIE = CreateObject("Scripting.Dictionary")

  'Get the windows shell application
  Set oWinShell = CreateObject("Shell.Application")
  'Get a collection all open explore windows,
  'Microsoft Explorer + Internet Explorer
  Set allWindows = oWinShell.Windows

  'Loop through each window
  For Each oWindow In allWindows
    'Check if it is internet explorer process then only add it
    If InStr(1, oWindow.FullName, "iexplore.exe",vbTextCompare) Then
      EnumerateIE.Add oWindow.hwnd, oWindow
    End if
  Next
End Function
```

Now we can use the above function to close all open IE windows

```
'Get the list of all IE window
Set allIE = EnumerateIE()

'Lets quit all the IE
For Each oIE In allIE.Items
  oIE.quit
Next
```

The code given above can work in pure VBScript (without QTP). But in QTP we can also close IE windows with a single line of statement:

```
'Close all iexplore.exe processes
SystemUtil.CloseProcessByName("iexplore.exe")
```

Finding an IE window

We can also use the enumeration method given above to search for an IE window based on its Window's handle using the following function.

```
'Function to get an IE COM interface using its Window's handle
Function GetIECOMByhWnd(ByVal iehWnd)
  'Return Nothing in case no IE windows are found
  Set GetIECOMByhWnd = Nothing

  Set allIE = EnumerateIE()

  For Each oIE In allIE.Items
    If oIE.hwnd = iehWnd Then
      'We found the associated IE window. Return its COM interface object
      Set GetIECOMByhWnd = oIE

      Exit Function
    End If
  Next
End Function
```

Similarly we can search for an IE window using its URL:

```
'Function to get a IE COM interface using its URL
Function GetIECOMByURL(ByVal ieURL)
  'Return Nothing in case no windows are found
  Set GetIECOMByURL = Nothing

  Set allIE = EnumerateIE()

  For Each oIE In allIE.Items
    If InStr(oIE.LocationURL, ieURL) Then
      'We found the associated IE window. Return its COM interface object
      Set GetIECOMByURL = oIE

      Exit Function
    End If
  Next
End Function
```

 NOTE: In case multiple browsers have been opened with the same URL, the function given above may return any one of the browser

Launching a new browser

When we launch an IE window through QTP, there is no identification of the window returned to us. In situations where there are already open IE windows we might not be able to determine which window was launched by QTP. We can create a workaround by opening the browser with a random number URL and then searching the COM interface by using the GetIECOMByURL function we just created.

```
'Generate a random string of digits of specified length
Function GetRandomNumberByLen(ByVal Length)
  GetRandomNumberByLen = ""

  'Generate the random number digit by digit
  For i = 1 To Length
    'Seed the radom generator with current timer
    Randomize Timer()

    'Generate and append the random number
    iRnd = CInt((9)*Rnd())
    iRnd = CStr(iRnd)
    GetRandomNumberByLen = GetRandomNumberByLen & iRnd
  Next
End Function


'Function to get a new browser
Function GetNewBrowser()
  Set GetNewBrowser = Nothing

  'This is to store the random browser id generated
  'which can be later used to recognize the browser
  'which was launched
  browserID = GetRandomNumberByLen(10)

  SystemUtil.Run "iexplore.exe", "about:" & browserID

  'Wait for few seconds to make sure the process launches
  Wait 3
  Set GetNewBrowser = GetIECOMByURL(browserID)
End Function

'Get a new browser
Set oBrowser = GetNewBrowser()

'Naviagte to a URL in the opened browser
oBrowser.Navigate2 "http://www.mywebsite.com"
```

In case we want to use the browser using QTP test object only, we can do that using the code given below

```
'Get a new browser
Set oBrowser = GetNewBrowser()

'If using OR then we can update the identification properties
Browser("Main Browser").SetTOProperty "hwnd", oBrowser.hwnd
Browser("Main Browser").Navigate "http://www.mywebsite.com"

'If using DP we can just use the handle to recognize the browser
sBrowser = "hwnd:=" & oBrowser.hwnd
Browser(sBrowser).Navigate "http://www.mywebsite.com"
```

Getting Web page DOM

The IE COM interface exposes the document object and thereby provides access to the entire web page. The following example shows how the DOM elements are accessed by using this technique:

```
'Create an IE application
Set oIE = CreateObject("InternetExplorer.Application")

'Make the application visible
oIE.Visible = True

'Navigate to a web site
oIE.Navigate2 "www.mywebsite.com"
While oIE.Busy: Wend

'Get DOM document object
Set oDOMDoc = oIE.Document

'Get all INPUT tag elements
Set allInput = oDOMDoc.getElementsByTagName("INPUT")

'Loop through all INPUT elements and
'set the value for all text boxes on the page
For Each oInput In allInput
  If oInput.type = "text" Then
    oInput.Value = "Set by IE COM/DOM access"
  End If
Next
```

 NOTE: The code given above does not need QTP and can be run purely in VBScript

More information on DOM can be found in the "HTML DOM" chapter.

Accessing webpage script variables

Consider the below HTML source code

```
<html>
    <SCRIPT language="JScript">var PageName2 = {};
        PageName2["val1"] = "Tarun1";
        PageName2["val2"] = "Tarun2";
    </SCRIPT>
    <body>
        <SCRIPT language="VBScript">
            Const PageName = "Tarun Lalwani"
            Dim arr(1)
            Arr(0) = "Array 1"
            Arr(1) = "Array 2"
            Public Sub Func1(a, b)
                Msgbox a + b
```

```
        End Sub
    </SCRIPT>
  </body>
</html>
```

The web page given above has 2 scripts, one in JScript and one in VBScript. The HTMLWindow object has access to all these variables and methods declared in these scripts. These variables can be accessed from QTP as shown in the following code:

```
'Get the Page test object
Set oPG = Browser("creationtime:=0").Page("micclass:=Page")

'Displays "Tarun Lalwani"
Msgbox oPG.object.parentWindow.PageName

'Displays "Array 1"
Msgbox oPG.object.parentWindow.arr(0)

'Displays "Tarun1"
Msgbox oPG.object.parentWindow.PageName2.Val1

'Displays a message box with value 5 in the browser
Call oPG.object.parentWindow.Func1(2,3)
```

 NOTE: There are differences in accessing the JScript and VBScript array

Using IE to get user input

VBScript provides the InputBox method to obtain input from a user. But it is very limited as we can only get plain text values. There is no option for the user to select values from a list or to enter a password with hidden characters. As a workaround to this problem, we can create an HTML web page which has all the input controls which are needed to obtain the desired user inputs. Consider the next HTML page:

```
'C:\Files.html
<SCRIPT language="vbscript">
    Dim userAction
</SCRIPT>

<P>UserName:
    <INPUT type=text name=username value="Enter user name">

<P>Password:
    <INPUT type=password name=password>

<P>Environment:
    <SELECT type=select name=env>
        <OPTION>Test1</OPTION>
```

```
        <OPTION>Test2</OPTION>
    </SELECT>
<P>

<INPUT type=button value="Submit" onclick="vbscript:userAction='Submitted'">

<INPUT type=button value="Cancel" onclick="vbscript:userAction='Cancelled'">
```

The above HTML page has fields to take username, password and environment from user as shown in the Figure 26-1

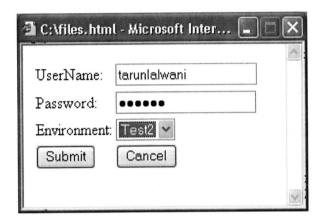

Figure 26-1. User Input using HTML

We can use the webpage given above in QTP to obtain user input as shown in the following code:

```
'Start a new browser
SystemUtil.Run "iexplore.exe", "C:\files.html"

Set oBrw = Browser("micclass:=Browser")
Set oPg = oBrw.Page("micclass:=Page")

oBrw.Sync

'Resize the browser
oBrw.Object.Left = 350
oBrw.Object.Top = 300
oBrw.Object.Height = 200
oBrw.Object.Width = 300

'Disable all other browser features
oBrw.Object.AddressBar = False
oBrw.Object.Resizable = False
oBrw.Object.StatusBar = False
oBrw.Object.ToolBar = False

'Activate the browser window
Window("hwnd:=" & oBrw.GetROProperty("hwnd")).Activate

'Set the user action to blank
```

```
oBrw.object.Document.parentWindow.userAction = ""

'When user click submit or cancel button this userAction
'variable will be populated with a value
While oBrw.object.Document.parentWindow.userAction = ""
  Wait 1
wend

If oBrw.object.Document.parentWindow.userAction = "Cancelled" Then
  'Check if user clicked cancelled
  Msgbox "User clicked cancelled"
Else
  'User clicked Submit. Get the values
  Msgbox oPg.WebEdit("name:=username").GetROProperty("value")
  Msgbox oPg.WebEdit("name:=password").GetROProperty("value")
  Msgbox oPg.WebList("name:=env").GetROProperty("value")
End If
```

IE Popup Dialogs

Depending on the user settings or the website being browsed, IE can generate several different popup dialogs. These dialogs may vary from machine to machine depending on user settings and network authentication parameters. For example, a web application might not ask for the user ID and password, if the user is already logged in using the Windows Domain account. The same application might ask for the required authentication credential when a local system user is logged in. Then there are several Security warning dialogs, Security information dialogs, and the list goes on. There are two ways to handle these types of popup dialogs. One is to write code which checks for various dialogs and then take necessary action to skip them. And the other way would be to change the IE settings manually or programmatically to disable display of these popups.

Disabling IE dialogs

We can disable the display of any IE dialog box using the silent property of the browser, as shown in the code given below

```
'Disable all popup dialogs
Browser("..").Object.Silent = True
```

The problem with the approach given above is that it will take the default action on the dialog. So when IE displays a dialog and the default button is No, then this will take action as if No was clicked. But often we want to click the Yes button. So this solution is seldom the appropriate one.

 WARNING: Using this technique will not allow browsing a website which requires authentication through the IE password dialog.

Changing IE settings using the Registry

The Window's Shell object provides the RegRead, RegWrite and RegDelete methods to access and modify the Window's registry. We can change registry settings using the methods shown in the following code example:

```
'Create a Window's shell object
Set WshShell = WScript.CreateObject("WScript.Shell")

'Write to the registry
WshShell.RegWrite "HKCU\Software\Microsoft\TestThis", "TESTValue", "REG_SZ"

'Read from the Registry
Msgbox WshShell.RegRead("HKCU\Software\Microsoft\TestThis")

'Delete a registry key
Msgbox WshShell.RegDelete("HKCU\Software\Microsoft\TestThis")
```

 WARNING: Accidentally deleting or modifying a key in the registry may crash your computer. These actions should be performed with caution. And before trying out any code the registry should be backed up

Let's discuss various different popup dialogs and how to disable them in the registry.

Popup Blocker

The IE popup blocker blocks popup windows generated by the web page. This sometimes causes problems when we need the popup to be launched. The popup blocker bar is shown in the Figure 26-2.

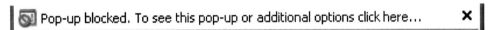
Pop-up blocked. To see this pop-up or additional options click here...   ✕

Figure 26-2. Popup blocker bar

This setting can be switched OFF or ON by using the following code to change the registry:

```
'Path to edit in registry
popupKeyPath = "HKCU\Software\Microsoft\Internet Explorer\New Windows\PopupMgr"

'Disable the IE pop-up blocker
WshShell.RegWrite popupKeyPath, "no", "REG_SZ"

'Enable the IE pop-up blocker
WshShell.RegWrite popupKeyPath, "yes", "REG_SZ"
```

We can also add a website to the "popup allowed" list by using the following code:

```
'Add website to pop-up allowed list
sDomain = "www.mywebsite.com"
popupAllowKey = "HKCU\Software\Microsoft\Internet Explorer\New Windows\Allow\"
WshShell.RegWrite  popupAllowKey & sDomain, 0, "REG_BINARY"
```

Disable Script Error dialog

If script error dialogs are enabled then any script error will be reported using an appropriate popup dialog. A typical script error dialog is shown in the Figure 26-3

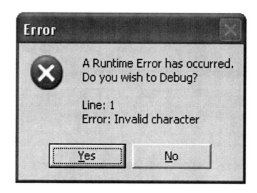

Figure 26-3. Script Error Dialog

These dialogs can be disabled using the following code:

```
'Disable all script debug dialogs
WshShell.RegWrite _
  "HKCU\Software\Microsoft\Internet Explorer\Main\Disable Script Debugger", _
  "yes" , "REG_SZ"

WshShell.RegWrite _
  "HKCU\Software\Microsoft\Internet Explorer\Main\DisableScriptDebuggerIE", _
  "yes" , "REG_SZ"

WshShell.RegWrite _
  "HKCU\Software\Microsoft\Internet Explorer\Main\Error Dlg Displayed On Every Error", _
  "no" , "REG_SZ"
```

Security Alert – Redirection popup

The dialog is shown in theFigure 26-4

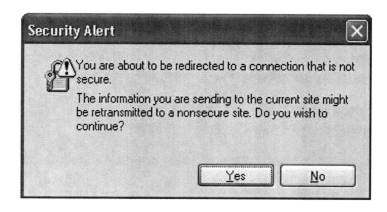

Figure 26-4. Security alert Redirection

The above popup can be disabled using the following code:

```
'Disable Security Alert - Redirection popup
WshShell.RegWrite _
  "HKCU\Software\Microsoft\Windows\CurrentVersion\Internet Settings\WarnOnPostRedirect", _
  "no" , "REG_SZ"
```

Security Alert – Certificate warning

The dialog is shown in the Figure 26-5

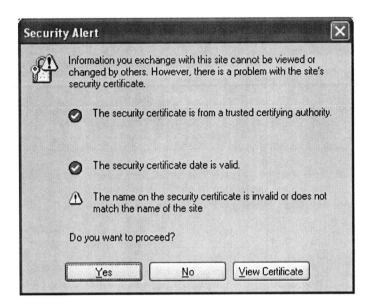

Figure 26-5. Security alert certificate

The above dialog can be disabled using the following code:

```
'Disable the Security Alert - Certificate popup
WshShell.RegWrite _
  "HKCU\Software\Microsoft\Windows\CurrentVersion\Internet Settings\", _
  "no" , "REG_SZ"
```

Security Alert – Secure Connection

This dialog shown in the Figure 26-6

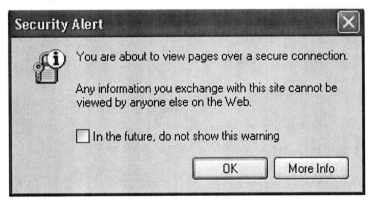

Figure 26-6. Security Alert – Secure connection

The above dialog can be disabled using the following code:

```
'Disable the Security Alert - Secure Connection popup
WshShell.RegWrite _
"HKCU HKCU\Software\Microsoft\Windows\CurrentVersion\Internet Settings\WarnOnPost", _
  "no", "REG_SZ"
```

Security Information – Secure and non-secure item

This dialog is shown in the Figure 26-7

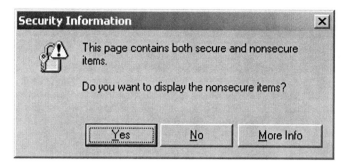

Figure 26-7. Secure Information – secure and non-secure popup

These settings are stored in a zone. There are five different zones in IE settings

- ⊙   My Computer

- ⊙   Local Intranet Zone

- ⊙   Trusted sites Zone

- ⊙   Internet Zone

- ⊙   Restricted Sites Zone

If we are not sure which zone we would be working on then we can disable the settings in all the zones. Each setting has its corresponding code. These codes can be found in Microsoft KB article 182569 (*http://support.microsoft.com/kb/182569*).

We can disable the above popup using the following code:

```
'Various zone codes
'Value    Setting
'------------------------------
'0        My Computer
'1        Local Intranet Zone
'2        Trusted sites Zone
'3        Internet Zone
'4        Restricted Sites Zone

'0 - enabled, 1 - prompt, 3 - disabled
newValue = 0

'Disable the Security information secure non-secure popup in all the Zones
SettingCode = "1609"

'Change the setting for all 5 zones
For i = 0 To 4
  ChangeIEZoneSetting CStr(i), SettingCode, newValue
Next

'Function to change specified setting in a specified zone
Function ChangeIEZoneSetting(ByVal ZoneCode, ByVal SettingCode, ByVal newValue)
```

```
Dim WshShell
Set WshShell = CreateObject("WScript.Shell")

keyPath = "HKCU\Software\Microsoft\Windows\CurrentVersion\Internet Settings\Zones"
WshShell.RegWrite keyPath & "\" & ZoneCode & "\" & SettingCode, newValue, "REG_DWORD"
End Function
```

Active content/Java Script Prompt

The active content/Java script is popup bar instead of a window as shown in the Figure 26-8:

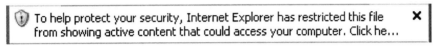

Figure 26-8. Active content bar

```
'Various zone codes
'Value     Setting
'-------------------------------
'0         My Computer
'1         Local Intranet Zone
'2         Trusted sites Zone
'3         Internet Zone
'4         Restricted Sites Zone

'Disable the above popup in all the Zones
'0 - enabled, 1 - prompt, 3 - disabled
newValue = 0

'Disable download information bar in all the Zones
SettingCode = "1400"

'Change the for all 5 zones
For i = 0 To 4
  ChangeIEZoneSetting CStr(i), SettingCode, newValue
Next
```

File download – Information bar

When we try to download a file, IE pops up an information bar as shown in the Figure 26-9

Figure 26-9. File download – Information bar

To disable the above information bar we can use the following code:

```
'Various zone codes
'Value     Setting
'-------------------------------
'0         My Computer
'1         Local Intranet Zone
'2         Trusted sites Zone
'3         Internet Zone
'4         Restricted Sites Zone
```

```
'Disable the above popup in all the Zones
'0 - enabled, 1 - prompt, 3 - disabled
newValue = 0

'Disable download information bar in all the Zones
SettingCode = "2200"

'Change the for all 5 zones
For i = 0 To 4
  ChangeIEZoneSetting CStr(i), SettingCode, newValue
Next
```

Handling popup dialog by using a code

We can also work with these IE popup dialogs by using a code when we know the dialog's title. The best way to handle this situation is to use QTP Descriptive programming (DP). We can interact with any dialog displayed in IE using the following DP code:

```
Public Function CleanBrowserPopups(oBrw)
  'Get the popup dialog
  Set oPopDlg = oBrw.Dialog("ispopupwindow:=True")

  CleanBrowserPopups = False
  If oPopDlg.Exist(0) Then
    'There is a popup dialog
    'Get its title
    sPopTitle = oPopDlg.GetROProperty("title")

    Select Case LCase(sPopTitle)
      Case "security information", "security alert", "security warning"  "error"
        'Either a OK button would be there or a yes button
        'Use a regular expression to cater both in a single statement
        oPopDlg.WinButton("text:=(&Yes|OK)").Click
        CleanBrowserPopups = True
        Reporter.ReportEvent micPass, sPopTitle, "Closed IE dialog popup"
      Case "enter network password"
        'CODE to handle enter network password widows
        'this is application to Windows 2000 OS
      Case Else
        If Left(LCase(sPopTitle),10) = "connect to" Then
          'CODE to handle enter network password windows
          'this is application to Windows XP OS
        Else
          MsgBox "Unknown dialog box - " & sPopTitle
        End If
    End Select
  End If
End Function

'We can register this as user defined user method
RegisterUserFunc "Browser", "CleanBrowserPopups", "CleanBrowserPopups"
```

```
If Browser("creationtime:=0").CleanBrowserPopups = True Then
  MsgBox "Cleaned all dialogs in the browser"
End if
```

It would make it more convenient to integrate the above function with the Browser and Page sync methods. We can do that by using the code given below

```
'New sync methods which will clear browser popups
'as well
Public Function NewSync(oObject)
    If oObject.GetTOProperty("micclass") = "Page" Then
          Set oBrw = oObject.GetTOProperty("parent")
    Else
          Set oBrw = oObject
    End If

    'Sync
    oObject.Sync

    'Clean browser popups
    Call CleanBrowserPopups(oBrw)

    'Re sync
    oObject.Sync
End Function

'Register them as user defined methods
RegisterUserFunc "Browser", "Sync", "NewSync"
RegisterUserFunc "Page", "Sync", "NewSync"
```

File Download – Security Warning popup

While downloading a file there are 3 dialogs which can occur:

- ⊙   File Download - Security Warning (Figure 26-10)

- ⊙   Save As

- ⊙   File download

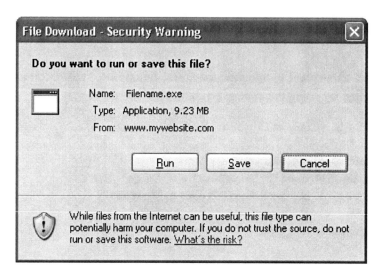

Figure 26-10. File download security warning

We can use the following code to download a file.

```
'Function to download a file from IE
Public Function IEDownloadFile(ByVal oDlg, ByVal sFileName, ByVal
bWaitComplete)
  sPopup = "ispopupwindow::true"
  sBtn = "nativeclass::button"

  'We will use window handle because the title will change later
  'From "File Download" to "Download Complete", but handle will remain
  'the same
  hWnd = oDlg.GetROProperty("hwnd")

With Dialog("hwnd::" & hwnd)
    'Get the value of the close on download complete checkbox
    sCloseAfterDownload=.WinCheckBox(sBtn,"text::&Close.*").GetROProperty("checked")

    'Check if the security wanring dialog is present
    If .Dialog(sPopup).Exist(0) Then
      'Two click events needed sometimes as the first one does not do anything
      .Dialog(sPopup).WinButton("text::&Save",sBtn).Click
      'Make the second click option in case the first one works
      'And to use OptionalStep we need to use the Complete statement
      OptionalStep.Dialog("hwnd::" &
          hwnd).Dialog(sPopup).WinButton("text::&Save",sBtn).Click
    End if

    'Enter the complete file name in the save windo
      hwnd=.Dialog(sPopup).GetROProperty("hwnd")
      .Dialog(sPopup).Activate
      .Dialog(sPopup).WinEdit("nativeclass::Edit","attached text::File &name\:").Set ""
      .Dialog(sPopup).WinEdit("nativeclass::Edit","attached text::File &name\:").Type
sFileName
      .Dialog(sPopup).WinButton(sBtn,"text::&Save").Click
```

```
'Check if the file already exist dialog has appeared
'We get the Save As dialog handle and then check for the
'File allready exist. Going by the normal way we would have used
'Dialog("hwnd:=" & hwnd).Dialog(sPopup).Dialog(sPopup).Exist(0)
'Which is expected to work but it does not. So  to reduce one level
'of hierarchy we take the hWnd and use it
If Dialog("hwnd:=" & hwnd).Dialog(sPopup).Exist(0) Then
  Dialog("hwnd:=" & hwnd).Dialog(sPopup).WinButton(sBtn,"text:=&Yes").Click
End If

If bWaitComplete Then
    'Once download is complete either the window is closed if the checkbox
    'was checked or the Open Folder on the window will change get enabled
    While .Exist(0) and Not .WinButton("text:=Open &Folder").
GetROProperty("enabled")
        Wait 1
    Wend

    'If the checkbox OFF then we need to close the dialog
    If sCloseAfterDownload = "OFF" then .Close
  End if
 End with
End Function
```

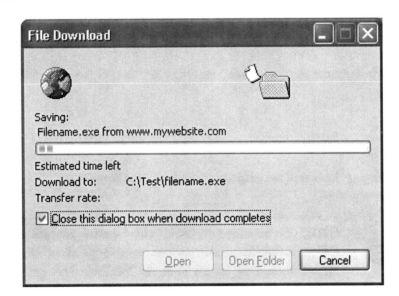

Figure 26-11. File download progress.

Usage:

```
'Get the dialog window
Set oDlg = Dialog("text:=File Download","Index:=0")

'Download the file synchronously
IEDownloadFile oDlg , "C:\Test.exe", True
Msgbox "Download Complete"
```

```
'Download the file asynchronously
IEDownloadFile oDlg , "C:\Test.exe", False
MsgBox "The download has started"
```

Checking for Broken images on a Web Page

QTP does not provided any direct method to check for broken images on a web page but there are certain properties in DOM which can be used for this purpose. A broken image has following property values:

- ⦿ fileSize = -1

- ⦿ readyState = "uninitialized"

```
'Function to Check for broken images on a page
Public Function CheckBrokenImages(oPage)
  pgTitle = oPage.GetROProperty("title")
  Set allImages = oPage.object.Images
  iCount = allImages.Length - 1

  For i = 0 To iCount
    Set curIMG = allImages.item(i)
    sHTML = "HTML = " & curIMG.outerHTML
    If curIMG.fileSize = -1 Then
      'The image did not load
      Reporter.ReportEvent micFail, pgTitle & "Broken Image", sHTML
    Else
      Reporter.ReportEvent micPass, pgTitle & "Valid Image", sHTML
    End if
  Next
End Function

'Usage
CheckBrokenImages Browser("micclass:=Browser","index:=0").
Page("micclass:=Page")
```

 NOTE: We have used the DOM in the example given above because QTP ChildObjects function will not search inside all the WebTable objects. Some of the images inside the WebTable might get ignored while using the ChildObjects method.

Using a Browser Object as a Window Object

A browser Window is treated as a Browser object by QTP because of the Web add-in. If we disable the Web add-in and try to work with a browser, all the actions will be recorded against the browser's Window object. Each Window has its own unique handle which can be used to identify it. We can use the following approach to work with a Browser as a Window object:

```
'Get the Browser object's unique Windows handle property
hwnd = Browser("").GetROProperty("hwnd")
```

```
'Get the browser as a window object
Set oBrowserWindow = Window("hwnd:=" & hwnd)
```

With this "conversion" technique we can then use all of the Window Test Object's methods, many of which are not directly supported by the Browser Test Object:

```
'Window methods being used with the Browser
Public Function BrowserType(oBrw, Text)
   Dim hwnd
   hwnd = oBrw.GetROProperty("hwnd")

   Window("hwnd:=" & hwnd).Type hwnd
End Function

Public Function BrowserMaximize(oBrw)
   Dim hwnd
   hwnd = oBrw.GetROProperty("hwnd")

   Window("hwnd:=" & hwnd).Maximize
End Function

Public Function BrowserMinimize(oBrw)
   Dim hwnd
   hwnd = oBrw.GetROProperty("hwnd")

   Window("hwnd:=" & hwnd).Minimize
End Function

Public Function BrowserDblClick(oBrw, X, Y, MouseButton)
   Dim hwnd
   hwnd = oBrw.GetROProperty("hwnd")

   Window("hwnd:=" & hwnd).DblClick X, Y, MouseButton
End Function

Public Function BrowserResize(oBrw, width, heigh)
   Dim hwnd
   hwnd = oBrw.GetROProperty("hwnd")

   Window("hwnd:=" & hwnd).Resize width, height
End Function

Public Function BrowserRestore(oBrw)
   Dim hwnd
   hwnd = oBrw.GetROProperty("hwnd")

   Window("hwnd:=" & hwnd).Restore
End Function

Public Function BrowserMouseMove(oBrw, X, Y)
   Dim hwnd
   hwnd = oBrw.GetROProperty("hwnd")
```

```
   Window("hwnd:=" & hwnd).MouseMove X, Y
End Function

Public Function BrowserMove(oBrw, X, Y)
   Dim hwnd
   hwnd = oBrw.GetROProperty("hwnd")

   Window("hwnd:=" & hwnd).Move X, Y
End Function

Public Function BrowserhWnd(oBrw)
   hwnd = oBrw.GetROProperty("hwnd")
End Function

RegisterUserFunc "Browser", "Maximize", "BrowserMaximize"
RegisterUserFunc "Browser", "Minimize", "BrowserMinimize"
RegisterUserFunc "Browser", "DblClick", "BrowserDblClick"
RegisterUserFunc "Browser", "Resize" , "BrowserResize"
RegisterUserFunc "Browser", "Restore", "BrowserRestore"
RegisterUserFunc "Browser", "MouseMove", "BrowserMouseMove"
RegisterUserFunc "Browser", "Move" ,"BrowserMove"
RegisterUserFunc "Browser", "hWnd" ,"BrowserhWnd"
```

Custom Browser Applications

Certain Windows applications host browsers inside them. By default QTP doesn't recognize the emebeded browser in applications and identifies the whole browser as WindObject. To identify an embedded browser we need to first register our application as a Browser. QTP provides a utility "Register New Browser Control" to register such applications. The tool is located at *Start Menu→All Prorgrams→QuickTest Professional→Tools→Register New Browser Control.*

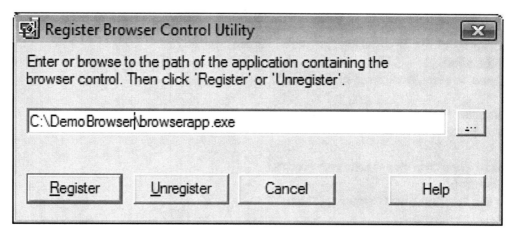

Figure 26-12. Resgiter New Browser Control

Reader's Note

Reader's Note

Chapter 27

Working with HP Quality Center

Quality Center (QC) is a test management tool from HP/Mercury. QC can be used to manage requirements, tests and defects. Many companies prefer storing their scripts within QC and later running them from QC. Scripts stored in QC do not behave exactly the same way scripts stored on Local or shared folders do. For our scripts to be able to run from either QC or Local, some modification in the code is required. These modifications depend on type of actions a script might be taking. The actions may include updating a file, creating a new test result file etc.

In this chapter we explore how to use QC with QTP test scripts.

Quality Center

QC can be used to store different types of tests. These types include Manual, WinRunner, and QuickTest. QC has four different primary tabs:

- ◉ Requirements – This tab is used to store requirements in a structured form
- ◉ Test Plan – This tab is used to store the tests
- ◉ Test Lab – This tab is used for executing tests
- ◉ Defects – This tab is to log defects and bugs found during testing

Connecting QTP with QC

To work with QC we first need to connect QTP to QC. To connect QTP to QC, Open QTP and go to menu Tools→*Quality Center Connection...* as shown in the Figure 27-1

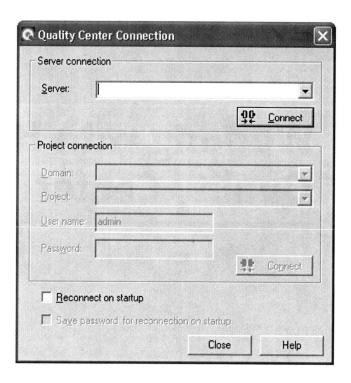

Figure 27-1. Quality Center Connection

Once connected, we can save the scripts in QC as shown in the Figure 27-2

In case there is a need to switch from the QC test plan to the file system then we can click on the *File System…* button as shown in the Figure 27-2

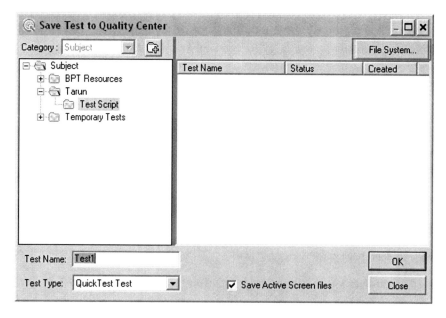

Figure 27-2. QC Save as dialog box

Saving scripts in QC provides a way to have a centralized repository for the scripts.

QC Paths

Once a test case is saved to the repository it will then be presented on the QC test plan tab. The root folder of this tab is named "Subject". So any QC path referenced in QTP will start with "[QualityCenter] Subject". Once the test scripts are moved to the QC repository all the folder paths on QTP's *Tools→Options...→Folder (Tab)* need to be changed to the appropriate QC path for the scripts to work correctly. By default QTP takes the <CurrentTest> location as one of the paths to search for various files. Any associated resources i.e. resource libraries, shared object repositories and data tables stored as an attachment in the Attachment tab of the script inside QC, will be available to the test. These paths are also used to resolve any external reusable action call.

QTP functions which use file path for reading purpose as parameter, can also use QC paths. All of the statements given below are valid in QTP:

```
'Import the data table from Quality Center
DataTable.Import "[QualityCenter] Subject\Input\TestCase1.xls"
DataTable.ImportSheet "[QualityCenter] Subject\Input\TestCase1.xls", "Global", "Global"

'Load the VBS file from Quality Center
ExecuteFile "[QualityCenter] Subject\ScriptConfigurator.vbs"
```

 NOTE: QC path won't work with functions like DataTable.Export, DataTable.ExportSheet etc. as they are writing files to QC and not reading

Relative Paths in QC

We can't directly use relative paths when working with QC for example if we use a path *"[QualityCenter] ..\Common\Common.vbs"* it is considered invalid. QTP tries to find the each required resource in all the folders specified in the tools folders options. Though we cannot specify a relative path in the folders options but we can do it for the resource itself. Which means that we can specify the path of the VBS library for example - *"..\Common\Common.vbs"* while the QC path mentioned in the Folder options would be the absolute path.

Resolving Relative Paths

Relative paths are based on "." (Current folder) and ".."(Parent folder). So a relative path like "C:\All Test\Tests\Test1\..\Common\.\Common.vbs" will finally resolve as "C:\All Test\Tests\Common\Common.vbs" using the following rules:

- Each "\.\" is replaced by a "\" as "." means the current folder only.

- Each "\..\" causes deletion of all text before it until a "\" character is encountered. In our case the "\Test1\..\" path portion is replaced by a single "\" .

We can implement the conversion rules given above by using the following function:

```
'Function to resolve the relative paths to absolute paths
Public Function ResolveRelativePath(ByVal sPath,ByVal sCurPath)
  ResolveRelativePath = sPath
```

```
'Replace [QualityCeneter] from the path
sPath = Trim(Replace(sPath, "[QualityCenter]","",1,-1,vbTextCompare))

'In case the first character is a \ to . the we need to start
'with current path
If Left(sPath,1) ="\" or Left(sPath,1) ="." Then
  sPath = sCurPath & "\" & sPath
End If

'\\ in paths have no meaning so replace them with \'
sPath = Replace(sPath, "\\","\")

Do
  'Replace all "\.\" with "\"
  sPath = Replace(sPath, "\.\","\")

  'Is there are relative parent folder in the path
  iRelPath = InStr(sPath, "\..\")
  If iRelPath <> 0 Then
    'Find the \ before the "\..\"
    iRelPath2 = InStrRev(sPath, "\", iRelPath-1)

    If iRelPath2 = 0 Then
      sPath = Left(sPath, iRelPath-1) & Mid(sPath, iRelPath + 3)
    Else
      sPath = Left(sPath, iRelPath2-1) & Mid(sPath, iRelPath + 3)
    End if
  End If
'Loop untill all relative paths are resolved
Loop while iRelPath <> 0
'Return the resolved path
ResolveRelativePath = sPath
End Function
```

This function can be used as shown in the following code:

```
'Displays "C:\Tests\Common\Common.vbs"
MsgBox ResolveRelativePath("C:\Tests\TestCase1\..\Common\Common.vbs","")

QCRelativePath = "[QualityCenter] Subject\Test Cases\..\Common\Common.vbs"
QCActualPath = "[QualityCenter] " & ResolveRelativePath(QCRelativePath,"")
'Displays "[QualityCenter] Subject\Common\Common.vbs"
MsgBox QCActualPath
```

QCUtil Object

QTP supports the QCUtil utility object which provides the following properties:

⦿ IsConnected – This is a Boolean value and indicates if QTP is connected to QC. This only indicates connectivity status and not whether a QC test case is running or not

⦿ TDConnection – returns a reference to the Quality Center COM object of the QC Open Test Architecture (OTA). Discussing the OTA is out of the scope of this book but we will take a look at few basics of OTA later in this chapter

- CurrentTest – returns a reference to the current QC OTA Test object. This is a reference to the test present in the Test Plan tab

- CurrentTestSetTest – returns a reference to the current QC OTA TSTest object, which represents an execution instance. The CurrentTestSetTest is present on the Test Lab tab

- CurrentTestSet – returns a reference to the current QC OTA TestSet object, which represents a group of tests. The CurrentTestSet is present on the Test Lab tab

- CurrentRun – returns a reference to the current QC OTA test Run object. The test Run contains properties of the Test (inside test sets) in the Test Plan tab

The properties discussed above are valid, depending on how a test is running, as defined in Table 27-1 :

Table 27-1. QCUtil properties existence

	CurrentTest	CurrentTestSetTest	CurrentTestSet	CurrentRun
Test not stored in QC	Error -<Cannot Evaluate>	Error -<Cannot Evaluate>	Error -<Cannot Evaluate>	Error -<Cannot Evaluate>
Test(in QC) running manually with results stored in temporary folder	OTA Object	Nothing	Nothing	Nothing
Test(in QC) running manually/ through QC with results stored in a QC Run	OTA Object	OTA Object	OTA Object	OTA Object

NOTE: In the table given above , if results are getting stored in QC then we cannot determine if the test was run through a QC TestSet or it was run through QTP. In case this information is required we can check if the test is opened in read only mode or not. Read-only mode would mean the test was run through a QC TestSet. To check if the test is opened in read-only mode, we can use 'Setting("isreadonly")'.

WARNING : This is not a foolproof method.

IsConnected can also be determined using the TDConnection property. If TDConnection property is not set then it means QTP is not connected to QC. All these properties can be used as shown in the following code:

```
'Are we connect to QC?
IsQCConnected = Not (QCUtil.TDConnection Is Nothing)

'Is the test stored in QC
IsTestPresentInQC = Not (QCUtil.CurrentTest Is Nothing)

'Is the test running from QC
IsTestRunningFromQC = Not (QCUtil.CurrentRun Is Nothing)
```

QC Open Test Architecture (OTA)

QC OTA provides a very large object model. Figure 27-3 shows a few selected objects from that model.

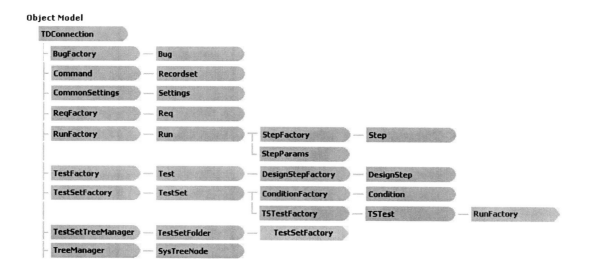

Figure 27-3. OTA Object Model

The TDConnection Object

TDConnection is the top level object in the model. This object is required to connect to the QC server and works with any project. In QTP we obtain a reference to this object using the following statement:

```
'Get the TDConnection OTA object reference
Set TDConnection = QCUtil.TDConnection
```

 NOTE: This has been renamed to QCConnection in QTP 9.x. Though for backward compatibility it would still work in QTP 9.x as QCUtil has a hidden object TDConnection

But if we are not connected to QC then the above statement won't work and returns 'Nothing'. There are two ways to connect to QC through QTP, one of them is to connect through the QTP UI which has already been discusses earlier. The second method is to connect using the QTP Automation Object Model (AOM), which is shown using the following code:

```
'Get the QTP AOM Application object
Set qtpApp = CreateObject("QuickTest.Application")

'Launch the App
qtpApp.Launch
qtpApp.Visible = True

Set oQCConnection = qtpApp.TDConnection
sServerURL = "http://qcserver"
sDOMAIN = "DEFAULT"
sProjectName = "QualityCenter_Demo"
sUser = "username"
sPassword = "password"

'Check if we are already connected to QC
If oQCConnection.IsConnected Then
  'Check if the connection parameters are same with the
  'the project which want to connect to
  If oQCConnection.Server<> sServerURL Or _
     oQCConnection.Project <> sProjectName Or _
     oQCConnection.User <> sUser Then
    'Disconnect from the project. we would like to reconnect
    oQCConnection.DisConnect
  End If
End If

'Connect only if we are not connected to QC
If Not oQCConnection.IsConnected Then
  'Sub Connect(ServerURL As String, DomainName As String,
  'ProjectName As String, UserName As String, Password As String,
  'EncryptedPW As Boolean)
  oQCConnection.Connect sServerURL, sDOMAIN,sProjectName,sUser ,sPassword,
False
End If

'Get the TDConnection OTA Object reference
Set TDConnection = oQCConnection.TDOTA
```

 NOTE: In case we are running the code given above in QTP then we can also replace the last line as Set TDConnection = QCUtil. TDConnection

The code given above first determines if we are already connected to the desired project and if not then it performs the required connection. If we don't want to use a plain text password then we can use the QTP Password Encoder tool located in the QTP programs folder menu. The code lines that would be changed are as follows

```
'Encrypted password
sPassword = "46c8c47fc7c4cdc8b310968680abb263967e14b5f4d0"

'Connect using the encrypted password
oQCConnection.Connect sServerURL, sDOMAIN,sProjectName,sUser ,sPassword, True
```

The method given above uses QTP AOM to get a TDConnection object reference, but it is also possible to create the object using the CreateObject function as follows:

```
'Create the TDConnection object using OTA COM object
Set TDConnection = CreateObject("TDAPIOle80.TDConnection")

'Connection details
sServerURL = "http://qcserver"
sDOMAIN = "DEFAULT"
sProjectName = "QualityCenter_Demo"
sUser = "username"
sPassword = "password"

'Connect to the Sever
TDConnection.InitConnectionEx sServerURL

'Connect to the give project
TDConnection.ConnectProjectEx sDOMAIN, sProjectName, sUser, sPassword

'Check the connection status
MsgBox TDConnection.Connected

'Disconnect from the project
TDConnection.DisconnectProject

'Release the connection to the server
TDConnection.ReleaseConnection
```

 NOTE: With the above code we cannot use an encrypted password

The Command and Recordset Objects

The Command and Recordset objects allow us to get data directly from the QC project's database. Details about the QC database tables are out of scope for this book but we will show how to make a simple query and process the results. The following code shows how to get the Design Steps (i.e. Manual Steps) present in test plan for the current test:

```
'Get the TD OTA object reference
Set TDConnection = QCUTil.TDConnection

'Get the ID of the current test in the Data base
TestID = QCutil.CurrentTest.Field ("TS_TEST_ID")

'Get all the design steps present in the Test and
'read the Step Description and Expected Text
Set TDCommand = TDConnection.Command
TDCommand.CommandText = _
  "Select DS_DESCRIPTION, DS_EXPECTED From DESSTEPS where DS_TEST_ID = " &
TestID

'Execute the query
Set TDRes = TDCommand.Execute

'Loop throuh all the results in the recordset
While Not TDRes.EOR
  Msgbox TDRes.FieldValue("DS_DESCRIPTION")
  Msgbox TDRes.FieldValue("DS_EXPECTED")

  'Move to the next row of the results
  TDRes.Next
Wend
```

We can use the above technique to pass parameters to the script using the design steps in an automated script. Note that in the example given above the description and expected value returned from the database is in HTML format. We can use the following function to convert the HTML to plain text:

```
'Function to convert HTML type text to plain text
Public Function ConvertHTML2PlainText(ByVal HTMLText)
  Dim oHTML
  'Create a HTML document object
  Set oHTML = CreateObject("htmlfile")
  oHTML.Clear
  'Write the HTML on to the document
  oHTML.write HTMLText

  'Get the outerText of the whole document
  ConvertHTML2PlainText = oHTML.documentElement.outerText
  Set oHTML = Nothing
End Function
```

The AttachmentFactory Collection

Attachments present in an object can be accessed through the AttachmentFactory collection. The Object can be one of the following:

- ⊙ Requirements Tab – Any requirement can have attachments

- ⊙ Test Plan Tab – Folder, Test in the folders and Design steps inside the tests can have attachments

- ⊙ Test Lab Tab – Folder, TestSet, Test in the TestSet, TestRun of a Test, TestStep inside a TestRun can have attachments

- ⊙ Defects – A defect can also have attachments

Downloading and uploading attachments to one of these objects is done in a similar manner.

But before we can download an attachment we need to locate a specific attachment in the collection. The following function shows how to find an attachment inside a selected object. The function returns an array of attachment objects which match the specified file name criterion:

```vbscript
'This function allows to find an attachment from a QC Object
'FromPlace is the object from where the attachments need to checked
Public Function FindAttachment(ByVal FromPlace,ByVal FileName)
    Set FindAttachment = Nothing

  'Get Attachments (AttachmentFactory)
   Set oAttachments = FromPlace.Attachments

 'Get a collection of all attachments present
   Set allAttachment = oAttachments.NewList("")

  'Array to retun the files found
  Dim filesFound: ReDim filesFound(0)

  'Object to match regular expresison in file names
  Dim regEx: Set regEx = New RegExp
  regEx.IgnoreCase = True

  'If there is a * present in the file name then treat it as regular expression
  '*.txt will be invalid r.e. in VBScript. So convert to .*.txt
  If InStr(FileName, "*") Then
    'It's regular expression
    regEx.Pattern = Replace(FileName,"*",".*")
  Else
    'Treat it as a complete file name by appending ^ at start and $ at end
    regEx.Pattern = "^" & Replace(FileName,".","\.") & "$"
  End if

  'Enumerate through all the attachments
  For Each oAttachment In allAttachment
   'Does the actual file name match with the search criteria
   'To get the actual file name we use tha paramter with name as 1
   If regEx.Test(oAttachment.Name(1)) Then
```

```
'Add the attachment object to the array
Set filesFound(UBound(filesFound))= oAttachment
ReDim Preserve filesFound(UBound(filesFound)+1)
End if
Next

'We create an extra element in the array for the last attachment. Removed
'the extra element
ReDim Preserve filesFound(UBound(filesFound)-1)

'Retrun the array of attachment objects
FindAttachment = filesFound
End Function
```

The function uses the NewList function to get the collection from an AttachmentsObject and then parses all attachments to get an array matching the file. Use the following function to download specific attachments:

```
'Function to download attachments from a QCObject
'to a specified folder
Public Function DownloadAttachments(ByVal FromPlace, ByVal TOPlace, ByVal
fileName)
    'function returns the # of attachments downloaded
    DownloadAttachments = 0

    'If there is no \ at the end of the folder path then add one
    If Right(TOPlace,1)<>"\" Then
        TOPlace = TOPlace & "\"
    End If

    'Find the attachment using the FindAttachment function
    Dim oFindAttachments
    oFindAttachments = FindAttachment(FromPlace, fileName)

    Set FSO = CreateObject("Scripting.FileSystemObject")
    Dim i

    For i = LBound(oFindAttachments) to UBound(oFindAttachments)
        'Load the attachment to local drive
        oFindAttachments(i).Load True,""

        'Copy the file from temporary downloaded location to the TOPlace folder
        FSO.CopyFile oFindAttachments(i).FileName, _
                    TOPlace & oFindAttachments(i).Name(1),True

        'Increment no. of files downloaded
        DownloadAttachments= DownloadAttachments + 1
    Next
End Function
```

We can use the above function in QTP as:

```
'Download all the VBS file attached to current test
'in the test plan tab
DownloadAttachments QCUtil.CurrentTest, "C:\Download", "*.vbs"

'Download all the VBS file starting with name as override from the
'current test set in which the test is present (test lab tab)
DownloadAttachments QCUtil.CurrentTestSet, "C:\Download", "Override*.vbs"

'Download TestData.xls from the current test (in the test lab tab)
DownloadAttachments QCUtil.CurrentTestSetTest, "C:\Download", "TestData.xls"
```

Simple way of Downloading files from QC

Downloading files from QC in QTP is not very complex. According to the QTP help, the PathFinder. Locate method returns the full file path that QTP uses for the specified relative path (resolves the path) based on the folders specified in the Folders tab search list (*Tools > Options > Folders tab*) of the Options dialog box Consider the paths present in the folders tab :

```
<CurrentTest>
[QualityCenter] Subject\All Test\Common
```

Assume we have a common.vbs file in the QC path's common folder and we execute the following code:

```
'Locate the common.vbs from current folders path
sFilePath = PathFinder.Locate ("common.vbs")
Msgbox sFilePath
```

We would intuitively expect the path to be "[QualityCenter] Subject\All Test\Common\Common. vbs". But after running the code we will find that the MsgBox statement displays something like this:

"C:\DOCUME~1\tarun\LOCALS~1\Temp\TD_80\de8007cd\Attach\QTPro\ALL_LISTS_730_ Common.vbs"

So, what happened in here? PathFinder.Locate does something which is not documented in the QTP help. In case a file is located inside QC then QTP downloads the file to a temporary location and returns that path. But what happens if we have to download a file located in the "[QualityCenter] Subject\All Test" folder or some other folder? If we use the file's complete path it too will be downloaded:

```
'Locate the common.vbs from current folders path
sFilePath = PathFinder.Locate ("[QualityCenter] Subject\All Test\numbers.jpg")
Msgbox sFilePath
```

NOTE: The technique mentioned above can only be used on folders or tests present in the test plan tab.

WARNING: The method described above will not always download the file. This happens when the file with same name is already present in the temporary folder. To fix this situation all the temporary files should be cleared.

Uploading Attachments to QC

The following function can be used to upload attachments to QC using the AttachmentFactory object:

```vbscript
'Function to Add an attachment to a specified object
Public Function AddAttachment(ByVal TOPlace,ByVal FileName,ByVal
overwriteExisting)
  Set AddAttachment = NOthing
  Dim oFindAttachment

  'Get attachments (AttachmentFactory)
   Set oAttachments = TOPlace.Attachments

   sFileName = GetLastNodeFromPath(FileName)

   'Find if any attachment with that name already exists
   oFindAttachment = FindAttachment(TOPlace, sFileName)

   'If the attachment already exists and we are supposed to overwirte the
attachement then
   'remove the attachment first
   If UBound(oFindAttachment) >= 0  and overwriteExisting Then
      oAttachments.RemoveItem oFindAttachment(0)
   End If

   'Now just upload the new one
   Set oNewAttachment = oAttachments.AddItem(Null)
   oNewAttachment.FileName = FileName
   oNewAttachment.Type = 1 'TDATT_FILE
   oNewAttachment.Post

   'Return the new attachment
   Set AddAttachment = oNewAttachment
End Function

'This function returns the last node text from a path
'For Ex - Last node in C:\Test\Test1\Test2.txt is Test2.txt
Public Function GetLastNodeFromPath(Byval Path)
    If Right(Path,1) = "\" Then Path = Left(Path, Len(Path) - 1)

    LastSlashIndex = InStrRev(Path, "\")
    If LastSlashIndex  Then
        GetLastNodeFromPath = Mid(Path, LastSlashIndex + 1)
    Else
        GetLastNodeFromPath = Path
    End If
End Function
```

When files are uploaded to QC and the file name already exists in the attachments then QC appends a number to the file. To avoid this behavior we need to first remove the old attachment and then upload the new one. To achieve this, set the overwriteExisting flag to True when using the AddAttachment function:

```
'Upload an attachment to the current test
AddAttachment QCUtil.CurrentTest, "C:\Test\File.txt", False

'The below will create File1.txt
AddAttachment QCUtil.CurrentTest, "C:\Test\File.txt", False

'This will delete old File.txt and upload the new copy
AddAttachment QCUtil.CurrentTest, "C:\Test\File.txt", True
```

Getting the Current Test Location

To get the current test's location we use the CurrentTest Object to locate for the test's parent folder path:

```
'Function to get the current test path is running from
Public Function GetCurrentTestPath()
  GetCurrentTestPath = ""

  'The test in not in QC
  If QCUtil.CurrentTest is Nothing Then Exit Function

  'Get the test name
  testName = CurrentTest.Name

  'Get the ID of the parent folder
  parentFolderID = CurrentTest.Field("TS_SUBJECT").NodeID

  'Get the complete path of parent folder
  parentFolderPath = QCUtil.TDConnection.TreeManager.NodePath(parentFolderID)

  GetCurrentTestPath = parentFolderPath & "\" & testName
End Function
```

Enumerating All Tests present in a TestLab folder

The QC OTA object model's TreeManager object manages the complete folder structure of the test plan tab. Each folder can contain sub folders and/or tests. Tests inside a folder are managed by a TestFactory object:

Figure 27-4. Test Plan related objects

We can enumerate the entire test inside a folder and its sub folders using the following function:

```
'Below function can enumerate through all tests present in a
'folder path specified. To enumerate through root node use "" or "subject"
'else use folder paths like "Subject\All Test"
Public Function EnumerateAllTestsinTestPlan(ByVal folderPathOrObject)
  If IsObject(folderPathOrObject) Then
    'We already have a reference to the folder object
    Set oTestPlanFolder = folderPathOrObject
  ElseIf folderPathOrObject = "" or lcase(folderPathOrObject) = "subject" Then
    'Get the root subject folder
    Set oTestPlanFolder = QCutil.TDConnection.TreeManager.NodeByPath("Subject")
  Else
    'Get the folder using the string path
    Set oTestPlanFolder = QCUTil.TDConnection.TreeManager.NodeByPath(folderPath
OrObject)
  End If

  'Get the TestFactory object for the current folder
  'And then use NewList on that object to get the collection
  'of tests present in the folder
  Set oTestFactory = oTestPlanFolder.TestFactory.NewList("")

  'Loop through all the test present in the current folder.
  For each oTest in oTestFactory
      MsgBox oTestPlanFolder.Path & "\" & oTest.Name
  Next

  'Recursively call this function for each sub folder
  'present in current folder
  Set allSubFolders = oTestPlanFolder.NewList()
  For each oFolder in allSubFolders
    'We can safely pass the oFolder object back to the function
    'as it checks that the folderPath is a string or a object
    'In case we were not checking that we would have to call
    'it using the oFolder.Path parameter
    EnumerateAllTestsinTestPlan oFolder
  Next
End Function
```

 NOTE: We can use any of the oTestPlanFolder or the oTest object with the DownloadAttachments function we created earlier in this chapter.

Enumerating all the Tests in a Test Lab Tab

The Test Lab folder structure is managed by a TestSetTreeManager object. These folders can further contain sub folders and/or TestSet objects. TestSet objects are managed by a TestSetFactory objects. Each TestSet object contains one or more test managed by a TSTestFactory object. This object model is shown in the Figure 27-5

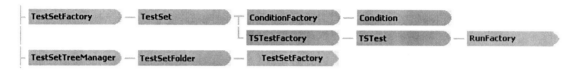

Figure 27-5. Test Lab relates objects

Now we will create two recursive functions to enumerate all the Tests located in the Test Lab tab, one function to enumerate all the test sets in a folder and another to enumerate all the tests present inside a test set:

```
'Function to enumerate all test sets in a folder and sub folders
Function EnumerateAllTestSets(ByVal FolderPath)
  'Check if the folder object has been passed or a string path
  If isObject(FolderPath) Then
    Set oTestSetFolder = FolderPath
  ElseIf FolderPath = "" or LCase(FolderPath) = "root" then
    'Root folder needs special handling
    Set oTestSetFolder = QCUtil.QCConnection.TestSetTreeManager.Root
  Else
    'Get the object from the path
    Set oTestSetFolder = QCUtil.QCConnection.TestSetTreeManager.
NodeByPath(FolderPath)
  End If

  'A root folder cannot have any test set. So we need not check
  'for any testsets in case of the Root Folder.
  If oTestSetFolder.name <> "Root" Then
    Print oTestSetFolder.Path

    'Loop through all the test sets present in the folder
    Set allTestSets = oTestSetFolder.TestSetFactory.NewList("")
    For each oTestSet in allTEstSets
      Print "Test Set - " & oTestSetFolder.Path & "\" & oTestSet.Name

      'Call another function to enumerate all the test inside
      'the current test set
      EnuemrateTestInTestSet oTestSet
    Next
  End If

  'Recuersively enumerate all test sets in sub folders
  Set allSubFolders = oTestSetFolder.SubNodes

  For each oSubTestSetFolder in allSubFolders
```

```
      'Enumerate all test sets in the current folder
      EnumerateAllTestSets oSubTestSetFolder
   Next
End Function


'This function can be used to enumerate all the test present
'inside a test. Function takes the OTA Object reference to the
'TestSet which needs to be enumerated
Public Function EnuemrateTestInTestSet(ByVal oTestSet)
   'Get all the tests in the test set
   Set allTests = oTestSet.TSTestFactory.NewList("")

   'Loop through all the tests present in the test set
   For each oTest in allTests
      Print "Test - " & oTest.name
   Next
End Function


'Usage
'Enumerate all test sets and tests inside them for test lab tab
EnumerateAllTestSets ""

'Enumerate all Test sets in the current test's test set
EnuemrateTestInTestSet QCUtil.CurrentTestSet
```

Getting the Current Test Set Location

We can use the CurrentTestSet object in QTP to get the location of the test set in the Test Lab tab. The root folder of this tab is named as "root" while the root folder in test plan is called "Subject". To get the test set location we can use the following function:

```
'Function to get the current test set path
Public Function GetCurrentTestSetPath()
    GetCurrentTestSetPath = ""
    'If current test set is nothing then exit
    If QCUtil.CurrentTestSet is Nothing Then Exit Function

    'Name of the test set
    testSetName = CurrentTestSet.Name

    'Path for the folder where the Test Set exists
    testSetFolder = CurrentTestSet.TestSetFolder.Path

    'Combine the two...
    GetCurrentTestSetPath = testSetFolder & "\" & testSetName
End Function
```

Reader's Note

Chapter 28

Advanced QTP

In this chapter We will discuss different advanced problems and their solution in QTP. Since this chapter uses concepts from various chapters discussed earlier, i have kept it near the end. We also look at the enumeration of the Settings object at run-time; this technique is results of lot of research to find features of QTP which have never been documented anywhere.

Synchronizing Script Execution between different machines

Some complex system testing scenarios require QTP to coordinate its code execution activities with other scripts and application which are executing independent of QTP. In this situation we need the various applications and QTP to work together through a synchronization semaphore described in this section.

To create this solution we need to get progress information from a running QTP script. The QTP Automation object model (AOM) exposes the Environment object, which we can use at run-time to implement a needed synchronization point (a semaphore) to coordinate and control the script's execution. The following code show's how to get the environment of a local or a remote PC using AOM:

```
'Get an object reference to the running QTP
Set qtpLocalPC = CreateObject("QuickTest.Application")
sRemoteIP = "10.1.1.1"
Set qtpRemotePC = CreateObject("QuickTest.Application", sRemoteIP)
'Then get its Environment object
Set qtpLocalEnv = qtpLocalPC.Test.Environment
Set qtpRemoteEnv = qtpRemotePC.Test.Environment

'Lastly, access the environment variables
MsgBox qtpLocalEnv("TestDir")
MsgBox qtpRemoteEnv("TestDir")
```

Now when we want to wait for QTP to reach a certain point in the script we have the script update an Environment variable after reaching that point. Consider the following QTP scripts:

QTP Script 1

```
'Script 1
'Create a SyncPoint environment variable here
Environment.Value("SyncPoint1") = False

Msgbox "Job 1 Completed"
'Do some operations
'<-- Another job waiting for execution to reach this point
Environment.Value("SyncPoint1") = True

Msgbox "Starting Job 2"
```

VBScript 2

This VBScript waits for QTP Script 1 to reach its SyncPoint1 state to start its execution:

```
'Local machine IP
strCompIP = "127.0.0.1"

Set qtpApp = CreateObject("QuickTest.Application", strCompIP)

'Wait till the script has not started
While Not qtpApp.Test.IsRunning
Wend

'Now wait for the SyncPoint environment variable to be true
While qtpApp.Test.Environment("SyncPoint1") <> True
Wend

MsgBox "Script 1 has passed the sync point."
```

Run Script 1 in QTP and Script 2 in the Windows Script Host (WSH) environment. We will see that the Script 2 waits until we dismiss the "Job 1 Completed" message box in the QTP script, thereafter Script 2 presents the "Script 1 has passed the sync point" message box..

Enumerating the Setting Variables

We have already seen in the "Utility Objects" chapters that there are several documented Setting variables:

- ◉ Setting("AutomaticLinkRun")

- ◉ Setting("DefaultLoadTime")

- ◉ Setting("DefaultTimeout")

- ◉ Setting.WebPackage("ReplayType")

- ◉ Setting("SnapshotReportMode")

- ◉ Setting("WebTimeout")

Now we can enumerate the settings at run-time or we can use the registry to determine what settings are available. We will notice how easier the job becomes after knowing these settings and things that were not looking possible earlier are possible now. Let's take a look at both the methods

Method 1 – Looking for settings in Registry

First launch *REGEDIT.exe* from the Windows Run dialog. There are two main keys where the settings variable exists

```
HKEY_LOCAL_MACHINE\SOFTWARE\Mercury Interactive\QuickTest Professional\MicTest\
SettingInfo
```

and

```
HKEY_LOCAL_MACHINE\SOFTWARE\Mercury Interactive\QuickTest Professional\MicTest\
Packages
```

Let's see how to access these settings. Browse to the key as shown in the Figure 28-1

```
HKEY_LOCAL_MACHINE\SOFTWARE\Mercury Interactive\QuickTest Professional\MicTest\
SettingInfo\TSRManager
```

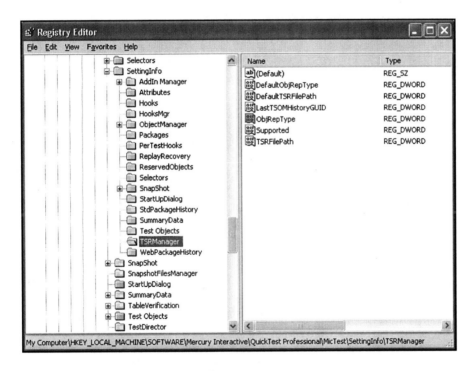

Figure 28-1. Registry Editor – QTP settings

Now if we want to access the ObjRepType data inside the TSRManager key, we need to use the following code

```
Msgbox Setting("TSRManager")("ObjRepType")
```

By changing the object repository type in the script and running the code mentioned above we will notice

0 = Per-Action repository

1 = Shared object repository

The format is using the all the child keys after SettingInfo and the last value name

```
'Access the setting value
Setting("Child Key1")("Child Key2")("...")("Child KeyN")("ValueName")
```

We believe QTP gets complete registry for the two specified keys (including sub keys). We can access any of the keys that we want by using the format specified earlier

WARNING: Changing some of these settings at run-time might cause unexpected behavior. These should always be used for ready only purposes.

Method 2 – Enumerating Setting Objects and Variables

The Setting object is actually the "Mercury.ScriptSetting" COM library. This library provides two undocumented arrays for enumeration. The arrays are named Keys (which contains all the keys) and items (returns all the object/value stored for a given index/key).

A Setting value can be an object or a plain variable, so it's important to use the TypeName function to make this determination.

The Setting.Keys property returns a 2 dimensional variant array with first dimension as 0. In the Figure 28-2 we enumerate all the keys and place them into the Global DataTable in the Key, Value and Type columns:

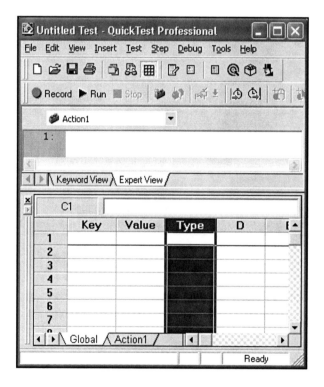

Figure 28-2. Data Table for Enumerate Setting

```
'ObjSetting is of Type
Public Function EnumerateSettings(objSetting)
  'Get arrays of key
  vKeys = objSetting.Keys

  'Get the 2nd dimenstion of the Keys array
  i_Count = UBound(vKeys,2)

On error resume next

  'Loop through all the keys and get the details
  For i = 0 to i_Count
    DataTable("Key",dtGlobalSheet) = vKeys(0,i)
    DataTable("Value",dtGlobalSheet) = objSetting.Item(vKeys(0,i))
    DataTable("Type",dtGlobalSheet) = TypeName(objSetting.Item(vKeys(0,i)))
    DataTable.GlobalSheet.SetCurrentRow i+2
  Next
End Function
```

To enumerate current setting we can call the function as given below

```
'Enumerate all settings under settings object
Call EnumerateSettings (Setting)
```

Run the code given above and the output will appear in the run-time data table. Export the sheet and open it. The sample enumerated sheet is shown in the Figure 28-3

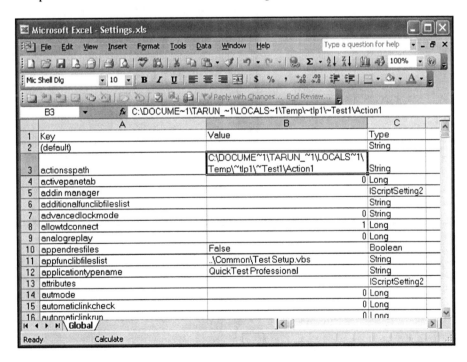

Figure 28-3. Enumerated Settings

If we notice the type of various keys we will notice that many of them have "IScriptSetting2" which is nothing but the Interface for "Mercury.ScriptSetting". This means we can also enumerate that object using the same method we used for the Setting object. Here is an example of how that is done:

```
'Enumerate all settings under attributes setting
Call EnumerateSettings (Setting("attributes"))
```

Table 28-1 shows some of the settings and the description for them

Table 28-1. Settings

Setting	Description/Value
Setting("FirstGlobalIteration")	Starting iteration row number of the global data table from the run settings
Setting("LastGlobalIteration")	Ending iteration row number of the global data table from the run settings
Setting("GlobalIterationMode")	The iteration mode in the run settings 1 = Run on all rows 2 = Run on single row/Run on specified rows
Setting("DisableReplayUsingAlgorithm")	Disable Smart Identification at run-time 0 = Smart Identification enabled 1 = Smart Identification disabled
Setting("OnReplayError")	Set what action needs to be taken in case an error occurs while replaying the script Following are the possible values: Dialog = pop up message box NextIteration = proceed to the next iteration Stop = stop run Skip = proceed to the next step
Setting("UseExternalDataTablePath")	Whether an external data table is being used or not. 0 = No external data table 1= External data table
Setting("ExternalDataTablePath")	Path of the external data table in case UseExternalDataTablePath is 1
Setting("SnapshotOnErrorActiveUI")	Save image to desktop when error occurs (if test run by mercury business process monitor) 0 = disabled 1 = enabled
Setting("TSRManager")("ObjRepType")	Type of object repository being used in the test 0 = Per-Action repository 1 = Shared object repository

Setting	Description/Value
Setting("TSRManager")("ObjRepType")	Type of object repository being used in the test 0 = Per-Action repository 1 = Shared object repository
Setting("TSRManager")("TSRFilePath")	File path of the shared object repository in case objRepType is 1. The value might be present even in case objRepType is 0 but it's not used in such a case
Setting("TSRManager")("DefaultObjRepType")	Default Type of object repository being used for all new test 0 = Per-Action repository 1 = Shared object repository
Setting("TSRManager")("DefaultTSRFilePath")	Default File path of the shared object repository in case objRepType is 1. The value might be present even in case objRepType is 0 but it's not used in such a case
Setting("ReplayRecovery")("Enabled")	Recovery scenarios 0 = Disabled 1 = Enabled
Setting("isreadonly")	Test scripts opened in the read only mode True – Read-only False – Read/write
Setting("actionsspath")	Current action's path on the local machine
Setting("launchreport")	View test results after run is completed 0 – Do not show any results 1 – Show the results We can use it to disable the display of test results after the run is completed but that cannot be re-enabled until QTP is closed and launched again

Setting Persistence

The Setting variables added at run-time in script are not destroyed when the test run completes. They are only destroyed when QTP is closed or a new script is opened.

 NOTE: Setting Persistence however is not mentioned in any of the QTP documentations.

The following code demonstrates this persistence:

```
'Check if setting exists or not
If Setting.Exists ("Session") Then
  Msgbox "The session exists"
Else
  Setting.Add "Session", "Session1"
  Msgbox "Session created"
End If
```

The first run displays the message "Session created" while all subsequent runs of the same QTP run display the "The session exists" message. This demonstrates that the settings are persisted in memory.

NOTE: Setting persistence only remains for a script session. Settings object is re-instantiated on closing of QTP or opening up of new script within the same QTP session.

Setting persistence allows us to create a session based test. Now we exploit this capability to implement code which can restart QTP programmatically.

Stop and Re-Run QTP using Code

Here are few situations where restarting QTP might be required:

- When a recovery scenario is added at run-time it doesn't get applied to the test until the test case is stopped and re-run

- When we are running multiple sessions for Terminal Emulator (TE). QTP does not allow running multiple TE sessions within a single script run. To run on multiple sessions the script needs to be stopped at the end of each session code and should be re-run from the point where the next session begins

The technique would be to call the restart QTP routine but only to run it for the first time. Now when we stop QTP we can't execute any code to re-run it. So we will run an asynchronous script which will check if QTP is not in running mode and then run it and the script will end.

```
'Function stop and restart QTP
Sub StopAndReRunQTP(restartFlag)
  'Only restart if the flag has not been used
  If Setting.Exists(restartFlag) = False then
    'Flag does not exist add. Settings added at
    'run-time are kept for whole session of QTP
    Setting.Add restartFlag,True
    'Call the routine for launching jon to
    're-run QTP after we have stopped QTP
    Call AsyncReRunQTP

    'Disable reporting failure
    Reporter.Filter = rfDisableAll

    'Change the setting to stop on any error
    Setting("OnReplayError") = "Stop"
```

```
        'Stopping Test by causing an intentional error
        Err.Raise vbObjectError + 1,"Stop", "Causing Error for Stopping QTP"
    End if
End Sub

Sub AsyncReRunQTP()
    'Create the re-run script at run-time
    Call CreateQTPRunScript()

    'Run the script asynchronously
    Set wShell = CreateObject("WScript.Shell")
    wShell.Run "ReRunQTP.vbs"
End Sub

Public Function CreateQTPRunScript()
    'Create script to wait for QTP to stop and then re run it
    Set fso = CreateObject("Scripting.FileSystemObject")
    set file = fso.OpenTextFile("ReRunQTP.vbs", 2, True)
    file.WriteLine "Set qtpApp = CreateObject(""QuickTest.Application"")"
    file.WriteLine "While qtpApp.Test.IsRunning"
    file.WriteLine "Wend"
    file.WriteLine "qtpApp.Test.Run ,False"
    file.close
    set file = nothing
    set fso = nothing
End Function
```

The StopAndReRunQTP function checks if the flag exists in the setting and stops QTP only if the flag does not exist in the setting. This is where Setting Persistence plays a key role. Without it, it would not be possible to skip the restart code.

The AsyncReRunQTP function creates and executes a VBScript. The created script can now re-launch QTP at run-time. Here is the code for the re-run

```
'Create the QTP Application object
Set qtpApp = CreateObject("QuickTest.Application")

'Wait whle the test is running
While qtpApp.Test.IsRunning
Wend

'Run the test
qtpApp.Test.Run ,False
```

Adding Recovery Scenarios at Run-time

Recovery scenarios can be added at run-time using QTP Automation Object Model (AOM), but we need to use the stop and re-run function as described above:

```
'Check if the setting exists or not
If Not Setting.Exists("AddingRecoveryScenario") then
    Dim qtpApp
    'Add the recovery scenario
    Set qtpApp = CreateObject("QuickTest.Application")
```

```
qtpApp.Test.Settings.Recovery.RemoveAll
qtpApp.Test.Settings.Recovery.SetActivationMode "OnEveryStep"
sRecoveryFileName = "C:\Program Files\Mercury Interactive\" _
                   & "QuickTest Professional\recovery\WebRecovery.qrs"
qtpApp.Test.Settings.Recovery.Add sRecoveryFileName, "Security Warning", 1
qtpApp.Test.Settings.Recovery.Item(1).Enabled = "True"
StopAndReRunQTP "AddingRecoveryScenario"
End If
```

Executing code when Script ends

QTP uses VBScript, which is not an event driven language, so we don't have script start or script end events. But executing some codes at the start of a script is easy which is done by adding that code in a VBS file and then associating it with the test resources.

Now we give an example of executing the code at the end of a script to export a data table; this is commonly done at the end of the last Action in a script. But the problem is that when we are using global iteration that code will get called again and again. On every iteration the sheet will get exported, which is something not desirable. The typical workaround is to execute the code at the last iteration only.

```
'Check if the current iteration is equal to the last one
If Environment.Value("TestIteration") = Setting("LastGlobalIteration") Then
  DataTable.Export "C:\Test.xls"
End if
```

The above code works fine in most situations but it fails when we have imported the global sheet as the 'Setting("LastGlobalIteration")' is not updated at run-time.

So next we describe a solution to this problem using code that will only be executed when the script terminates. We know that a VBScript class has a built-in Initialize and Finalize subroutines, which are executed when the class is created and destroyed respectively, as in:

```
'place this code into the C:\LoadUnload.vbs file
Class LoadUnload
  Sub Class_Initialize()
    MsgBox "Initialized"
  End Sub

  Sub Class_Terminate()
    MsgBox "Terminated"
  End Sub
End Class

Dim oLoadUnload
Set oLoadUnload = New LoadUnload
```

If we run the code given above using the Windows Script Host (WSH) host we will be presented with both the "Initialized" and "Terminate" message boxes. We didn't destroy the oLoadUnload object but still it was destroyed automatically by the WSH Host.

Now we add this VBScript file to a QTP script on its Test Settings Resource tab and run the script for 3 or 4 iterations. We will observe that only the "Initialized" message box is presented. QTP (version 8.x) didn't implicitly destroy the oLoadUnload object after the test script was terminated. The finalized event does not fire which makes it even more important for it to be able to execute a finalization code in QTP.

NOTE: This issue is present in QTP 8.x but has been resolved in QTP 9.x, so no special additional coding is needed while using version 9.x.

The following code provides a solution that works with both QTP 8.x and 9.x, because the built-in QTP Environment object is always destroyed when a script terminates. So we change the code given above to store the oLoadUnload object reference in a new QTP Environment variable:

```
'Create a load unload class
Dim oLoadUnload
Environment.Value("oLoadUnload") = New LoadUnload
```

Now if we run the QTP script we will be presented with both the "Initialized" and the "Terminate" messages.

NOTE: If we need to access any of the methods or properties of the class we can use
Environment.Value("oLoadUnload").MethodName
Environment.Value("oLoadUnload").Property = Value

WARNING: If we assign the object from the Environment variable to another variable then this technique won't work in QTP 8.x as the there will be multiple references to the object and only the reference stored in the Environment object will be destroyed when the script ends.

For the optimal utilization of the above concept, the LoadUnload class should only be used to Load and Unload other objects. Consider the following code:

```
'Variable declaration
Dim FSO
Dim xlApp
Dim oMyClass

Class MyClass
  '....
End Class

Class LoadUnload
  Sub Class_Initialize()
    Set FSO = CreateObject("Scripting.FileSystemObject")
    Set xlApp = CreateObject("Excel.Application")

    Set oMyClass = New MyClass
  End Sub
```

```
Sub Class_Terminate()
  On Error Resume Next
  'Clean up all the objects
  Set FSO = Nothing

  'Close all open sheet and quit excel
  For Each workBook In xlApp.Workbooks
    'Close the work book and dont save changes
    workBook.Close False
  Next

  'Quit the Excel application
  xlApp.Quit

  Set xlApp = Nothing

  Set oMyClass = Nothing
  End Sub
End Class

Dim oLoadUnload
Environment.Value("oLoadUnload") = New LoadUnload
```

 NOTE: The best thing about the approach mentioned above is that even if we click the stop button and the test is aborted, the class termination sub routine will be called.

Making an Object visible on a Web Page

A Browser snapshot taken normally through QTP will only include that area of the web page which is visible on the screen. This may not include our object of interest which is on the web page. QTP provides an undocumented MakeObjVisible method for each TestObject which can be used to ensure that the object is visible in the displayed portion of the screen:

```
'Bring object to focus and capture ths screenshot
Browser("..").Page("..").WebEdit("UserName").MakeObjVisible
Browser("..").CaptureBitmap "C:\Snap1.bmp", True

'Bring object to focus and capture the screenshot
Browser("..").Page("..").WebEdit("Submit").MakeObjVisible
Browser("..").CaptureBitmap "C:\Snap2.bmp", True
```

Advanced Text Checkpoints

To create text checkpoints on the fly, we implement a custom checkpoint using classes. Consider the following information we need about a Text checkpoint:

- ⊙ Name – Name of the checkpoint

- ⊙ Parameter – The parameter we want to verify

- ⊙ ExpectedValue – Expected value of the parameter

- ⊙ ComparisonType – This can determine the type of comparison, for example few of the possible values can be CONTAINS, EQUALS, CONTAINS, REGULAREXPRESSION

Since a page can have multiple checkpoints we will allow multiple checkpoints with same name.

Table 28-2. Sample Checkpoints

Name	Parameter	ExpectedValue	ComparisonType	TreatFailAs	TreatWarningAs
oPgLogin	url	Login.do	Contains	Warning	
oPgLogin	innerText	Welcome to the Login System	Contains		
oPgLogin	innerText	Click Here to Login!	Contains		

We use the following class to implement a single row of checkpoint as shown in Table 28-2

```
'Class to store checkpoint information
Class TextValidation
  Public Name
  Public Parameter
  Public Value
  Public ComparisonType
  Public TreatFailAs
  Public TreatWarningAs
End Class
```

The TreatFailAs and TreatWarningAs flag allows us to disable checkpoints. Setting these flags to Pass will force a checkpoint to pass even when the checkpoint fails. Now we can create a TextValidations class which has a dictionary of all TextValidation type objects. This class is used to store checkpoints with the same name.

```
'Class to support text validation checkpoints
Class TextValidations
  'Dictionary to store all the text validation information
  Public oValidations

  Sub Class_Initialize()
    'Create the Dictionary
    Set oValidations = CreateObject("Scripting.Dictionary")
  Ens Sub

  'Add functions allows to add a checkpoint
  'either using a TextValidation class object
  'or and Array containing all the information
  Public Sub Add(pValidation)
```

```
        'this will eventually call the AddByParam
        'method as it contain all validation
        'for adding an checkpoint
        If TypeName(pValidation) = "TextValidation" Then
          Set pValidation = New TextValidation
          AddByParam pValidation.Name, _
                pValidation.Parameter, _
                pValidation.ExpectedValue, _
                pValidation.ComparisonType, _
                pValidation.TreatFailAs, _
                pValidation.TreatWarningAs
      Else
        AddByParam pValidation(LBound(pValidation)), _
            pValidation(LBound(pValidation) + 1), _
            pValidation(LBound(pValidation) + 2), _
            pValidation(LBound(pValidation) + 3), _
            pValidation(LBound(pValidation) + 4), _
            pValidation(LBound(pValidation) + 5)
      End If
    End Sub

    'Add checkpoint by parameter
    Public Sub AddByParam(pName, pParameter, pValue, pComparisonType,
    pTreatFailAs, pTreatWarningAs)
      Dim pVal
      Set pVal = New TextValidation
      pVal.Name = pName
      pVal.Parameter = Trim(pParameter)
      pVal.Value = pValue
      pVal.ComparisonType = UCase(Trim(pComparison))

      'Make sure the comparison type is valid
      'else assum CONTAINS comparisontype
      Select Case pVal.ComparisonType
        Case "EQUALS","CONTAINS", "NOTCONTAINS"
        Case Else
          pVal.Comparison = "CONTAINS"
      End Select

      pVal.TreatFailAs = UCase(Trim(pTreatFailAs))

      'Make sure the flag is from a valid
      'set of values else assume Fail to be
      'treated as Failed
      Select Case pVal.TreatFailAs
        Case "MICPASS","PASS","PASSED"
          pVal.TreatFailAs = micPass
        Case "MICWARNING","WARNING"
          pVal.TreatFailAs = micWarning
        Case "DONE", "NOT", "NOTHING", "DONOTHING","DISABLED"
          pVal.TreatFailAs = micDone
```

```
      Case Else
         pVal.TreatFailAs = micFail
      End Select


   pVal.TreatWarningAs =  UCase(Trim(pTreatWarningAs))


   'Make sure the flag is from a valid
   'set of values else assume Warning to be
   'treated as Warning
   Select Case pVal.TreatWarningAs
     Case "MICPASS","PASS","PASSED"
        pVal.TreatWarningAs = micPass
     Case "FAIL","FAILED", "FAILS"
        pVal.TreatWarningAs = micFail
     Case "DONE", "NOT", "NOTHING", "DONOTHING","DISABLED"
        pVal.TreatFailAs = micDone
     Case Else
        pVal.TreatWarningAs = micWarning
   End Select

   'Add the validation
   oValidations.Add CStr(oValidations.Count +  1), pVal
  End Sub


  Sub Class_Terminate()
    oValidations.RemoveAll
    Set oValidations = Nothing
  End Sub
End Class
```

A single validation is executed using the following function within the class:

```
'Function to execute text validation
Function TextValidation(pObject, pValidation)
  TextValidation = False
  Dim sActual, sExpected, sReport, compRes

  'Get the propety value
  sActual = pObject.GetROProperty(pValidation.Parameter)

  'In case blank and it's a page object then use
  'the HTML body
  If sActual = "" And pObject.GetROProperty("micclass") = "Page" Then
    sActual = pObject.WebElement("html tag:=BODY","index:=0").GetROProperty(pVa
lidation.Parameter)
  End if


  sExpected = pValidation.ExpectedValue

  'Which type of comparison needs to be done
  Select Case UCase(Trim(pValidation.ComparisonType))
    Case "EQUALS"
      compRes = CompStr(sActual, sExpected)
```

```
        Case "NOTCONTAINS", "CONTAINS"
          compRes = InStr(sActual, sExpected)
      End Select

      'Create the checkpoint text to be reported
      sReport = "&lt;<B>Checkpoint Name</B>&gt;: " & pValidation.Name & vbNewLine
      sReport = sReport + "<P><B>Type</B>: " & pValidation.Comparison & vbNewLine &
        vbTab & vbTab
      sReport = sReport + "<P><B>Property</B>: " & pValidation.Parameter &
        vbNewLine & vbTab & vbTab
      sReport = sReport + "<P><B>Expected Value</B>: " & sExpected & vbNewLine &
        vbTab &
      sReport = sReport + "<P><B>Actual Value</B>: " & sActual

      'Report the status based on comparison type
      Select Case pValidation.ComparisonType
        Case "NOTCONTAINS", "EQUALS"
          Select Case compRes
            '0 means not found or a Equal match based on the
            'function used
            Case 0
              Reporter.ReportEvent micPass, pValidation.Name, sReport
              TextValidation = True
            Case Else
              Reporter.ReportEvent pValidation.TreatFailAs, pValidation.Name,
    sReport
              TextValidation = False
          End Select
        Case "CONTAINS"
          Select Case compRes
            Case 0
              Reporter.ReportEvent pValidation.TreatFailAs, pValidation.Name,
    sReport
              TextValidation = False
            Case Else
              Reporter.ReportEvent micPass, pValidation.Name, sReport
              TextValidation = True
          End Select
      End Select
End Function
```

Since we can have more than one validation with same name stored in the TextValidations class we need to have one more function which will execute all of them one at a time. The following function is used for that purpose within the class:

```
'Function to execute multiple validations for a given
'keyword
Function Check(pObject)
    Dim i, iCount
    Check = True

    If Not pObject.Exist(0) Then
```

```
         Check = False
         Reporter.ReportEvent micFail, oValidations("1").Name, "Object does not exists"
         Exit Function
  End if


  iCount = oValidations.Count

  'Enumerate the Keys inside the dictionary
  Dim sKeys
  sKeys= oValidations.Keys
  For i = 0 To iCount - 1
         'Execute the check validation on the object
         Check = TextValidation(pObject, oValidations(sKeys(i)) And Check
  Next
End Function
```

We load these checkpoints from an excel spreadsheet using the following function:

```
'Function to load set of checkpoints from a give excel file
Public Sub AddCheckpointsFromXLS(ByVal oChecks,ByVal sFileName,ByVal
sSheetName)
  Dim xlApp,xlWorkSheet, xlWorkBook
  Dim iColCount, i, iRowCount, j

  'Open excel sheet
  Set xlApp = CreateObject("Excel.Application")

  'Do the processing in back ground
  xlApp.Visible = False

  '
  If xlApp is Nothing Then
         Err.Raise vbObjectError + 2, "Unable to open excel","AddObjectsFromXL"
         AddObjectsFromXLS = False
         Exit Sub
  End If

  'Open the workbook
  Set xlWorkBook = xlApp.Workbooks.Open (sFileName,,True)

  'In case sheet name is not specified then load the first one
  If IsEmpty(sSheetName) Or IsNull(sSheetName)  Then
         Set xlWorkSheet = xlWorkBook.Sheets(1)
  Else
         Set xlWorkSheet = xlWorkBook.Sheets(sSheetName)
  End If

  'Get the non-blank row count
  Dim allRows
  allRows = xlWorkSheet.UsedRange
  iColCount = UBound(allRows, 2)
```

```
        'Get the last non-blank row
        iRowCount = UBound(allRows,1)

        'Populate all the records
        For i = 2 to iRowCount
                If allRows(i, 1)<>"" Then
                        If Not oChecks.Exists(allRows(i,1)) Then
                                oChecks.Add allRows(i,1), GetNewValidations()
                        End If
                        'Assume the excel sheet columns to be in order
                        'Name, Parameter, ExpectedValue,
                        'ComparisonType, TreatFailAs, TreatWarningAs
                        oChecks(allRows(i,1)).AddByParam allRows(i,1), _
                                                        allRows(i,2), _
                                                        allRows(i,3), _
                                                        allRows(i,4), _
                                                        allRows(i,5), _
                                                        allRows(i,6)
                End If
        Next

        'Close workbook and application
        xlWorkBook.Close
        xlApp.Quit
        Set xlWorkBook = Nothing
        Set xlWorkSheet = Nothing
        Set xlApp = Nothing
End Sub
```

We now combine the functions described above as shown in the following code:

```
'Create a dictionary to store checkpoints
Dim mChecks
Set mChecks = CreateObject("Scripting.Dictionary")
mChecks.CompareMode = vbTextCompare

'Load the checkpoints
AddCheckpointsFromXLS mChecks, "C:\Validations.xls", ""

Set oPg = Browser("..").Page("..")

'Execute Checkpoint 1 on oPg object
mChecks("Checkpoint 1").Check oPg
```

NOTE: mChecks("Checkpoint I") return an object of type
TextValidations which may further contain series of checkpoints

Extending Test Objects using Classes

We can put an arbitrary number of functions into a custom class to extend test object functionality, as in:

```
'Class to extend WebTable functionality
Class extendWebTable
  Private oWebTable

  Public Property Set Item(pObject)
    Set oWebTable = pObject
  End Property

  Public Property Let Item(pObject)
    Set Item = oWebTable
  End Property

  'Click using QTP objects
  Sub Click(ByVal Row, ByVal Col)
    Set oCell = oWebTable. _
        WebElement("html tag:=TR","index:=" & (Row - 1)). _
        WebElement("html tag:=TD","index:=" & (Col - 1))
    oCell.Click
  End Sub

  'Click using DOM objects
  Sub ClickDOM(ByVal Row, ByVal Col)
    Set oCell = oWebTable.Rows(Row-1).Cells(Col-1)
    oCell.Click
  End Sub

  'GetCellData from QTP methods
  Public Function GetCellData(ByVal Row, ByVal Col)
    GetCellData = oWebTable.GetCellData (Row, Col)
  End Function

  'GetCellData from QTP methods
  Public Function GetCellDataDOM(ByVal Row, ByVal Col)
    GetCellDataDOM = oWebTable.object.rows(Row-1).Cells(col-1).outerText
  End Function

  'Returns the Index of a column by looking up for a given text in the header
row
  Public Function GetColIndex (ByVal Col)
    'Check if input is string or a number
    If VarType(Col) = vbString Then
      Col = "Text:=" & Col
      'Check if a column with given text exist in the header row
      If oWebTable.WebElement("html tag:=TR","index:=0").WebElement("html
tag:=TD|TH",Col).Exist(0) Then
        Set oCell = oWebTable. _
            WebElement("html tag:=TR","index:=0"). _
            WebElement("html tag:=TD|TH",Col)
```

```
          GetColIndex = oCell.GetROProperty("attribute/cellindex") + 1
        Else
          GetColIndex = 0
        End if
      Else
        GetColIndex = Col
      End If
  End Function

   Function FindTextBySearch(ByVal SearchText, ByVal matchIndex, ByRef Row,
ByRef Col)
      'CODE TO SEARCH INDSIDE THE TABLE
      'GOES HERE
  End Function
End Class
```

Now we can use the above class in one of two ways:

Method 1

```
'Create a extend WebTable class object
Set exWebTable = New extendWebTable

'Assign the table we would be working on
Set exWebTable.Item = Browser("..").Page("..").WebTable("..")

'Click in cell 2,3
exWebTable.Click 2,3

'Get the data in cell 3,4
MsgBox exWebTable.GetCellDataDom (3,4)
```

Method 2

This method registers the class as a function using the QTP RegisterUserFunc function.

```
'Get the extendWebTable object
Public Function exWebTable(pObject)
   Set exWebTable = Nothing
  Set exWebTable = New
   Set exWebTable.item = pObject
End Function

'Register the Extend function as one of the methods for WebTable object
RegisterUserFunc "WebTable","Extend","exWebTable", True
'Now we can use extend function as
Msgbox  Browser("..").Page("..").WebTable("..").Extend.GetCellDataDOM(4,4)
```

This approach provides means to extend QTP Test object functionality in a consistent way. And we still have the original methods available to be used.

Using JScript in QTP

As it is mentioned in the QTP Help, "The QTP Automation Object Model (AOM) can be used in any programming language that supports COM components (VBScript, JScript, VB, VBA, VC, .NET Languages etc.)". But some people confuse this statement and tend to believe that QTP test scripts themselves can be written in any language. QTP only supports writing scripts in VBScript language. Though we can use a workaround and write partial code in JScript for a QTP Script. Before we start doing that first let us see what we would gain if we were to use the JScript code in QTP:

- JScript (JS) allows variable number of arguments to be passed to a function

- Provides Try/Catch/Finally block to catch exception for give block of code

- Object oriented scripting language

- Provides continue statement and allows usage of labels in the code

- Provides conditional compilation of code

- Allows custom objects to be extended during run-time

There are few other differences between JScript and VBScript but those above are the only ones we will discuss in this section. Since QTP uses VBScript as its main scripting engine, it is not possible to introduce JScript code inside the current scope or context of a script. To be able to use JScript we need an external host which allows us to execute JScript code at run-time and also allow us to make calls to the code added. Internet Explorer is one such host application which allows the use of both JScript and VBScript within an HTML page. It allows accessing variables and methods inside any scripting code using the window object of HTML. Let's first see how we execute a simple java script within QTP:

```
'Create a HTML file object
Set oHTML = CreateObject("htmlfile")

'Get the object reference to the window object
'this object would allow us to execute JavaScript
'as well as VBScript code inside the host html file
Set JS = oHTML.parentWindow

'Execute some code in host application
JS.execScript "var JSTest; JSTest = 10;"

'Access the variable declared in the java script
'execute above
MsgBox JS.JSTest
```

 NOTE: For all future examples we will use the JS object directly

The code given above creates an HTML file in the memory and then gets the window object for the same. The window object provides execScript method which is used to load JScript or VBScript code. By default the code is taken as JScript; to use VBScript we need to pass another parameter to execScript:

```
'Execute some VBS code in host application
JS.execScript "Dim VBSTest: VBSTest = ""VBScript""","VBScript"

'Access the variable declared in the VBscript
'executed above
MsgBox JS.VBSTest
```

Passing variable number of arguments to a function

The JScript function that takes a variable number of parameters in JScript and return there sum is given below:

```
//Function to return sum of all given parameters
function SumAll()
{
   var i, argslength, sum = 0;
    argslength = arguments.length;
    for (i = 0; i <argslength;i++)
        {
          sum = sum + arguments[i];
        }
   return sum;
}
```

We can then use this JScript function in a VBScript environment using the following code:

```
'Execute some JS code in host application
JS. execScript "function SumAll() {var i, argslength, sum=0; argslength = arguments.
length; for (i = 0; i <argslength;i++) {sum = sum + arguments [i];}return sum;}"

'Call SumAll function with variable number
'of parameters
MsgBox JS.SumAll(1,2,3)
MsgBox JS.SumAll(1,2,3,5)
MsgBox JS.SumAll(1,2,3,4,5)
```

Scope differences

It is critical to understand the difference in Scope between QTP and the JavaScript code being executed. Since JScript code executes in an external host, it has no access to any of the QTP objects like SystemUtil, Window, Browser, Print, QCUtil etc. This does not imply that we cannot pass these variables to create them in JS scope. Consider the following example which allows adding SystemUtil support to the JScript code

```
'Create a SystemUtil variable in JS scope
JS.execScript "var SystemUtil;"

'Pass on the actual SystemUtil object to JS Scope
Set JS.SystemUtil = SystemUtil
```

```
'Execute code in JS and use SystemUtil
JS.execScript "SystemUtil.Run ('iexplore.exe');"
```

Similarly, to use OR objects or DP objects we need to pass the top most object into the JS scope. The following code would throw an error because of the Browser object not being in scope

```
'Execute some DP code in JS
JS.execScript "var pgURL; pgURL =
Browser('micclass:=Browser').Page('micclass:=Page').GetROProperty('url')"
```

To make the above code work we need to introduce the Browser object into the JScript scope. This can be done using the following code:

```
'Create a SystemUtil variable in JS scope
JS.execScript "var Browser;"

'Introduce browser into the scope of JS
'no need to do that for any child objects like
'Page, WebEdit etc...
Set JS.Browser = Browser
```

Using Try...Catch block

One big advantage of JScript over VBScript is the functionality of the JScript Try/Catch/Finally construct for effectively processing errors. The following code demonstrates the usage of this construct:

```
'Introduce Print object in JS scope
JS.execScript "var Print;"
Set JS.Print = Print

'Try catch block
JS.execScript "try{Print('inside try block');Browser.click;}" & _
        "catch(ex){Print ('inside catch block');}" & _
        "finally{Print('inside finally block');}"
```

This script would generate output in the print window as shown in the Figure 28-4

Figure 28-4. Try/Catch/Finally output

Working with JScript Arrays

JScript arrays differ from VBScript arrays. So an array created in JScript can't be accessed in QTP like normal VBScript arrays. The following code demonstrates how to use a JScript array in QTP:

```
'Create a JS array
JS.execScript "var arrTest = new Array(4,1,5,2);"

'Print the all the element in the array
Print "Printing initial array"
For i = 0 to JS.arrTest.length - 1
   Print JS.eval ("arrTest[" & i & "]")
Next

'Sort the array
JS.arrTest.sort

'Print the all the element in the array
Print "Printing sorted array"
For i = 0 to JS.arrTest.length - 1
   Print JS.eval ("arrTest[" & i & "]")
Next
```

There is another way to enumerate through the elements of the array, using enumerators. The following code shows this technique:

```
'Create a JS array
JS.execScript "var arrTest = new Array(1,2,3);"

'Get a array enumerator
set arrEnum = JS.eval ("new Enumerator(arrTest)")

'Run through all elements in the enumerator
While Not arrEnum.atEnd()
   Print arrEnum.item()
   arrEnum.moveNext()
Wend
```

Working with JS classes

JScript supports creating classes using this object. The following code demonstrates the same

```
//constructor to new person class
function person()
   {
         this.FirstName = '';
         this.LastName = '';
   }

//create a new person object
var me = new person();

'Assign values to object properties
me.FirstName = 'Tarun';
me.LastName = 'Lalwani';
```

We can also assign methods to the class. The code given below demonstrates how to add Display method to a person class

```
//function display to be used as object method
function Display()
    {
            alert(this.FirstName + ' ' + this.LastName);
    }

//constructor to new person class
function person()
    {
            this.FirstName = '';
            this.LastName = '';
            this.Display = Display
    }

//create a new person object
var me = new person();

//Assign values to object properties
me.FirstName = 'Tarun';
me.LastName = 'Lalwani';
me.Display()
```

 NOTE: All the above methods need to be loaded using JS.execScript as done in the previous examples of this chapter.

Object Class Mapping

At times, QTP does not recognize an object correctly. We can force QTP to map these objects to a specific QTP object type by updating a few details in the system registry *HKEY_LOCAL_MACHINE\ SOFTWARE\Mercury Interactive\QuickTest Professional\MicTest\Packages\StdPackage\ClassMap* setting. A class mapping is shown in the Figure 28-5.

Figure 28-5. Object class map

To create a mapping we need to create a REG_SZ entry with the object's class name (as shown by the Object Spy) and an entry value which is the mapped-to QTP Test Object name. So if there is a Tree View object in a .NET application which is being recognized as a SwfObject then we use the following steps to map this object to a QTP SwfTreeview Test Object:

- Find the object class using Object Spy. In this example it will be a "Company.Shared.Controls.TreeView" object

- Open regedit.exe

- Navigate to HKEY_LOCAL_MACHINE\SOFTWARE\Mercury Interactive\QuickTest Professional\ MicTest\Packages\SwfPackage\ClassMap

- Create a value named "Company.Shared.Controls.TreeView" and assign a value "Mercury.SwfTreeView" to the same as shown in the Figure 28-6

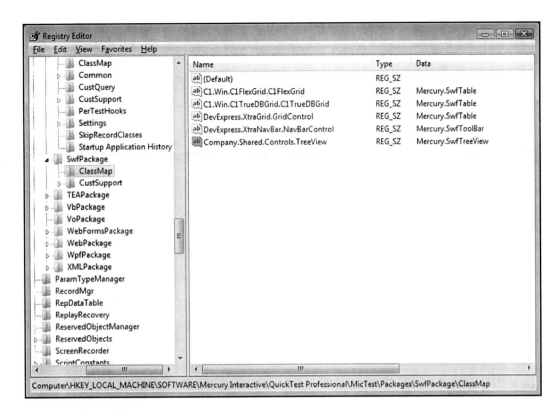

Figure 28-6. .NET SwfTreeView mapping

 WARNING: Troublesome objects might appear to function like a particular QTP Test Object, but infact they are not internally implemented using standard methods and therefore class mapping may not always work. Editing the system registry can cause harm to the system, so always backup the registry before making any changes to it.

```
'Store the object reference
Set oPg = Browser("Browser").Page("Page")
Set oSearch = oPg.WebEdit("name:=q")

'Use the object reference to the operation
oSearch.Set "Test"

'Refresh the page
Browser("Browser").Refresh

'Refresh the object cache
oSearch.Init

'Would throw an error that object cannot be
'identified.
oSearch.Set "Test"
```

Reader's Note

Chapter 29

What's New in QTP 9.2

QTP 9.x saw many changes from QTP 8.x. These changes ranged from UI re-organization to functionality changes. It is important for all us to know which features are available in which version of QTP. This chapter will walk through most of these changes. .

IDE Enhancement

QTP 9.2 IDE enhancements are described in this section.

Comment Block

We can now comment and uncomment on the selected blocks of code. This is done through the Edit toolbar or we can use the shortcut hotkeys,, which are Comment Block - 'CTRL + M' and Uncomment Block - 'CTRL + SHIFT + M', after selecting a block of code.

Improved Intellisense

QTP 9.2 has an improved Intellisense as compared to the previous versions. Now Intellisense also works while using Descriptive Programming which was not the case with QTP 8.x.

Run to Step

QTP 9.2 now allows us to run code from the script's starting point to a specified line. This is in addition to the "Run from step" feature which allows us to run code starting from a given step.

Enable/Disable Breakpoints

QTP 9.2 now allows us to disable and later re-enable existing breakpoints. In QTP 8.x we had to clear all breakpoints to disable them but in QTP 9.2, after disabling the breakpoint, they are still present but remain inactive until re-enabled.

Renaming Checkpoints

QTP 9.2 allows renaming checkpoints which was not allowed in QTP 8.x.

Function Definition Generator

QTP 9.x now provides a function definition generator which is used to define functions as shown in the Figure 29-1

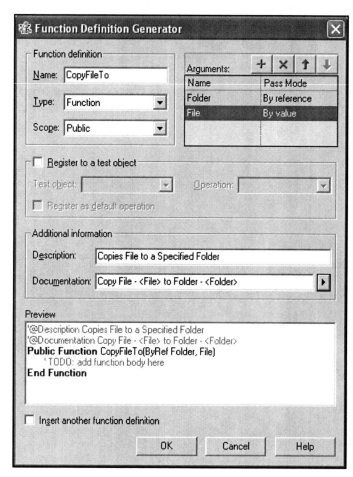

Figure 29-1. Function Definition Generator

The string added to the Description text box appears as a tool tip when we select the function from the Intellisense list. The Documentation text is displayed in the documentation column while working in the Keyword View. The function parameters <File> and <Folder> are replaced with the actual values for the Documentation text. To add description and/or documentation it is not necessary to declare the function through Function Definition Generator only. If we type the function manually into the IDE, then also it works:

```
'@Description Copies File to Specified Folder
'@Documentation Copy File - <File> to Folder - <Folder>
Public Function CopyFileTo(ByRef Folder, File)
        ' TODO: add function body here
End Function
```

Library Support Enhancements

QTP 9.2 allows editing multiple libraries at the same time. It now allows debugging any library added to the Test Settings Resource tab. Debugging libraries loaded using the ExecuteFile statement is still not supported.

Local Functions List

QTP 9.2 supports a new function that only lists the local functions present inside the current Action/ Library. This list is displayed when the 'ALT + "."' key combination is pressed. A sample list is shown in the Figure 29-2

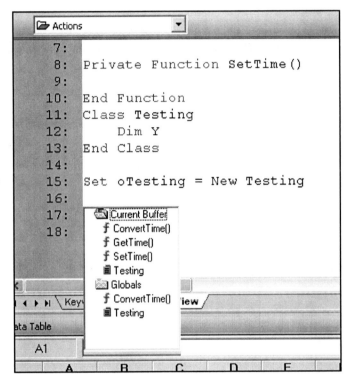

Figure 29-2. Local Functions List

The Current Buffer folder shows all the functions and classes present in the Action/Library while the Globals folder does not list any private functions.

NOTE: This functionality is also present in QTP 8.x, but it is not documented.

Object Spy

The QTP 9.2 Object Spy displays test object properties when the mouse cursor is placed over a GUI object. This allows interrogating multiple objects in a single spying session by just pointing the cursor at the objects of interest.

Web Drag and Drop Support

QTP 9.2 now supports performing drag and drop operation on web objects. This can be done by use the Drag and the Drop method on the test object.

Menu updates

QTP 9.2 has added many changes to the IDE Menu structure. Table 29-1 shows the difference between menu structure of QTP 8.2 and QTP 9.2:

Table 29-1. Menu changes from QTP8.x to QTP 9.x

QTP 8.x	QTP 9.x
Step▫	Edit Action
▸▸ Action Properties…	▸▸ Action Properties…
▸▸ Action Call Properties…	▸▸ Action Call Properties…
▸▸ Split Action…	▸▸ Split Action…
Step	Edit Step Properties
▸▸ Object Properties…	▸▸ Object Properties…
▸▸ Checkpoint Properties…	▸▸ Checkpoint Properties…
▸▸ Output Value Properties…	▸▸ Output Value Properties…
Step Optional Step	Edit Optional Step
Test Settings…	File Settings…
Test	Automation
▸▸ Record…	▸▸ Record…
▸▸ Run…	▸▸ Run…
▸▸ Stop	▸▸ Stop
▸▸ Run From Step…	▸▸ Run From Step…
▸▸ Update Run…	▸▸ Update Run…
▸▸ Analog Recording	▸▸ Analog Recording
▸▸ Low Level Recording	▸▸ Low Level Recording
▸▸ Record and Run Settings…	▸▸ Record and Run Settings…
▸▸ Results…	▸▸ Results…
Tools Recovery Scenario Manager…	Resources RecoveryScenario Manager…

New Configuration Options

QTP 9.2 adds a few configuration updates in the Tools→Options dialog.

Ignore Browser

We can now configure QTP to ignore the Quality Center as well as other browsers, using settings on the Options Web tab as shown below in the Figure 29-3:

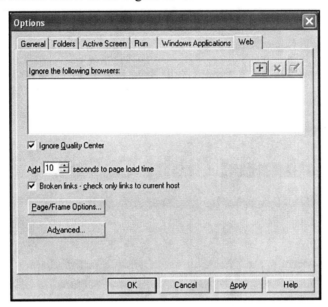

Figure 29-3. Ignore Browser options

Movie Capture to Results

QTP 9.2 can be configured to capture a movie of a test run. This configuration is done using the Options Run tab as shown in the Figure 29-4:

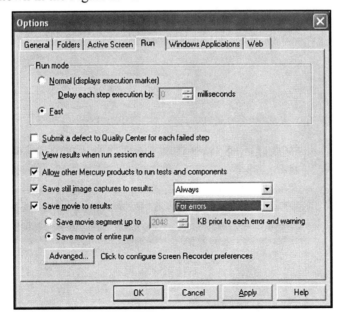

Figure 29-4. Movie to Results

Object Repository Enhancements

Object repository feature of QTP 9.x saw major changes from QTP 8.x. A brief overview of these changes is listed below

- Multiple Shared Object Repository can now be associated with the test

- Shared Object Repositories now map to individual actions instead of the whole test

- Repository Parameters for creating parameterized objects in Shared Object Repository

- Drag and drop objects in Object Repository

- Merge Object Repository tool now integrated with Object Repository manager

- Export Object Repository as XML

- Ability to define objects manually

Added and Enhanced Utility Objects

This section describes Utility objects that have been added and/or enhanced in QTP 9.2.

QCUtil

We had used the QCUtil object in the "Working with Quality Center" chapter. The only change made to this object is that the TDConnection property has now been renamed as QCConnection. Hence, instead of using 'QCUtil.TDConnection', we now need to use 'QCUtil.QCConnection'. If we want to create version independent scripts we can use the following approach:

```
'Check the version of QTP on which code is running
Select Case Environment("ProductVer")
  Case "8.0", "8.1" , "8.2"
    Set TDConnection = QCUtil.TDConnection
  Case "9.0", "9.1", "9.2"
    Set TDConnection = QCUtil.QCConnection
End Select
```

SystemUtil

QTP 9.2 adds two new methods to the SystemUtil object: BlockInput() and UnBlockInput().

The BlockInput method allows us to block input from the PC's keyboard and mouse while the script is running. This allows us to avoid any accidental keystrokes or the mouse events.

NOTE: BlockInput method is recommended when we are using methods like Type or Set (with replay type set to mouse)

Input is blocked until one of the following events occur:

- The UnBlockInput method is called

- CTRL + ALT + DEL key is presses

- The test run ends

- Any error is encountered during the test run

- A Breakpoint is reached

- A System error occurs

The following code shows a typical use of these methods:

```
'Launch the calculator app
SystemUtil.Run "calc.exe"

'Wait Max 10 seconds to calculator window to appear
bWait = Window("title:=Calculator").Exist(10)

With Window("title:=Calculator")
  'Block any user input
  SystemUtil.BlockInput

  'Activate the application
  .Activate

  'Type a event
  .Type "2"
  .Type "+"
  .Type "3"
  .Type "="
  .Type "-10="

  'Allow user inputs
  SystemUtil.UnBlockInput

  'Display the output
  Msgbox .WinEdit("nativeclass:=Edit").GetROProperty("text")
End with
```

The Print Log Utility

This is a new utility added to QTP 9.2 that allows messages to a QTP dialog in real-time, most often for the purposes of debugging. It can be used as shown in the following code:

```
'Print something on to the Print Log
Print "Tarun Lalwani"
```

This code opens the QTP Print Log window and displays the Print message as shown in the Figure 29-5

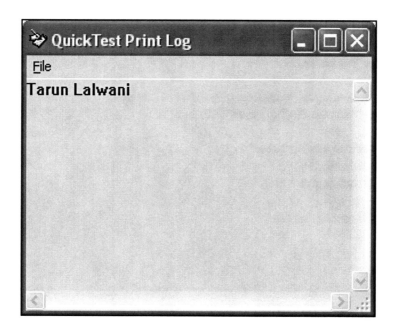

Figure 29-5. Print Log window

Once the log window is open, each additional call to the Print function adds a new line in the log window. The only control available in the Print Log window itself is a Clear All command. This new print utility has some limitations as mentioned below:

- Its log window can't be cleared programmatically

- Its log window's contents can't be saved directly to a file (but we can interactively cut and paste the window contents to a text editor and then save the file)

- Its log window can't be configured to run in hidden mode

It is easy to overcome these limitations by writing some code as described in the next section.

Hiding the Print Window

We can use the ShowWindow API to hide and show the print log window programmatically. The code for this is shown below:

```
'API declaration for ShowWindow API
Extern.Declare micLong,"ShowWindow","user32","ShowWindow",micLong,micLong
```

```
'ShowWindow constants
Const SW_HIDE = 0
Const SW_SHOW = 5

'Function to hide the print log window
Public Function HidePrintWindow()
   Set QTPlogWindow = Window("regexpwndclass:=Mercury::Qtprn::PrintWindow")

   'Check if the LOg window exist
   If QTPlogWindow.Exist(0) Then
         hwnd = QTPlogWindow.GetROProperty("hwnd")
         'Hide the window
         Extern.ShowWindow hwnd, SW_HIDE
   End if
End Function
```

Now running the code given above will hide the log window.

Showing the Print window

We can also create a function to re-display a hidden log window using the following code:

```
'Function to print the log window
Public Function ShowPrintWindow()
   Set QTPlogWindow = Window("regexpwndclass:=Mercury::Qtprn::PrintWindow")
   'Check if the LOg window exist

   If QTPlogWindow.Exist(0) Then
         hwnd = QTPlogWindow.GetROProperty("hwnd")
     'Show the window
         Extern.ShowWindow hwnd, SW_SHOW
   End if
End Function
```

If we attempt to use the code given above when the print log window is hidden, the window is not re-displayed. If we observe closely we will notice that QTPlogWindow.Exist(0) always returns a False value. This happens because QTP usually does not work on hidden windows unless it has been instructed to do so explicitly. So we change the 'Window' object in the function as described below:

```
'Specify using visible:=False that we are looking for a hidden window
Set QTPlogWindow = Window("regexpwndclass:=Mercury::Qtprn::PrintWindow", "visible:=False")
```

The code given above fails if the window is currently visible. We don't need to do anything in case the window is already hidden. And in case, we want to check the existence of the log window, regardless of it being visible or hidden, we can use the following approach:

```
'Specify visible:=True|False ensures we get the window
'regardless if it is visible/invisible
Set QTPlogWindow =
Window("regexpwndclass:=Mercury::Qtprn::PrintWindow", "visible:=True|False")
```

Clearing the Print Window

In the following functions, we use the "visible:=True|False" approach for all the objects so that our functions are compatible regardless of the visibility of the window.

```
'API Declaration for SendMessage
Extern.Declare micLong,"SendMessage","user32","SendMessageA",micLong,micLong,mi
cLong,micRef+micLong

'Message to Set text of a window
Const WM_SETTEXT = &HC

'Function to clear the print Log window
Public Function ClearPrintWindow()
  'Check if the print Log window exists or not
  Set QTPlogWindow =
   Window("regexpwndclass:=Mercury::Qtprn::PrintWindow","visible:=True|False")
  If QTPlogWindow.Exist(0) Then
    'Get the handle of edit box
    'It is important to use "visible:=True|False" here also as the
    'for a hidden window the edit is also hidden
    hwnd = QTPlogWindow.WinEdit("nativeclass:=Edit","visible:=True|False").
GetROProperty("hwnd")

    'Send a message to clear the text box text
    Extern.SendMessage hwnd, WM_SETTEXT, 0, 0
  End if
End Function

'Use the function to clear the window
Call ClearPrintWindow

'Print on to the log
Print "Tarun Lalwani"
```

Programmatically Capturing the Print Log text

```
'Function to get the text from the QTP Print Log Window
Public Function GetPrintWindowText()
  GetPrintWindowText = ""
  Set QTPlogWindow = Window("regexpwndclass:=Mercury::Qtprn::PrintWindow",
"visible:=True:False")
  'Check if the Log window exist

  If QTPlogWindow.Exist(0) Then
    'Get the text from of edit box
    GetPrintWindowText =
QTPlogWindow.WinEdit("nativeclass:=Edit","visible:=True:False").GetROProperty("text")
  End if
End Function

Msgbox GetPrintWindowText
```

micRegExpMatch

This is a new utility object that is hidden by default in QTP Intellisense and does not show up in the Intellisense list. This object is intended to be used with the WaitProperty methods as shown in the QTP help file. This object can still be used in QTP directly. The object has three methods:

Initialize: Assigns the regular expression pattern to be tested.

Compare: Compares it with a value and return True or False

ToString: Gets the string description of the operation

The following code shows how to use this object and its methods:

```
'Initialize the base value
micRegExpMatch.Initialize("test.*")

'Prints 'True'
Print micRegExpMatch.Compare("testing")

'Prints 'False'
Print micRegExpMatch.Compare("System testing")

'Prints 'regular expression match with "test.*"'
Print micRegExpMatch.ToString()
```

 NOTE: There is a difference between RegExp and micRegExpMatch behavior. RegExp matches the pattern anywhere inside the string while micRegExpMatch matches the pattern against the whole string.

There are additional and related objects which do not seem to provide much value. These are:

- ⊙ micGreaterThan
- ⊙ micGreaterThanOrEqual
- ⊙ micLessThan
- ⊙ micLessThanOrEqual
- ⊙ micNotEqual

All these objects work in a manner similar to micRegExpMatch. These objects otherwise can be used with WaitProperty method available for any test object.

MercuryTimers

MercuryTimers is a new utility objects that allows us to create various timers. A timer is automatically created when it is first used. An instantiated timer can then be accessed as shown in the following code:

```
'Get a timer using Timer property
Set newTime = MercuryTimers.Timer("Time1")
```

```
'Timer is the default property of MercuryTimers
'so we don't need to specify Timer
Set newTime = MercuryTimers("Time1")
```

A MercuryTimer object provides the following methods:

- Start: Start the timer

- Stop: Stop the timer

- Reset: Reset the timer

- Continue: Continue a stopped timer

- ElapsedTime: Time elapsed till last stop (in milliseconds)

The following code shows how to use these methods:

```
'Start the timer
MercuryTimers("Time1").Start
Wait 2
'Stop the timer
MercuryTimers("Time1").Stop


'Print elapsed time - On my machine prints '2012'
Print MercuryTimers("Time1").ElapsedTime


Wait 1


'Continue with the timer
MercuryTimers("Time1").Continue
Wait 1
'Print the Elapsed Time - On my machine prints '3014'
Print MercuryTimers("Time1").ElapsedTime
Wait 1
'Stop the timer - On my machine prints '4025'
Print MercuryTimers("Time1").Stop


'Start the timer (this is equivalent to using Reset and then start)
MercuryTimers("Time1").Start
Wait 2
'Stop the timer
MercuryTimers("Time1").Stop


'Print the elapsed timer - On my machine prints '2012'
Print MercuryTimers("Time1").ElapsedTime


'Reset the timer
MercuryTimers("Time1").Reset


'Print the elapsed time - prints '0'
Print MercuryTimers("Time1").ElapsedTime
```

RepositoriesCollection

RepositoriesCollection is new utility object added in QTP 9.2. This object allows us to add any number of shared object repositories at Run-time to the current action, in addition to any object repositories associated with the Action as well. The RepositoriesCollection object provides the following methods:

- Add: Add a shared repository

- Find: Find a shared repository

- MoveToPos: Move shared repository to a give position in the priority order

- Remove: Remove a shared repository

- RemoveAll: Remove all shared repositories

- Count: Count of shared object repositories

- Item: Get path to the shared object using a specified index

```
'Remove all the object repositories
RepositoriesCollection.RemoveAll

'Add the new object repository
RepositoriesCollection.Add "C:\CompleteObjectRepository.tsr"
```

The code given above will add the object repository to the Action in which the code is being executed. These changes are for run-time only and get reverted when the test run ends.

 WARNING: If we use the above mentioned code in an Associated library file then it will only associate the repository to the first action of the script and also the changes will not be reverted when the script stops. This means the object repository will actually be added to the test and running the code again may throw an error as the object repository is already associated

DotNetFactory

QTP 9.2 adds the new DotNetFactory utility object which allows creating instances of .NET classes in QTP. The object provides only one method, CreateInstance:

```
'Function Syntax
Set var_CreateInstance = DotNetFactory.CreateInstance (TypeName [,Assembly] [,args])
```

The method takes the following parameters

- TypeName: Type name of class to be instantiated, for example "System.Windows.Forms.Form", "System.Net.Mail.MailMessage", etc.

- Assembly: Name of the Assembly class, for example "System.Windows" etc.

- Args: Parameters to be passed to the .NET object constructor. This is needed to create object instance when there is no parameter-less constructor

⊙ The DotNetFactory utility has greatly enhanced what we can achieve in QTP and that's why this book has a chapter dedicated to discussing this feature in detail

Generating Object name from the object

Each QTP Test Object now supports two new properties

⊙ TestObjName: Returns the name of the object in the repository

⊙ TestObjGenType: Returns the generic type of the object. For example, text box, list box, table, text label, etc.

These new properties prove very useful for debugging and logging purposes. The TestObjName property gives us the power to regenerate the whole object statement from an object. We created a function GetObjectSTR in the "Recovery Scenarios" chapter which allowed us to convert an object to its string definition. Now we enhance that function to include the TestObjName property in the following code:

```
'Function to convert a QTP test object into its string
'description.
Public Function GetObjectSTR(pObject)
    Dim sProps()
    ReDim sProps(0)

    'Get the name property from TestObjName
    sProps(0) = pObject.GetTOProperty("TestObjName")

    'Get the type of the objecy
    sClass = pObject.GetTOProperty("micclass")

    'If the name contains [ in the start and ] in the end
    'then it is not from object repository
    If Left(sProps(0),1) = "[" and Right(sProps(0),1) = "]" Then
            'The object is not from the OR. Continue the normal method
            'to get the description of the object

            'Get all the test object identification properties
            Set oTOProps = pObject.GetTOProperties

            iCount = oTOProps.Count - 1
            'Loop through and create a array for string description
            For i = 0 to iCount
                    sProps(UBound(sProps)) = oTOProps(i).Name & ":=" & oTOProps(i).
Value
                    ReDim Preserve sProps(UBound(sProps) + 1)
            Next

            ReDim Preserve sProps(UBound(sProps)-1)
    End If

    'Create the string object description of current object
    sObjectStr = sClass & "(""" & join(sProps,""",""") & """)"
```

```
    'Check if the object is a top level object
    If TypeName(pObject.GetTOProperty("parent")) = "Empty" Then
         GetObjectSTR = sObjectStr
    Else
      'Get the parent object of the current object
         Set    oParent = pObject.GetTOProperty("parent")
         'Recursivly call the function to get the complete description
         GetObjectSTR = GetObjectSTR(oParent) & "." & sObjectStr
    End If
End Function

'Prints "Dialog("Run").WinEdit("Open:")"
Print GetObjectSTR(Dialog("Run").WinEdit("Open:"))

'Prints "Dialog("Run").WinEdit("text:=Open:")"
Print GetObjectSTR(Dialog("Run").WinEdit("text:=Open:"))
```

The TestObjGenType might not be required generally and has no use in the above function.

Reader's Note

Chapter 30

Working with .NET Classes

We saw in the last chapter that QTP provides a new utility object named DotNetFactory. The Dot NET framework provides several built-in libraries which can be used to enhance QTP test cases. But since we are working in a VBScript environment and not .NET, there are a few things that need to be handled differently. This chapter provides the examples of useful .NET libraries as well as how to handle a few specific situations.

Using the DotNetFactory Object

The DotNetFactory object itself only provides a single method, CreateInstance, used to create a specific .NET object instance. CreateInstance is the default method so we do not need to use its name explicitly when we create a new .NET object:

```
'Create the form
Set oForm = DotNetFactory("System.Windows.Forms.Form", "System.Windows.Forms")
```

CreateInstance also supports a third optional parameter, ParamArray, which is used to pass an unlimited number of values to the specified object's class Constructor when required.

Passing Parameters to Class Constructors

Some class constructors require passing objects as parameters. Consider the following code:

```
'Create a .NET Form object
Set oImageFormats = DotNetFactory("System.Drawing.Imaging.ImageFormat","System.Drawing")
```

The code given above creates an ImageFormat .Net object. But attempting to execute this code throws the following error:

```
Constructor of type 'System.Drawing.Imaging.ImageFormat' not found.
```

When we inspect the constructor for the ImageFormat class in .NET documentation, it mentions:

```
'Constructor for ImageFormat
Public Sub New(ByVal guid As Guid)
```

The constructor takes a GUID structure object. The problem of passing a GUID object to the above function is that the GUID is .NET structure and not a class. With the DotNetFactory we can only create .NET classes and not the structures. But we know that an object can always be set to 'Nothing'. Now we can pass a dummy parameter equal to 'Nothing' to create the ImageFormat object:

```
'Create a .NET Form object
Set oImageFormats = DotNetFactory("System.Drawing.Imaging.ImageFormat","System.Drawing",
Nothing)
```

Passing Parameters to .NET Objects

When we pass a parameter to a .NET object, .NET will search for the function/property whose definition matches the passed data type. Consider the following code:

```
'Create a text box
Set oTextBox = DotNetFactory("System.Windows.Forms.TextBox","System.Windows.Forms")

'Set the password character
oTextBox.PasswordChar = "*"

'Destroy the textbox
Set oTextBox = Nothing
```

But attempting to execute this code produces the following error:

```
External object System.Windows.Forms.TextBox::PasswordChar has thrown the
following exception:
Method 'System.Windows.Forms.TextBox.PasswordChar' not found.
```

This error occurs because Password Char property expects a .Net character parameter and we are passing it a VBScript string parameter. There are two possible workarounds for this issue.

Method 1

The first method is to convert the "*" string to a single byte/character:

```
'Set the password character. Use Asc to get the int code of *
'And then use CByte to convert it to a Character
oTextBox.PasswordChar = CByte(Asc("*"))
```

Method 2

Another method is to use a .NET Convert object method to convert the VBScript string to a .Net character:

```
'Create a convert object
Set Convert = DotNetFactory("System.Convert","System")
oTextBox.PasswordChar = Convert.ToChar("*")
Set Convert = Nothing
```

Passing Enums

The following code in a .NET module displays a .NET form on the center of the screen:

```
'Create a new Form
Dim oForm as System.Windows.Forms.Form = New oForm

'Center the from on the screen
oForm.StartPosition = FormStartPosition.CenterScreen
```

But we can't use this code in QTP because we do not have access to the FormStartPosition. CenterScreen .NET constant. To develop a solution we need to see how the Enum FormStartPosition is defined in .NET:

```
'Definition of FormStartPosition in .NET
Public Enum FormStartPosition
    ' Fields
    CenterParent = 4
    CenterScreen = 1
    Manual = 0
    WindowsDefaultBounds = 3
    WindowsDefaultLocation = 2
End Enum
```

Now that we know that the CenterScreen constant has a Value 1, we can try to execute the following code in QTP to assign the StartPosition:

```
'Create a .NET Form object
Set oForm = DotNetFactory("System.Windows.Forms.Form")

Const CenterScreen = 1
oForm.StartPosition = CenterScreen
```

But attempting to execute the code given above throws the following exception:

```
External object System.Windows.Forms.Form::StartPosition has thrown the
following exception:
Method 'System.Windows.Forms.Form.StartPosition' not found.
```

This exception occurs because in .NET everything is an object and that includes enum values. So when we attempt to assign a numeric value, the conversion from numeric to enum object does not occur and hence we get an exception. But we can use a workaround here; we know that everything is an object in .NET which means if we use the StartPosition property on right side of an assignment we get the needed Enum object:

```
'Create a .NET Form object
Set oForm = DotNetFactory("System.Windows.Forms.Form")

'Get the enum FormStartPosition
Set StartPosition = oForm.StartPosition
oForm.StartPosition = StartPosition.CenterScreen
```

The above technique works by first getting the StartPosition object which is of Type System. Windows.Forms.FormStartPosition. So whenever we need to pass a .Net enum object to a function, we should try to find a property that is a child of another object which returns the required data type.

Working with .NET Arrays

.Net arrays are not similar to QTP arrays, and therefore can't use functions like Ubound or LBound with them. They also do not support the 'For Each' iteration construct either.

```
'Create the .NET screen object
Set Screen = DotNetFactory("System.Windows.Forms.Screen")

'Get an array of Screens (all available monitors)
Set allScreens = Screen.AllScreens

Print "Total available screens - " & allScreens.Length

'ERROR: returns an empty value
screen1 = allScreens(0)

'ERROR: causes Object required: 'allScreens(...)'
Set screen1 = allScreens(0)
```

The last two statements, which fail to access array values demonstrate that we cannot enumerate the .NET arrays in the typical manner in QTP. To successfully access .Net array elements, we need to use the array's .Net Enumerator object as follows:

```
'Create the .NET screen object
Set Screen = DotNetFactory("System.Windows.Forms.Screen")

'Gets an array of all the screens connected to the system.
Set allScreens = Screen.AllScreens

'Get the enumerator for current array
Set enumScreen = allScreens.GetEnumerator()

'Call the <Enumerator>.MoveNext until the the MoveNext
'returns a False value. The current element can be accessed
'Using the current property of the enumerator
While enumScreen.MoveNext
  Set oScreen = enumScreen.Current

  'Display the screen information
  Print "Device Name - " + oScreen.DeviceName
  Print "Bounds - " & oScreen.Bounds.ToString()
  Print "Type - " & oScreen.GetType().ToString()
  Print "Working Area - " & oScreen.WorkingArea.ToString()
  Print "Primary Screen - " & oScreen.Primary.ToString()
  Print vbNewLine
Wend
```

The code mentioned above produces the following output on my machine:

```
Device Name - \\.\DISPLAY1
Bounds - {X=0,Y=0,Width=1024,Height=768}
Type - System.Windows.Forms.Screen
Working Area - {X=0,Y=0,Width=1024,Height=708}
Primary Screen - True
```

So far we have discussed solutions for some of the commonly faced issues when DotNetFactory is used. Now we will look at some additional examples and explore various .NET classes.

Playing a Wav File

```
'Create a .NET Audio object
Set Obj = DotNetFactory("Microsoft.VisualBasic.Devices.Audio","Microsoft.VisualBasic")

'Play a wav file
Obj.Play "C:\WINDOWS\Media\Windows XP Shutdown.wav"

'Destroy the object
Set obj = Nothing
```

Working with the Clipboard

```
'Create a .NET computer object
Set Obj = DotNetFactory("Microsoft.VisualBasic.Devices.Computer", "Microsoft.VisualBasic")

'Get the clipboard's text
Print "Clipboard Text - " & Obj.Clipboard.GetText()

'Clear the clipboard
Obj.Clipboard.Clear()

'write a new value to the clipboard
Obj.Clipboard.SetText "This is a test"
Print "Clipboard Text - " & Obj.Clipboard.GetText()
```

Getting Computer Information

```
'Get the .NET Computer object
Set Obj = DotNetFactory("Microsoft.VisualBasic.Devices.Computer", "Microsoft.VisualBasic")

'Get the computer info object
Set compInfo = Obj.Info

'Print details about system
Print "AvailablePhysicalMemory - " & compInfo.AvailablePhysicalMemory
Print "AvailableVirtualMemory - " &  compInfo.AvailableVirtualMemory
Print "OSFullName - " &  compInfo.OSFullName
Print "OSPlatform - " &  compInfo.OSPlatform
Print "OSVersion - " &  compInfo.OSVersion
Print "TotalPhysicalMemory - " &  compInfo.TotalPhysicalMemory
Print "TotalVirtualMemory - " &  compInfo.TotalVirtualMemory

'Destroy the object
Set Obj = Nothing
```

Accessing the Registry

```
'Get the .NET Computer object
Set Obj = DotNetFactory("Microsoft.VisualBasic.Devices.Computer", "Microsoft.VisualBasic")

Set Registry = obj.Registry
IEPathKey = "HKEY_LOCAL_MACHINE\SOFTWARE\Microsoft\Windows\CurrentVersion\App
Paths\IEXPLORE.EXE"

'Get the path of iexplore.exe from registry
Print "Internet explore location - " & Registry.GetValue(IEPathKey, "","")

'Set a value in registry
Registry.SetValue "HKEY_CURRENT_USER\Software\MyApp", "Path", "C:\Test.exe"
```

Ping an IP Address

Before discussing the code to ping an IP address, let's first explore the IIf function, which reduces the lines of code we need to evaluate several If/Else conditions:

```
'Function IIf. Returns TrueValue if Condition is True
'Else returns false value
Public Function IIf(condition, TrueValue, FalseValue)
  If Condition Then
    IIf = TrueValue
  Else
    IIf = FalseValue
  End If
End Function
```

The remaining examples in this chapter will use the 'IIf()' function without further comments.

```
'Create a .NET network object
Set obj = DotNetFactory("Microsoft.VisualBasic.Devices.Network", "Microsoft.VisualBasic")

pingSuccess = obj.Ping ("127.0.0.1")

Print IIf(pingSuccess, "Ping was Successful", "Ping was UnSuccessful")

'Max wait for 10 sec for ping
pingSuccess = obj.Ping ("127.0.0.1" ,10000)

Set obj = Nothing
```

Evaluating Keyboard Control Key Status

```
'Create the .NET object keyboard
Set obj = DotNetFactory("Microsoft.VisualBasic.Devices.Keyboard","Microsoft.VisualBasic")
'Check the status of various control keys
Print IIf(obj.AltKeyDown ,"Alt Key is down", "Alt key is NOT down")
Print IIf(obj.CapsLock, "Caps lock is ON", "Caps lock is OFF")
Print IIf(obj.CtrlKeyDown ,"CTRL Key is down", "CTRL key is NOT down")
```

```
Print IIf(obj.NumLock, "Num lock is ON", "Num lock is OFF")
Print IIf(obj.ScrollLock,"Scroll Lock is ON", "Scroll Lock is OFF")
Print IIf(obj.ShiftKeyDown, "Shift key is down", "Shift key is not down")

Set obj = Nothing
```

The code given above checks the status of various keyboard Control keys, which can prove useful in the different testing scenarios. For example, if the CTRL key is kept pressed during the start of a test we can a take special action like setting an internal DEBUG flag to either True or false, or ask for the data input from a user etc.

.Net Arrays Revisited

```
'Instantiate an Array List
Set arrArray = DotNetFactory("System.Collections.ArrayList","System")

With arrArray
  'Add few elements
  .Add "e"
  .Add "b"
  .Add "c"
  .Add "a"
  .Add "d"

  'Get the Index of A
  Print "Index of A - " & .IndexOf("a")

  .Sort
  Print "Index of A after Sorting array - " & .IndexOf("a")

  .Reverse
  Print "Index of A after reversing array - " & .IndexOf("a")

  Print "Value at index 1 - " & .Item(1)
End With

Set arrArray = Nothing
```

The code mentioned above produces the following output

```
Index of A - 3
Index of A after Sorting array - 0
Index of A after reversing array - 4
Value at index 1 - d
```

Working with .Net Stacks

```
'Instantiate a Stack object
Set Stack = DotNetFactory("System.Collections.Stack","System")

'Add objects to Queue
Stack.Push "Tarun"
Stack.Push "Varun"
```

```
x = Stack.Pop
'Prints Varun
Print x

x = Stack.Peek
'Prints Tarun
Print x

x = Stack.Pop
'Prints Tarun
Print x

Set Stack = Nothing
```

Working with .Net Queues

```
'Instantiate a Queue object
Set Queue = DotNetFactory("System.Collections.Queue","System")

'Add objects to Queue
Queue.Enqueue "Tarun"
Queue.Enqueue 1

x = Queue.Dequeue
'Prints Tarun
Print x

x = Queue.Peek
'Prints 1
Print x

x = Queue.Dequeue
'Prints 1
Print x

Set Queue = Nothing
```

Working with .Net Date and Time Formatting

```
'Create the DateTime object
Set DateTime = DotNetFactory ("System.DateTime")

'GMTTime
Print "GMT Time (MM/dd/yyyy hh:mm tt) - " & DateTime.Now.ToUniversalTime.
toString("MM/dd/yyyy hh:mm tt")

'Current Time
Print "Date (dd-MMM-yyyy) - " & DateTime.Now.toString("dd-MMM-yyyy")
Print "Date (dddd, dd-MMMM-yyyy) - " & DateTime.Now.toString("dddd, dd-MMMM-
yyyy")
Print "DateTime (dd-MMM-yyyy hh:mm:ss tt) - " & DateTime.Now.toString("dd-MMM-
yyyy hh:mm:ss tt")
Set DateTime = Nothing
The code given above produces the following output on my machine
```

```
GMT Time (MM/dd/yyyy hh:mm tt) - 08/26/2007 11:52 PM
Date (dd-MMM-yyyy) - 26-Aug-2007
Date (dddd, dd-MMMM-yyyy) - Sunday, 26-August-2007
DateTime (dd-MMM-yyyy hh:mm:ss tt) - 26-Aug-2007 04:52:48 PM
```

Sending Emails using .NET

We earlier saw how to send emails from QTP using the Outlook COM object in the "Working with Outlook" chapter. Outlook has security issues wherein security warning popups whenever the code attempts to send a mail or read email addresses. We will now see how to send an email in QTP which does not produce any security warning dialogs.

We do this by first creating a .NET MailMessage object and then populating it with the necessary details:

```
'Create a .NET MailMessage object
Set oMailMessage = DotNetFactory("System.Net.Mail.MailMessage")

'Set the From mail address with a display name also
Set oMailMessage.From = DotNetFactory("System.Net.Mail.MailAddress","System",
"nobody@nowhere.com", "No Where Dot Com")

'Add a recipient to TO list with email address only
oMailMessage.To.Add DotNetFactory("System.Net.Mail.MailAddress","System",
"noone@nowhere.com")

'Add a recipient to CC list with mail address and display name
oMailMessage.CC.Add DotNetFactory("System.Net.Mail.MailAddress","System",
"someone@nowhere.com","I am someone")

'Add a recipient to BCC list
oMailMessage.BCC.Add DotNetFactory("System.Net.Mail.MailAddress","System",
"hidden@nowhere.com")

'Subject line of the email
oMailMessage.Subject = "Test Mail from QTP"

'Body of the email
oMailMessage.Body = "<h1>Test E - Mail from QTP"

'Mark the body as a HTML type
oMailMessage.isBodyHTML = True

'Add and attachment to the email
oMailMessage.Attachments.Add
DotNetFactory("System.Net.Mail.Attachment","System","C:\TestAttachment.txt")
```

Once the MailMessage object has been constructed we can send the message using a SmtpClient object as shown in the following code:

```
'Create the SmtpClient
Set oSmptClient = DotNetFactory("System.Net.Mail.SmtpClient","System")
```

```
oSmptClient.Host = "smtp.nowhere.com"
oSmptClient.Port = 25

'Send the email message
oSmptClient.Send oMailMessage
```

We can also use a simpler and shorter technique to send a single recipient a plain text email message using the following code:

```
'Send a plain text email
oSmptClient.Send "from@nowhere.com", "to@nowhere.com" ,"Test Subject", "Test Body"
```

We can also set the priority of the email to high using the following code:

```
'Set the priority to High
oMailMessage.Priority = oMailMessage.Priority.High
```

Converting Images to other File Formats

Converting a file from one format to another is a simple task using .NET objects described in this section:

```
'Convert image from one format to the another format
Public Function ConvertImage(ByVal fromFile, ByVal toFile)
  Dim oImageLib ' as System.Drawing.Image

  'Create the .NET image object
  Set oImageLib = DotNetFactory.CreateInstance("System.Drawing.Image")

  Dim oImage

  'Get the Image from file
  Set oImage =  oImageLib.FromFile(fromFile)

  'Convert the file
  oImage.Save toFile, GetImageFormat(toFile)

  'Destroy the image
  oImage.Dispose

  'Clean up objects
  Set oImage = Nothing
  Set oImageLib = Nothing
  Set oImageFormats = Nothing
End Function

Public Function GetImageFormat(byVal fileName)
  'Get the file extension from the destination file name
  'Pass a dummy Nothing parameter to the constructor in place of Guid
  Set oImageFormats = DotNetFactory.CreateInstance
("System.Drawing.Imaging.ImageFormat", "System.Drawing", Nothing)

  newFileExtension = GetFileExtension(lcase(fileName))
```

```
'Get the image format based on the file name
Select Case newFileExtension
  Case "jpg", "jpeg"
    Set oNewImgFormat = oImageFormats.Jpeg
  Case "gif"
    Set oNewImgFormat = oImageFormats.gif
  Case "tiff"
    Set oNewImgFormat = oImageFormats.Tiff
  Case "wmf"
    Set oNewImgFormat = oImageFormats.wmf
  Case "emf"
    Set oNewImgFormat = oImageFormats.emf
  Case "exif"
    Set oNewImgFormat = oImageFormats.Exif
  Case "bmp"
    Set oNewImgFormat = oImageFormats.Bmp
  Case "png"
    Set oNewImgFormat = oImageFormats.Png
  Case Else
    Set oNewImgFormat = oImageFormats.Png
End Select

Set GetImageFormat = oNewImgFormat

Set oImageFormats = Nothing
End Function

'Get the file extenstion of a given file name
Public Function GetFileExtension(ByVal FileName)
  lastDot = InStrRev(FileName,".")
  If lastDot Then
    GetFileExtension = Mid(FileName, lastDot + 1)
  Else
    GetFileExtension = ""
  End If
End Function
```

To do the conversion of the source image this function first loads it and then does the conversion based on the destination filename extension. Following is an example showing how to use these functions:

```
'Capture the current desktip snap
Desktop.CaptureBitmap "C:\Testing.bmp", True

'Convert images to various format
ConvertImage "C:\Testing.bmp", "C:\Testing.jpg"
ConvertImage "C:\Testing.bmp", "C:\Testing.gif"
ConvertImage "C:\Testing.bmp", "C:\Testing.png"
ConvertImage "C:\Testing.bmp", "C:\Testing.tiff"
```

Getting user Input using .NET Forms

We can create and then display a .NET form using the following code:

```
'Create the .NET form object
Set oForm = DotNetFactory("System.Windows.Forms.Form","System.Windows.Forms")

With oForm
   'Title of the form
   .Text = "Enter environment details"

   'Make it the top most window
   .TopMost = True

   'Set the startup position a CenterScreen
   .StartPosition = .StartPosition.CenterScreen

   'Set the form style as fixed tool window
   .FormBorderStyle = .FormBorderStyle.FixedToolWindow

   'Set the size of the window
   .Size = GetSize(300,150)

   .Show()

   'Displaye the form for a few seconds
   Wait 5

   'Close the form
   .Close
End With

'Function to get a Size object
Public Function GetSize(x,y)
   'Create a Size object with constructor int, int
   Set GetSize = DotNetFactory("System.Drawing.Size","System.Drawing", x, y)
End Function
```

The code given above creates and then displays a .Net form in the center of the screen for 5 seconds and then closes the form. But to obtain user input from the form we need to display the form until the user has entered some data. To do this we use the ShowDialog method instead of the Show method. The ShowDialog method displays the form as a modal dialog and inhibits QTP code execution until the form is closed. We create controls on the form using .NET classes and add them at run-time. But since we are not executing in a pure .NET environment we cannot handle form events, like adding a button and then responding to its click event. So the only option available to us is to add the needed controls and let the user close the form after they have added the requested data.

The following code creates a form which requests a user to enter a login name, password and environment:

```
'Function to get a Point object
Public Function GetPoint(x,y)
   'Create a POINT object with constructor int, int
```

```
    Set GetPoint = DotNetFactory("System.Drawing.Point","System.Drawing", x, y)
End Function

'Function to get a Size object
Public Function GetSize(x,y)
    'Create a Size object with constructor int, int
    Set GetSize = DotNetFactory("System.Drawing.Size","System.Drawing", x, y)
End Function

'X, Y coordinate for a Label
lStartX = 15
StartY = 20
labelWidth = 75

'Width and height of each control
controlWidth = 160
controlHeight = 25

'X coordinate of a control in front of the variable
cDelta = lStartX + labelWidth + 10

'Difference in height between two controls
deltaHeight = 30

'Create a Label object for the requested user name
Set oLabelUserName = Dotnetfactory("System.Windows.Forms.Label","System.
Windows.Forms")

'Set the properties of the user name Label
With oLabelUserName
    'Set the Size of the Label
    .Size = GetSize(labelWidth, controlHeight)

    'Set the location of the Label on the form
    .Location = GetPoint(lStartX, StartY)

    'Text to display for the Label
    .Text = "&User Name:"

    'Tab index. Since we are using &UserName
    'When user press ALT + U the label will get the focus
    'But since a label cannot take focus the focus is passed
    'on to the control with a higher tab index
    .tabIndex = 0
End with

'Create an input text box object for the requested user name
Set oTxtUserName = DotNetFactory("System.Windows.Forms.TextBox","System.Windows.Forms")
```

```
'Set the text box properties
With oTxtUserName
   'name of the text box
   .Name = "txtUserName"

   'Size and location
   .Size = GetSize(controlWidth, controlHeight)
   .Location = GetPoint(lStartX + cDelta, StartY)
   .TabIndex = 1
End with

'Increase the Y coordinate to displace the new controls
StartY = StartY + deltaHeight

'Create the password label object and set its properties
Set oLabelPassword = Dotnetfactory("System.Windows.Forms.Label","System.Windows.Forms")
With oLabelPassword
   .Text = "&Password:"
   .Size = GetSize(labelWidth, controlHeight)
   .Location = GetPoint(lStartX, StartY)
   .TabIndex = 2
End with

'Create the text box object for the requested password
Set oTxtPassword = DotNetFactory("System.Windows.Forms.TextBox","System.Windows.Forms")
With oTxtPassword
   .Name = "txtPassword"
   .Size = GetSize(controlWidth, controlHeight)
   'Set the password character property. PasswordChar only
   'accepts a char parameter, so convert the * string to a Byte
   .PasswordChar = Cbyte(Asc("*"))
   .Location = GetPoint(lStartX + cDelta, StartY)
   .TabIndex = 3
End with

'Increase the Y coordinate for the new controls
StartY = StartY + deltaHeight

'Create a Label for the requested Environment and set its properties
Set oLabelEnvironment = Dotnetfactory("System.Windows.Forms.Label","System.Windows.Forms")
With oLabelEnvironment
   .Text = "&Environment:"
   .Size = GetSize(labelWidth, controlHeight)
   .Location = GetPoint(lStartX, StartY)
   .TabIndex = 4
End with

'Create a combo box object for the the requested Environment
Set oLstEnvironment = DotNetFactory("System.Windows.Forms.ComboBox","System.Windows.Forms")
```

```
With oLstEnvironment
   'Name the list box
   .Name = "lstEnvironment"
   .Size = GetSize(controlWidth, controlHeight)
   .Location = GetPoint(lStartX + cDelta, StartY)
   .TabIndex = 5

   'Clear all items in the combo box list
   .Items.Clear

   'Add items to the combo box list
   .Items.Add "Local Environment"
   .Items.Add "Testing Environment"
   .Items.Add "Staging Environment"
   .Items.Add "Production Environment"

   'Set the default as the Testing environment
   .SelectedIndex = 1
End with

'Create the .NET form object
Set oForm = DotNetFactory("System.Windows.Forms.Form","System.Windows.Forms")

With oForm
   'Title for the form
   .Text = "Enter environment details"

   'Make it the top most window
   .TopMost = True

   'Set the startup position a CenterScreen
   .StartPosition = .StartPosition.CenterScreen

   'Set the form style as a fixed tool window
   .FormBorderStyle = .FormBorderStyle.FixedToolWindow

   'Set the size of the window
   .Size = GetSize(300,150)

   'Add the controls we just created to the form
   .Controls.Add oLabelUserName
   .Controls.Add oTxtUserName

   .Controls.Add oLabelPassword
   .Controls.Add oTxtPassword

   .Controls.Add oLabelEnvironment
   .Controls.Add oLstEnvironment

   'Show the form as a modal dialog. Code execution will advance to
   'next line after the user closes the form
   .ShowDialog()
```

```
'Pause for one second
Wait 1

'Get the user specified values from each form control
sUserName = oTxtUserName.Text
sPassword = oTxtPassword.Text
sEnvironment = oLstEnvironment.Text

'Close the form
.Close
End With

'Dispose of all the .Net objects
oLabelUserName.dispose
oTxtUserName.dispose
oLabelPassword.dispose
oTxtPassword.dispose
oLabelEnvironment.dispose
oLstEnvironment.dispose
oForm.dispose

'Destroy all of the object reference
Set oLabelUserName = Nothing
Set oTxtUserName = Nothing
Set oLabelPassword = Nothing
Set oTxtPassword = Nothing
Set oLabelEnvironment = Nothing
Set oLstEnvironment = Nothing
Set oForm = Nothing
```

The code given above creates a dialog as shown in the Figure 30-1

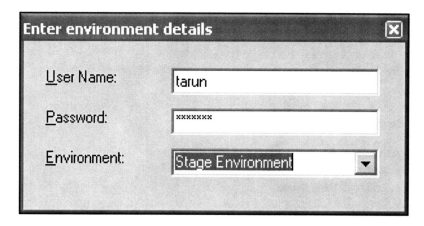

Figure 30-1. User Input using .NET forms

  NOTE: This method is not preferred over the user input method discussed in the "Working with Internet explorer" chapter, because the IE approach is simpler and faster.

Reader's Note

Reader's Note

Chapter 31

Designing Frameworks

A Framework defines a set of guidelines for all phases of test automation: Requirement Analysis, Script Design, Execution, Reporting and Maintenance. A framework can be seen as a wrapper around some complex internal architecture which makes it easy to use for the end user. It also enforces a set of standards for implementation. There is no standard set of guidelines available on developing a framework and what all considerations need to be taken during the development of the same. There are different white papers which go over types of framework and how they work. But none of them defines what all factors go in to the design of the same

Design guidelines

This section covers different desirable requirements of a good framework design.. This may not be an exhaustive list for all the project needs; we can add or remove more requirements as the need arises

Selection of a framework

Different types of frameworks that exist are:

- **Data Driven framework** – It is used when flow of the application remains constant, only the data changes. The data is provided by external medium e.g. - excel sheet, XML etc...

- **Keyword driven framework** – This framework provides generic keywords that can be used with any type of application. It also provides abstraction from the type of automation tool used and the type of application being tested, e.g. - it can test a similar Web and Windows application with the same test case

- **Hybrid framework** - A hybrid framework is the one which takes advantage from both Data Driven and keyword driven frameworks. These frameworks do not implement generic keywords but implement business logic keywords based on the application being tested. For example – Login, Logout could be application specific keywords that can be used

Don't reinvent the wheel

A framework should try and use the power of the automation tool rather than re-defining the whole language by implementing new keywords. Developing a keyword driven framework is time consuming and costly. A Hybrid framework can be developed in a shorter time period and with less cost.

Reusability

The framework should allow highest possible reusability. Combining individual actions into business logic provides re-usability. E.g. – Combing actions like "Enter username", "Enter password" and "Click Login" into one re-usable component "Login".

Support of different application versions

A framework should allow re-use of baselines scripts in case different versions or flavors of an applications are to be tested. There are two different ways to support different applications

- ⊙ **Copy and Modify** – This method involves creating copies of the baseline scripts and modifying them for a specific application version

- ⊙ **Re-use and Upgrade** – This method involves re-using baseline script and providing an upgrade code for the specific version of an application. This ensures maximum re-usability and should be preferred

Support of Script Versioning

Scripts should be stored in a version control system like CVS, Microsoft® VSS etc…This ensures recovery from any disaster.

Different Environment for Development and Production

Automation should be considered as any other development project. Test scripts should be created and debugged in Test environment.. It should be deployed to the production environment after the testing is complete on the test environment. This holds true for any emergency releases also

Externally Configurable

Configurable items of a script should be kept in an external file. This would contain configuration like Application URL, version, path etc. This allows running the same script against different environment. Ensure that the location of the configuration file is not hard coded. Hard coded files would allow running on any environment, but only one at a time. Keeping the configuration relative to current test path allows overcoming this limitation

Self configurable

Ideally a framework should be self configurable. Once deployed to a system, no manual configuration changes should be required and scripts should automatically configure the required settings.

Minimal changes required for any object changes

Most common issues faced during automation are object identification changes. Framework should be able to patch such changes easily. This can be achieved by storing all object identification settings at a shared location. This could be an external XML file, excel file, database or automation proprietary format. There are two possible way to load this object identification configuration

⊙ Static – In this all the object definitions are loaded into the memory at the start of the test. Any changes made to object definition can only be loaded by stopping and re-running the test

⊙ Dynamic –Object definition is pulled as per request. This approach is a bit slow as compared to the static one. But in case of huge scripts where the fix needs to be made at run-time this approach is suitable

Execution

Framework might need to cater to the requirements (on need bases) given below:

⊙ Execution of a individual test case

⊙ Execution of a test batch (combination of tests)

⊙ Re-execution of only failed test cases

⊙ Execution of a test case/test batch based on result of another test case/test batch

There could be many other needs, based on the project requirement. A framework might not implement all of them, but should be flexible enough to accommodate such requirements in future.

Status monitoring

A framework should allow monitoring the execution status in real time and should be capable of sending alerts in the case of failure. This ensures quick turnaround time in event of a failure.

Reporting

Different applications have different reporting needs. Some require combined results for a test batch and some require individual level test report for each test case in test batch. The framework should be flexible enough to generate required reports.

Minimum dependency on Automation tool for changes

Some fixes can only be made by opening the script in the automation tool and then saving it. Scripts should be developed in such a way that modification is possible even without the unavailability of the automation tool. This deflates company cost by reducing the number of licenses required. It also allows anyone to make changes to the script without having the need to setup the tool.

Easy debugging

Debugging takes a lot of time during automation and hence special care needs to be taken for this part. Keyword driven frameworks which use external data source, like an Excel Spreadsheets to read and process script keywords might be difficult to debug.

Logging

Log generation is an important part of execution. It is very important to generate debug information at various points in a test case. This information can help find the problem areas quickly and reduce the time to make the bug fixes at the same time.

Easy to Use

The framework should be easy to learn and use. It is time consuming and costly to train the manpower on a framework. A well documented framework is easier to understand and implement.

Flexible

Framework should be flexible enough to accommodate any enhancements without impacting existing test cases.

Impacts on Performance

A framework should also consider its impacts on the overall performanceof the automation scripts. A complex framework which increases the load time or the execution time of the scripts is never desirable. Techniques like caching, compiling all libraries into a single library during execution etc. should be used to improve performance whenever possible.

Framework Support Tools

External Tools can be developed to perform tasks that help in framework design. Some example tasks would be

- Uploading scripts from local folder to HP Quality Center

- Associating library files to currently open scripts

- Synchronizing local files with HP Quality Center

Coding Standards

Coding standards ensure scripts that are consistent, readable and easily maintainable. Coding standard should define all the things listed below

- Naming convention for variables, subs, functions, file names, script names etc. Ex – i_VarName for integer, fn_i_FuncName for function returning integer

- Library, subs, functions comment header. This should include information like version history, , description, parameters, example(s), created by, last modified by, last modified date etc

- Object naming conventions. Ex - txt_FieldName for a text box

QTP Examples

This section discusses implementation details of the few design guidelines discussed earlier. The implementation would be based on automation tool HP QuickTest Pro 9.2

Reusability

Consider the following code implementing the Login functionality

```
'Developer version of function
Function AppName_PageLogin_Login(UserName, Password)
    '....
    'Some code to do the login
    '....
End Function

'Wrapper around developer version to create
'simple english language keyword for Login
Function Login(UserName, Password)
    'Call the actual function
```

```
    Login = AppName_PageLogin_Login(UserName, Password)
End Function

'Default calling format of the function
Function LoginDef()
    'Call using the default parameters
    LoginDef = Login (DataTable("UserName",dtGlobalSheet), _
                            DataTable("Password",dtGlobalSheet))
End Function
```

In the code given above, three functions were created

- ◉ **AppName_PageLogin_Login** – This function is what does the actual job. The naming convention for this is followed in such a way that it is easy for a developer to locate the code

- ◉ **Login** – This function is a wrapper around AppName_PageLogin_Login and allows an English based keyword for implementation

- ◉ **LoginDef** –Most of the time, a script would call Login with parameters being taken from the same location. To increase reusability we make a LoginDef function which knows which location to pick the parameters from. This allows us to modify all scripts at the same time by just modifying the LoginDef function. It also gives flexibility to directly call Login when parameters are not to be taken from the default location

Support for different application versions

This can be achieved by using concepts of Override Files. An Override File is loaded just before the start of the test. This Override File would contain any changes to the old functionality in addition to the new functionality.

For example – In QTP we load Override Files using the code given below

```
'Get current test path
currentPath = Environment.Value("TestDir")

'Create the FileSystemObject
Set FSO = CreateObject("Scripting.FileSystemObject")
'Flag to check for loading
'of override files

Dim filesOverLoaded
filesOverLoaded = False

Set oFolder = FSO.GetFolder(currentPath)
'MAX 3 folder level

Const MAX_FOLDERLEVEL = 3

Dim iFolderCount : iFolderCount = 0

'Look in current test folder
'and 2 more parent folder and
'execute any override file
```

```
Do
    Set allFiles = oFolder.Files
    If iFolderCount > MAX_FOLDERLEVEL Then
    Exit Do
    End if
    iFolderCount = iFolderCount + 1

    'Check for any override
    'files in current folder
    For Each oFile In allFiles
            If InStr(oFile.Name,"override") Then
                    'Load the cureent file
                    ExecuteFile oFile.Path

                    'Set the flag and exit the loop
                    filesOverLoaded = True
            End If
    Next

    'Get current test folder
    Set oFolder = oFolder.ParentFolder

    'No more parent folders found
    If oFolder Is Nothing Then
            filesOverLoaded = True
    End If
Loop until filesOverLoaded
```

Externally Configurable

Script should use the Environment variable to launch the application

```
'Navigate to application URL
Browser("Browser").Navigate Environment("APP_URL")
```

Now this APP_URL can be defined in an External XML file, which is loaded at run time

```
'Locate and load the AppSetting.xml file using currently
'set folder paths
Environment.LoadFromFile PathFinder.Locate("AppSettings.xml")
This APP_URL can also be updated using the concept of override files discussed
earlier in the paper
'Set the application URL
Environment.Value("APP_URL") = "http://dev.mycompany.com/login.do"
```

Logging

The following Pseudo code shows how to log information

```
'Function to Login into the APP
Function DoLogin(UserName, Password)
 'Log debugging information
 LogDebugInfo "Enter Function DoLogin()"
```

```
If UserName = "" Then
  'Log debugging info
  LogDebugInfo "User Name is blank"
End If
Set Obj = Browser("Browser")
Set Obj = obj.Page("Page")
'Set user name and password
Obj.WebEdit("username").Set userName
Obj.WebEdit("password").SetSecure password
Obj.WebButton("Login").Click
  'Log debugging info
  LogDebugInfo "Exit Function DoLogin()"
End Function
```

Self configurable

A self configurable framework would make sure that all configurations needs for a script to run correctly would be done automatically by the script itself. Let see two different examples for the same

Using a 3rd Party ActiveX Library

Our script might be using a 3rd party library which if not installed on destination system would fail the script. To make such scripts self configurable, check if the object can be created or not, if not then register the DLL file on the current system and create the object. The code given below, demonstrates the same

```
'Disable error popups
On Error Resume Next
Err.Clear

'Create the custom object
Set oCustom = CreateObject("Company.CustomObject")

'The DLL is not installed on current system
If Err.Number <> 0 Then
    'Get the path of DLL from current folder locations
    sDLLPath = PathFinder.Locate("MyCustom.dll")

    If sDLLPath = "" Then
        MsgBox "Failed to locate required custom DLL"
    Else
        Set FSO = CreateObject("Scripting.FileSystemObject")
        'Get SystemFolder
        Const SystemFolder = 1
        sysFolder = FSO.GetSpecialFolder(SystemFolder)

        'Copy the DLL to system folder
        FSO.CopyFile sDLLPath, SystemFolder, True
        'Register the DLL
        Set WShell = CreateObject("WScript.Shell")
        WShell.Run "regsvr32 """ & sysFolder & "\MyCustom.dll"""

    End If
End If
```

Internet Explorer (IE) Popup blocker

Some application launch popup and IE popup blocker might block them up. In such a case before launching the application we should make sure that Popup blocker is disabled. This can be done through disabling the same in the registry.

```
'Create WScript shell
Set WshShell = CreateObject("WScript.Shell")

'Path to edit in registry
popupKeyPath = "HKCU\Software\Microsoft\Internet Explorer\New Windows\PopupMgr"

'Disable the IE pop-up blocker
WshShell.RegWrite popupKeyPath, "no", "REG_SZ"

'Enable the IE pop-up blocker
WshShell.RegWrite popupKeyPath, "yes", "REG_SZ"
```

Reader's Note

Reader's Note

Chapter 32

Useful Tools

No Automation tool will serve all the features which might be required during test automation. Add-on or 3rd party tools allow increasing capabilities of QTP. They can also help us improve efficiency during automation. In this chapter we will walk through various tools that I have found useful while doing Automation with QTP

QTP Script Editor

QTP 9.x comes with external QTP Script Editor which allows editing multiple QTP test scripts and libraries externally. It lists all the functions available in the currently open library as shown in the Figure 32-1

Figure 32-1. QTP Script Editor

VBSEdit

VBSEdit is another popular VBS file editor which has the following salient feature

- Intellisense for COM object created using CreateObject, and also for the user defined classes

- List available classes and methods available in the script as shown in the Figure 32-2

- Allows editing single VBS file at a time

- Comes with many sample source codes for various categories

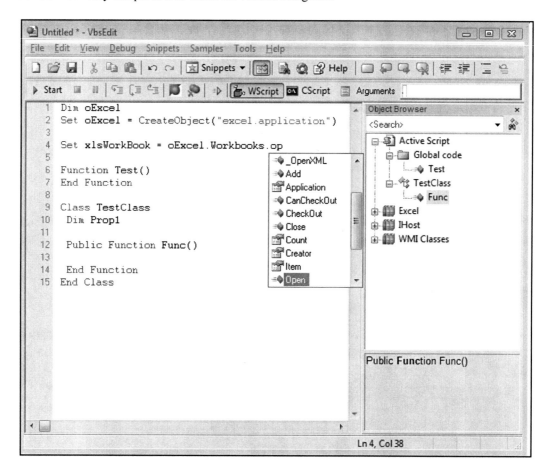

Figure 32-2. VBSEdit

Notepad++

Notepad++ is open source editor available at location given below

http://notepad-plus.sourceforge.net

The editor has the following key features for the QTP users

- Syntax highlighting for various languages

- Allows editing multiple files

- Lists available function as shown in the Figure 32-3

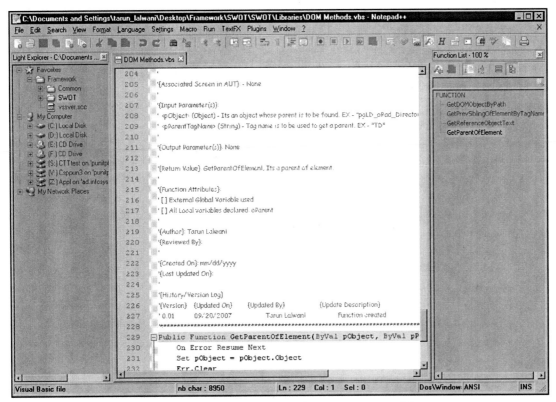

Figure 32-3. Notepad++ with Function List add-in

QTP Uninstaller

Uninstalling QTP using the usual uninstall option from a system's control panel does not remove QTP completely. Many of QTP keys are left in the system registry and cause issue while upgrading or re-installing QTP. The process of cleaning the registry manually is a time consuming task and could be dangerous in case wrong keys get deleted. QTP Clean uninstaller automates the process of deleting the information left in QTP registry even and also un-installing QTP and any of it's Add-ins. It deletes all the traces of QTP from the system for doing a fresh install, as shown in the Figure 32-4.

The tool is a freeware and available on my website at the following location

http://KnowledgeInbox.com/downloads/qtp/

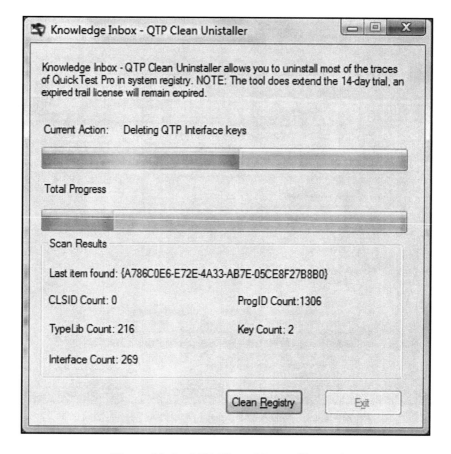

Figure 32-4. QTP Clean Uninstaller tool

ScreenCapture API

ScreenCapture API from KnowledgeInbox is a COM library developed in .NET which can be used to:

- Capture the desktop screen

- Capture the active window

- Capture a region on the screen

- Capture a window using the window handle

- Capture a region of the window using the window handle

- Convert an image from one format to the another format

- Get Internet Explorer object from the window handle

- Capture complete web pages in Internet explorer, including the invisible screen areas using vertical and horizontal scrolling screen captures.

- Compare two images and get the difference between them

- Combine different images

More details can be found at the following location

http://KnowledgeInbox.com/dowloads/general/

KnowledgeInbox IE Session Cookies Helper

Cookies are used by websites to store information on a client machine, they are of 2 types, Persistent and Non-Persistent. Persistent cookies are stored on the machine as files and can be cleared by deleting the files. Non-Persistent cookies are stored in the browser memory and are cleared only when the browser is closed. Non-persistent cookies might prevent using the same browser for different logins.

KnowledgeInbox IE Session Cookies Helper can be used to delete the non-persistent cookies from a running IE browser without closing it. The COM API library is available on my website at the link given below

http://KnowledgeInbox.com/downloads/general

VB 2 QTP API Converter

QTP provides extern object for declaring Windows API, but converting normal Windows API definitions to QTP extern declaration statements can take a good amount of time. This tool can be used to convert VB API definitions to QTP Extern declarations as shown in the Figure 32-5

This tool is available at the following location

http://knowledgeinbox.com/downloads/qtp/

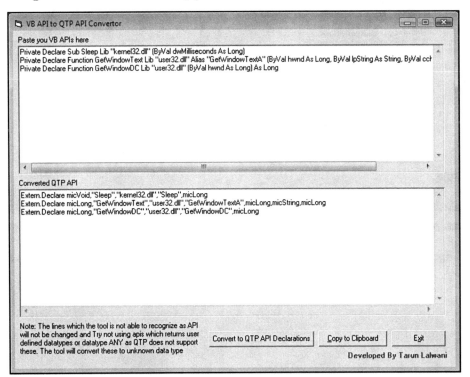

Figure 32-5. VB 2 QTP API Converter

IE WebDeveloper

IE WebDeveloper is an add-on for Microsoft Internet Explorer. The rich web debugging toolset allows you to inspect and edit the live HTML DOM and current cascaded styles, evaluate expressions and display error messages, log messages, explore source code of a webpage and monitor DHTML Event and HTTP Traffic.

The tool allows QTP developers to look at the DOM tree of the webpage and see how to access an object on the page in QTP. The tool is available as a 14 days trial version on

http://www.ieinspector.com/dominspector/

WebPage Inspector

WebPage Inspector tab allows viewing the tree DOM structure of the webpage and also allows selecting an object in the hierarchy by clicking anywhere in the document as shown in the Figure 32-6. Object style information can also be viewed in this tool.

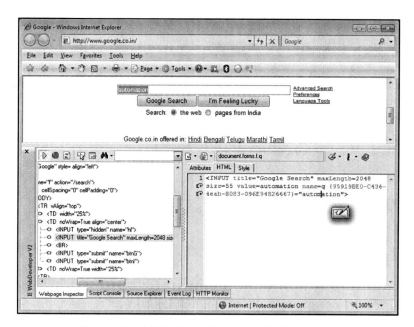

Figure 32-6. WebPage Inspector DOM viewer

Script Console

Script console allows evaluating JScript expression on the current web page. It is useful when trying to explore various DOM object options that can be used in the QTP code.

I won't be discussing the rest of the features of this tool as they are not needed in respect with QTP.

Test Design Studio (TDS)

TDS is the enhanced IDE for WinRunner and QTP, a product of Patterson Consulting, LLC. It provides a Visual Studio style editor which provided enhanced code editing experience. This review will walk you through some of the key features of the TDS

The tool has many features. Some of them are listed below

◉ Solution - A solution allows you to group various types of files into one solution. This includes QTP, WinRunner, VBS, text, ini etc...

◉ Expand/Collapse functions

◉ Smart Indentation

◉ Track Modification

◉ Split Windows

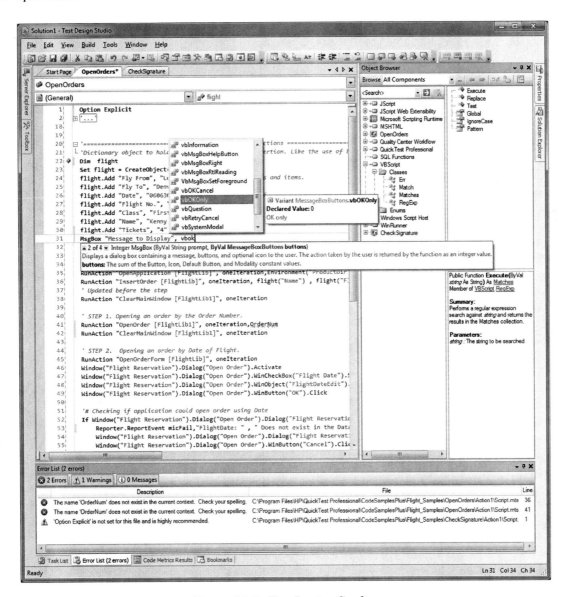

Figure 32-7. Test Design Studio

- Enhanced Intellisense - TDS provides Intellisense for almost everything. It provides Intellisense for all QTP object even when the machine does not have QTP installed. This allows automation developers to easily code there scripts on any machine without being dependent on QTP. TDS also provides Intellisense on COM libraries available to be used with the CreateObject function.

- Object Browser - Object Browser provides an easy reference to all the methods and properties available for a class/library in the current solution.

- Quality Center Support - TDS allows adding different quality center servers. Once the server is added, you can access any of the projects to which you have access.

- Supports scripted Business Process Components

- Inbuilt Browser

RAD Regular Expression Designer

RAD Software Regular Expression Designer is a free tool that helps programmers learn, develop and test Regular Expressions. It is an interactive Windows application that is designed to be simple and easy to use. The tool is available at following location

http://www.radsoftware.com.au/regexdesigner/

The tool can be used to test a regular expression that may be needed in QTP to identify an object or match a pattern. Figure 32-8 shows how to match a date pattern in a string using the tool

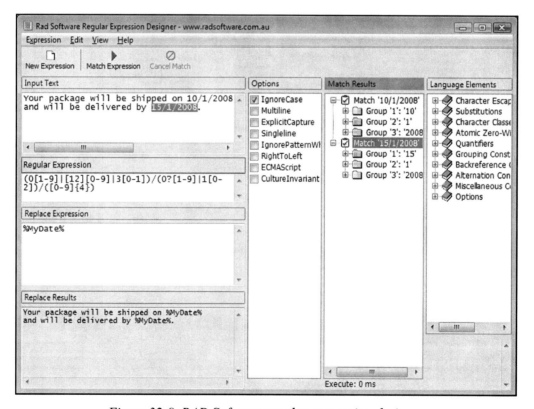

Figure 32-8. RAD Software regular expression designer

Reader's Note

Reader's Note

Appendix A: Problems discussed in the book

Appendix B: Index